✳ BIRDING WHILE INDIAN

MACHETE
Joy Castro, Series Editor

BIRDING WHILE INDIAN

A MIXED-BLOOD MEMOIR

THOMAS C. GANNON

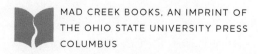
MAD CREEK BOOKS, AN IMPRINT OF
THE OHIO STATE UNIVERSITY PRESS
COLUMBUS

Library of Congress Cataloging-in-Publication Data
Names: Gannon, Thomas C., author.
Title: Birding while Indian : a mixed-blood memoir / Thomas C. Gannon.
Other titles: Machete.
Description: Columbus : Mad Creek Books, an imprint of The Ohio State University Press, [2023] | Series: Machete | Includes bibliographical references. | Summary: "Catalogs a lifetime of bird sightings to explore the part-Lakota author's search for identity and his reckoning with colonialism's violence against Indigenous humans, animals, and land."— Provided by publisher.
Identifiers: LCCN 2022057434 | ISBN 9780814258729 (paperback) | ISBN 0814258727 (paperback) | ISBN 9780814282908 (ebook) | ISBN 0814282903 (ebook)
Subjects: LCSH: Gannon, Thomas C. | Lakota Indians—Great Plains—Biography. | Indians of North America—Mixed descent—Great Plains—Biography. | Racially mixed people—Great Plains—Biography. | Bird watching—Great Plains. | Bird watchers—Great Plains—Biography. | BISAC: BIOGRAPHY & AUTOBIOGRAPHY / Cultural, Ethnic & Regional / Indigenous | NATURE / Essays
Classification: LCC E99.T34 G36 2023 | DDC 978.004/9752440092 [B]—dc23/eng/20230207
LC record available at https://lccn.loc.gov/2022057434

Cover design by Melissa Dias-Mandoly
Text design by Juliet Williams
Type set in Adobe Caslon Pro

"January 1968, Rapid Creek: Common Goldeneye" includes excerpts from "Immigration as Cultural Imperialism: An Indian Boarding School Experience or the Peer Gynt Suite and the Seventh Cavalry Cafe," originally published in the *Great Plains Quarterly* (34.2 [Spring 2014]: 111–22). "May 2003, Clay County Park: Bald Eagle" was originally published in a different version as "An Essay on Eagles," in the *South Dakota Review* (42.3 [Fall 2004]: 142–49). Several sections of this work incorporate excerpts from "Birding While Indian" (*South Dakota Review* 53.3&4 [Fall/Winter 2017], 80–90).

To all the birds I've seen and heard on my various drives through the Great Plains; and to all my family, friends, and colleagues who had faith that I would find a reason to ever come back.

✳ CONTENTS

Great Horned Owl, North Lake Basin Wildlife Management Area, 2 Sept. 2019

✳ PREFACE: *The Lifelook*

The immediate impetus for this book was an American Birding Association blog post by Frank Izaguire, in which he coins the term "lifelook." Different from a lifer (that first glimpse a birder gets of a particular species), a lifelook is "simply the best look you've ever had at a species, whether or not the bird was a lifer. [. . .] I've even heard birders talk about this experience before, and yet there's no concise way to describe the phenomenon of the lifelook. The linguistic niche is waiting to be filled."

I would modify this concept of the "lifelook" via William Wordsworth's notion of "spots of time." The birding moments in this book are not necessarily my "best look" at a certain species of bird, but more characteristically involve that birding moment in which a particular species became forever entwined in my life and mind as a "distinct pre-eminence," an epiphany that lies outside "the round / Of ordinary discourse,"[1] an epiphany outside my ordinary existence—a memory of psychic recuperation—or trauma—from that point on. The quality of this ornithic "spot of time" is thus dependent as much upon the human-all-too-human subject as it is upon the birding "object," itself really a brilliantly inscrutable subjectivity, an intrinsically wonderful world-of-worth, that hardly deserves the often inimical human projections foisted upon it.

This book could best be described as the untoward anti-memoir of a mixed-blood fellow who began birding around age eight, when he discovered that he was a neurotic introvert who preferred to be away from other people. Birding was a ready escape from hearing his food-stamp-welfare part-Lakota mother called a "squaw." And nor could suddenly being sent to a Catholic Indian boarding school be an especially fortuitous event for any healthy continuity of ego consciousness.

Worse yet: since this work is by a part-Native, lifelong inhabitant of the Great Plains (about "birding while Indian," to coin a phrase), it must also be a cultural critique of a Christo-Custer colonialism, as I have dubbed it—the imperialist ideology that still dominates the very names and signage of the state parks and tourist traps of the northern Plains that have been my stomping grounds. To paraphrase Leslie Marmon Silko's wonderful question: How can you write about birds *without* being "political?"[2] There may exist those blithe early "feathers of time," those childhood moments with that haunting Great Horned Owl, with that Wood Duck of impossibly gaudy pastels; but soon enough, human politics inevitably raises its interestingly ugly head. The result here, genre-wise, is something of a Frankenstein's monster mélange, part personal narrative framed around birding and part eco-poco-psycho-ethnic cultural criticism erupting now and again and again.

And so, even worse yet, the unsympathetic reader will find this book to be incoherent mishmashes of discordant voices, and tones, and discourses. "I" would claim this effect and affect to be intentional, an act of deconstruction of a Self that has served too long as the transcendental signified of all such memoir-esque writing. Indeed, in those places where "I" seem to be most personally vulnerable, another "I" is standing in the background, whispering "irony," whispering "distance," whispering "you can't really know 'me' because 'I' do not even know 'myself.'"

As a crossblood person, I feel inordinately pulled towards such a cross-genre form; and so I would ask the reader to be open in navigating the nonlinearity that is often the case in these essays—and poetry, and personal reminiscences, and ecocritical remonstrances, and dream-journal entries, and . . . . Furthermore, following various feminist and critical race theorists, I would claim that to tell a story of Native American genetic and cultural hybridity is itself a theoretical act. It is certainly a political one.

And so it may indeed turn out that this book is as much about birds and birding as *Zen and the Art of Motorcycle Maintenance* is about motorcycles, or *Flaubert's Parrot* is about a parrot—or even Flaubert. Alternatively, within the confines of Native American literary precedents, I have sometimes conceived of this project as Linda Hogan meets Gerald Vizenor meets obsessive birder nut. And as with many authors of Native heritage, there probably lurks somewhere in the background of this text the influence of N. Scott Momaday, the father of contemporary Native literature, that venerable "man made of words." (One need look no further than *The Way to Rainy Mountain*, both a Native American and modernist masterpiece via its skillful interweaving of personal narrative, of Native American history, and of Kiowa mythology.) The present project is under no illusion that it contains such skillful interweaving: that organic whole that Momaday learned from his great white mentors can no longer be my aesthetic ideal. But this will be a (more postmodernist) juxtaposition of four deep-map layers of—say—a sedimentary rock cliff: a top stratum involving birding, the book's ostensible "plot"; a second layer of personal memoir, of growing up part-Native in the racist politics of western South Dakota; beneath that, a third stratum of Great Plains history, of colonization and the Indian Wars. This third layer also involves both history and mythology, since it must largely be a critique of ideologies, especially Christo-Custer colonialism. Then there is a fourth and lowest—because most repressed—stratum, the *real* of the land, the birds themselves (flying us back to the top layer). This deepest history involves the interactions of human and non-human, of buffalo slaughter, bird extinctions, and habitat destruction—beyond the intramural conflicts of colonizer and colonized. If Momaday was the man made of words, I would be a man made of birds—and at least a bit of all four of these layers.

One of the earliest titles for this book was "Great Birding Moments I Have Known," intended as a tongue-in-cheek-and-cheesy tribute to Ernest Thompson Seton's early twentieth-century animal books. But I must insist that most of those moments have been earnestly heartfelt. Indeed, birding is the one thing that still gives my life meaning, that has kept me from checking out of a world of fucked-up humans that includes myself. But and so, as I have said, this book is just as much, if not more so, about one very fucked-up human being. Oh: and about birds.

✳ MARCH 1965, PISS HILL: *Great Horned Owl*

I jumped off an Iowa City bridge into the Iowa River my freshman year of college because I had been reading too much William Blake and Walt Whitman and William Butler Yeats. I jumped because I was on an ROTC scholarship and I suddenly realized that I didn't want to have to go and kill anybody on behalf of a jingoistic nationalism that I already didn't believe in. I jumped because I was a mixed-up mixed-blood who had already grown tired of trying to figure out who the hell I was—white or Indian.

It may have all begun when my best friend in the fourth grade asked me, "Do you know that your mom's a squaw?" That's the moment I began my retreat from the cruel racial politics of western South Dakota by taking weekend birding excursions to the dark pine hills just on the edge of town. A SoDak Huck Finn with a lot more personal baggage, I only had to walk a few miles through the dilapidated housing of North Rapid City, climb a chain-link fence along the interstate that led out of town, dodge across the interstate traffic, walk a few more dilapidated blocks— and there I was, at the foothills of the beautiful Black Hills of South Dakota.

I called the first steep hill that I had to climb Piss Hill because that's what I usually did when I reached the top of it. When my younger brothers came along, that communal piss became a manly (however boyish) initiation ritual of Campbellian proportions, given the relative immensity of the hill—and perhaps the

1

relatively small size of young boys' bladders. Then only a steep ravine of scattered small pines and yucca plants divided us from the next much more substantial pine hill, which was the actual goal of my bird ramblings. This was the primal Wordsworthian spot of ground of my formative years. There I honed my two-tone chickadee imitations—*fee-bee,* a whistled fall of a whole tone—and saw and heard for the first time a good majority of the bird species that made up the first fifty birds or so of my life list.

This was my home (away from a troubled home), where I could negotiate and navigate the contents of my grade-schooler consciousness, where I could map some order and reason onto my experiential universe. I needed something more "outside," less human, maybe: here I was beyond human borders and definitions.

"Do you know that your mom's a squaw?" No, I didn't want to know it, and maybe I was avoiding that self-recognition when I became that avid fourth-grade birder. After all, a Black-capped Chickadee was simply a Black-capped Chickadee.

But my will to order required some expenditure, and as the eldest boy of a single Indian woman on welfare, I couldn't buy such frivolities with food stamps. But there was Christmas, and I could also save my fifty-cents-a-month allowance; I could even interest my younger brothers in my hobby, thereby "borrowing" their allowances to procure the birding essentials that "we" needed. Our initial acquisition was that crucial first bird guide, Robbins, Bruun, and Zim's *Birds of North America,* about six bucks for the hardcover first edition. And the Christmas previous to my first Great Horned Owl brought me that essential pair of 7x35 binoculars, from K-Mart.

Years later, when I was a high school senior applying for

admission to West Point, a well-wishing friend of my mom typed up a "LIST OF ACHIEVEMENTS OF TOM GANNON." One item read, "Started a neighborhood bird club and published an ornithological journal, which only lasted one issue, due to member apathy." What this sentence doesn't convey is that the "bird club" consisted of just me and my two younger brothers, and that the "journal" was a one-page fold job made up of a few amateurish paragraphs by me about the local birds and a few paragraphs probably copied out of one of my bird books, for the edification of the masses. Copies—for my brothers—were laboriously created by hand on carbon paper.

Other items in that "list of achievements" included the following:

- Was advanced from third to fourth grade at the semester mark at Holy Rosary Mission.
- Was elected class president in the fourth grade of Garfield Elementary School.
- Studied the cello in the fifth grade.
- Won the Rapid City Boys Club spelling championship in the fifth grade; and went to the Regional Tournament in Omaha where he won second place.
- Have [sic] been an avid birdwatcher since the fourth grade.
- Is a book collector, specializing in poetry and classics, and owns over 50 volumes of poetry alone.

I remember that the cello lasted only for a month or two. For my lone recital, at a school assembly, I played the low obbligato to some awful faux-Native tune called "Arapaho Indians."

The same work friend of my mom's wrote a subsequent supporting letter to Senator George McGovern, on behalf of my application:

> Mr. Gannon is a non-service connected disabled Veteran. Alcohol became a serious disabling factor and he has intermittently been hospitalized. Mr. and Mrs. Gannon were separated in 1964 and divorced in 1969.
>
> In 1964 Mrs. Gannon was left with [. . .] four small sons, as well as the additional financial disadvantaged [*sic*] of being both a woman and a member of a minority group. She is 1/4 Sioux Indian.
>
> It became necessary for her to receive Aid to Dependent Children, and it was through Title V that she came to us. [. . .]
>
> [. . .] Vacations have been camping trips with the four boys in order to expand their geographical and ecological knowledge and increase their self reliance.
>
> Tom Gannon has taken much responsibility for the younger members of the family. School activities have been financially dictated. [. . .] Nature study involves hiking and climbing. Little brothers may be included.

Little brothers were welcome, in fact. I needed their allowances for that green army-surplus-store backpack I had my eye on.

"Do you know that your mom's a squaw?"

I looked at my mom again, closely. She was indeed a quite dark-skinned woman. My radiant fourth-grade class presidency seemed now a faint glorious memory, as I realized that I was just a poor Indian boy, doomed for years to live on food stamps and commodities and to hide, out of pure shame, from being seen with my more obviously Indian mother whenever we went to K-Mart.

One of the first jokes I remember was in a children's edutainment rag called *Golden Magazine,* in a regular monthly column titled "Jokes by Cracky": "What did the Indian boy say when his dog fell off the cliff?" the joke asked; the reply: "Dog gone!" I remember finding this hilarious and retelling it over and over to friends, ignorant of the fact that the joke's humor depended upon the racist stereotype that Natives speak in a substandard "Tonto" English. Growing up in South Dakota, I heard a lot of jokes about Indians, most involving class. "Q: What are the very first words a little Indian boy learns? A: Attention, K-Mart shoppers." Others involved not only poverty, but Natives' stereotypical laziness: "Q: How do you get seven Indians into a station wagon? A: Toss a welfare check into it. Q: How do you get them out? A: Throw in a job application form."

I heard many of these jokes from casual white acquaintances who didn't know I was part Indian. But I heard as many or more from my "skin" (Native) friends, who were telling offensive jokes about their own ethnicity. (I didn't have a name for it then, though we know this phenomenon today as internalized racism, the unconscious adoption of the mainstream culture's negative attitudes towards one's own minority ethnicity.) As Sherman Alexie said, "What is a real Indian? Someone who at some point in their life didn't want to be an Indian." Chickasaw author Linda Hogan's confession that "we often dislike ourselves" is especially applicable to mixed-bloods. Mary Crow Dog speaks of feeling "down" for "just being Indian [. . .] surrounded by an alien, more powerful culture"; but even worse "is being an iyeska, a half-blood, being looked down upon by whites and full-bloods alike."[1] (The Lakota word *iyeska* literally means "translator," but it is now used as a derogatory word for "half-breed" or mixed-blood.)

As for myself: I'm a tribe of one—and there's still a civil war going on. When those who bird while Indian—or rather, bird while mixed-blood—are confronted with hybrid birds like the Indigo Bunting/Lazuli Bunting cross I once saw at Lake McConaughy, they must wonder, with me, do these birds experience anything similar to the human torture of being a crossblood—of being shit upon by both sides? At one point in my twenties, I even declared myself "aracial," finally utterly frustrated by a species that created such cruel categories, categories that discipline and punish those who cannot help that they have a white dad and an Indian mom.

I often looked longingly at the pictures of the Great Horned Owl in my bird guide. It is *the* iconic horned, or eared, owl of North America, the owl that most schoolchildren would immediately approximate if you said, "Students, take out your crayons and draw me an owl." My early reading had already included a snippet of verse from Stephen Vincent Benét, which I conscientiously memorized in grade school and recited to myself in my spare time. It was about John James Audubon, who—rather than "live for warlike deeds" or "women's words"—lived only "to look at birds." These included "All our native fowl / From the little cedar waxwing / To the Great Horned Owl." Doggerel, to be sure, but to a grade-schooler with both literary and ornithological yearnings, it was a totally apt, even magical, mix of words and birds.

One day I was walking back down the bigger pine hill west

of Piss Hill, listening to the calls of nuthatches and chickadees and the like when, from behind me, a huge form sailed directly over my head, only a few feet above me, a shadow with no sound, and I immediately saw the real bird in front of me, flying away in the same halo of silence, very obviously a huge Great Horned Owl. Maybe I even felt a shiver at this point in the presence of silent deity.

Later I dreamed about this bird in flight, over and over again. Almost a decade later, in my late teens, I had an eerie dream in which Rapid City's Main Street was deserted, empty of humans and cars, and one huge Great Horned Owl was flying, forever, winging down the street, wings spread almost as wide as the street. Silently.

✳ JULY 1967, PISS HILL: *Lewis's Woodpecker*

On my many birding trips back to western Nebraska and to the South Dakota Black Hills from my university job in eastern Nebraska, I'm always reminded how much a mere several-hundred-miles difference in geography changes the very birds. But the old French saying *"plus ça change, plus c'est la même chose"* still rings true, as similar niches are taken over by different but closely related birds. Eastern Bluebirds become more airily blue Mountain Bluebirds, for instance. In the place of White-Breasted Nuthatches, I see and hear the smaller, more pine-happy Red-breasted species; the Violet-Green Swallow zips over mountain lakes and streams instead of the Tree Swallow. No more Eastern Meadowlarks at all—only the more effusive melodies of the Westerns.

Another two of these western birds, however, remind me of

something else—the fact that the names of American birds are often themselves acts of Western imperialism, of a discursive will to power. As the early Adamic namers and colonial eyes/I's for the Euro-American encounter with the American West, Lewis and Clark have each been fittingly memorialized with a native bird named after him. From a Native point of view, I would rather imagine the birds themselves encountering our intrepid explorers:

I: LEWIS'S WOODPECKER
They call me Lewis's Woodpecker.
I didn't choose that name, but after millennia of me
hammering at the dead wood of these pine hills . . .
they came: with maps, and a native woman, and a
whole mind's-load of old-world naturalist terms &
      knowledge.

In fact, I guess my real name is Latin now, but I can't even
begin to pronounce it—so just call me "Lewie," after that
guy who kept looking around and writing things down,
      in a
fine script, as if he were capturing my feathered soul.
I heard that he killed himself, only a few years later.
Why he did is beyond my understanding, but then,
I am only a bird.

II: CLARK'S NUTCRACKER
Well, this Lewis fellow's sidekick was named Clark, and so
here I am, or how you know me. The only thing else you
need to know, apparently, is that I crack open
pine cones for a living.

But did you also know that my nickname is "camp robber"?
Yes, tourists, I'll steal your picnic table blind. But hey, that's
nothing, compared to what Lewis &
Clark started, halfway on their
way to stealing a continent.

I wouldn't see a Clark's Nutcracker until a work trip to Yellowstone in 1981. But Lewis's Woodpecker was one of my boy-
hood pleasures on that hill beyond Piss Hill. My brothers and
I came to call that second hill Packing Plant Hill, because there
the acrid, rancid smell of the Black Hills Packing Plant "wafted"
up that hill to insult our nostrils and to remind us of the sor-
did origins of our commodity beef. My first Lewis's Woodpecker
flapped leisurely to the side of a huge telephone pole down by the
packing plant along Rapid Creek, a large, dark-backed bird aptly
nicknamed the "crow woodpecker," and indeed I first assumed
that it was a crow. But a K-Mart binoculars' examination of an
impossible ruby-colored face and salmon-flecked belly ended
that illusion. Perfect in its incredibility, "Lewie" was one of those
minor brilliancies that all birders come to cherish on their own
spot of ground as one of the peculiar handful of birds that make
that place a *place*, unique and magical.

My Mnikoju Lakota grandmother's 1943 photograph is perplex-
ing, to say the least. A Native woman wearing a male Lakota
chief's headdress is certainly plain *wrong*, a bogus Indian representation coerced by the white townsmen powers-that-be who
were in charge of a Pierre, South Dakota, public parade. And it
was a spectacle largely spurred, I assume, by World War II American patriotism: "Hey, let's get some local Injuns all dressed up in

Mollie Hackett, Lewis & Clark Centennial Pageant, Pierre, SD, 1943

their full regalia, too!"—as further moral support for an implicit agenda that these "defeated people" might serve as fine reminders of US military might. I have wondered many times what Grandma Mollie really thought about the whole thing. Above all, I just really, truly hope that she wasn't entirely happy about her role in the "ceremony."

The irony of the masquerade only gets worse: responding to my curiosity about the photo, my mom recently informed me that it was a *Lewis and Clark* parade—or "pageant"—and that Grandma was supposed to represent—*gasp*—Sacajawea! Never mind that this fact made the Native garb even more outrageously (tribally) inappropriate: I was confronted again with untoward thoughts of the Lewis and Clark expedition, and of bird names as emblems not only of Western epistemic violence, but of the physical colonial domination and decimation of both Indigenous birds and peoples.

Outside the Great Plains Art Museum in Lincoln, Nebraska, is yet another tribute to Lewis and Clark: a set of statues representing the expedition that I often have to walk by on my way to teach Native literature. Yes—as I told my fellow board members when I was on the Museum's board of directors—"it's therefore also another tribute to Euro-American colonialism and to all the tragedy that ensued. So what are we going to do about it?" It wasn't as if I were saying, "Hey, that 1916 statue is quaint and all, but are you sure it's the message we want to send in this multicultural twenty-first century?" No, the set of statues was created in 2004. It is called "On the Trail of Discovery." Beside the statues of Lewis and Clark is a Native man extending his hand into the distance, as if to say (I like to tell people seeing it for the first time): "See this land? Take it—it's *all yours!*"

Standing apart from the main figures is a little Indian boy proudly spreading a US flag—in a celebratory mood, certainly. It especially angers me that it is a child. Such a blatant iconographic act of colonialist wishful thinking, of coercive co-optation this is. Such a sad, presumptive emblem of a conquered people, of cultural assimilation and interpellation and deicide.

Planted as a part of the statue display are some tall natural grasses. This is actually the only part of the project for which I have some affection. But I've overheard a patron complain, as she walked out of the museum, "You'd think they cared more about *grass* than *art!*" This attitude, too, is part of a settler-colonial worldview.

When I shared my story about the statues and my interpretation thereof with visiting Dakota poet and activist John Trudell, he begged to differ with my reading of the boy with the flag: "I'd like to think it's a *captured* flag," he said. "They forgot to add the dead American soldier lying at his feet!"

At a lunch for Trudell the next day, a UNL student commented that there seemed to be "something sleazy" about the current US political process. John once again rose to the occasion: "Western Civilization is something sleazy."

✳ JANUARY 1968, RAPID CREEK:
Common Goldeneye

> Like the slaughter of the buffalo, the removal of Native American children to boarding schools was a calculated act of cultural genocide.
>
> —Leslie Marmon Silko[2]

I'm still not sure why I was so driven my grade-school days. To keep going. Maybe it just seemed a way to get away from my family, me half-still-believing my preschool paranoid suspicions that there was no way in hell I could possibly be the offspring of my mother and father, that I had actually been secretly placed with a random human family by aliens—for what purpose I have yet to figure out. I was a neurotic kid, and that neurosis included an obsessive compulsiveness that had me counting my steps to school well into junior high school. And not by ones, but by *fives* (that is, counting each toe): "*five, ten, fifteen, twenty,*" the ever-droning mantra in my head ran on and on, like a fever bird that never reached the height of its musical gamut, that kept going on and up and on. In the same way I used to walk to Mass as if saying a rosary with my feet. And to Confession, with a glib yet earnest "Bless me, Father, for I have sinned; my last Confession was one week ago. I fought with my brothers, and lied to my mother, and swore sometimes." Then ten Hail Marys and a relieved walk home to five, ten, fifteen, twenty, and God's good graces.

I had been told in preparation for Catholic Confirmation that a trip to the Confessor at least every two weeks was necessary to be held in the Lord's highest regard. However, I was the last of our family who kept up Mass attendance, walking to the church every Sunday when the rest of the family was watching *My Favorite Martian* or something. For one thing, Church Latin was so reassuringly maternal, with all the *-um* endings—as if the Good Mother Church had you covered, in a blanket of long *oom* sounds, from womb to tomb.

So on one occasion when I became a bit careless, and quite by accident the third week since my last unburdening arrived, a sudden fear for the sanctity of my immortal soul overtook me. Oh, the incredible embarrassment that I would have incurred by having to admit, "Bless me Father, for I have sinned—and worse yet, my last confession was *three* weeks ago!" Then it was four weeks, then five, then several months: that shame was even more painful than the fear of eternal damnation, being more immediate, and I eventually reconciled myself to the fact that my soul was henceforth doomed to the nether regions of eternity. Five, ten, fifteen, twenty.

I have no idea how I got the idea into my head to walk from my house on Haines Avenue in North Rapid City to Canyon Lake Park, on the outskirts of southwest Rapid, on an extremely cold day over winter break in grade school. (An old journal entry claims that it was "19 below, with wind chill," though this may have already been the beginnings of some creative mis-memory on my part.) According to Google Maps, it's only about a five-mile walk to Canyon Lake, but I was just a kid, and one with very little common sense, apparently; my brothers must have been aware of this truth when they could not be coerced into making the trip with me. I'm sure I owned no hat, and my threadbare Salvation Army coat was hardly a secure respite from the cold. I remember feeling my cheeks go numb just a few blocks into the trek from the icy South Dakota wind, but on I went. Why, when winter is the worst time for birds, for pretty much the same reason that it's the worst time for a human to go on a five-mile bird walk in the first place?

For years, I kept track of how much time had elapsed since my Catholic lapse. I'm sure I even said to myself at the appropriate juncture in time, "Bless me, Father: my last confession was seventeen years ago." Today, as if in some inane attempt at closure, when people ask me what I've given up for Lent, I say, attempting levity, "Mass and Confession."

The seeds of my monomaniacal monotheism (and its end, too, I think) were planted at Holy Rosary Mission, where I spent the third and fourth grades. And I was at Holy Rosary Mission because my mom was divorcing my "sonsabitch" of a dad (to use one of Dad's own favorite terms of endearment), and she sent us boys away for a year to a Jesuit Indian boarding school on the outskirts of Pine Ridge so she could get her life together in a flurry of restraining orders and flights from my abusive father.

Five, ten, fifteen, twenty.

They've subsequently changed the name from Holy Rosary Mission to Red Cloud Indian School, and ostensibly the name change is a good thing, a reinscription "by (or for) the Native," as it were, and I've heard some good things from other educators about how progressive it now is. Former Oglala tribal chairperson Cecelia Fire Thunder, for one, has personally told me that it gave her the organizational turn of mind and intellectual rigor to succeed in her bureaucratic career choice. But let's look at the Red Cloud "History" web page itself:

In 1969, Holy Rosary Mission School officially changed its name to Red Cloud Indian School, both as a token of respect for the man whose work had made it possible to found the school, and as a part of a program of *reidentification* meant to demonstrate to the world that Red Cloud was *not* meant to be an organization of *cultural imperialism*, but rather the product of a lasting bond formed between groups of two separate cultures, hoping to enhance the best parts of both [like hell that was their intention] and serve the people of the Pine Ridge Reservation.

To this day, Red Cloud Indian School, Inc. looks forward towards a brighter future for the children of the Pine Ridge Reservation. The schools [*sic*] work towards achieving Chief Red Cloud's dream of a Lakota youth who are able to walk *equally* in both worlds—a Lakota people who are educated and able to do whatever they want [REALLY?], on the reservation or off, and who will choose to live in a *good* way and strive to *succeed* [of course, because isn't that the Western way?] wherever their path may take them. [emphases mine]

Such a clever discourse of power this is, pretending towards complete equity, attempting to efface its very cultural imperialism. The words "good" and "succeed" invoke those tried-and-true Euro-American Christian and capitalist ideals, belying any equality of worldviews. And notice that they didn't name it *Crazy Horse* Indian School—for that *other* Oglala Lakota, that off-the-rez renegade who was still putting up a fight before the massacre at Wounded Knee and who was never Christianized. Red Cloud, as mighty a Lakota warrior that he was as a young man, became an emblem of assimilationism in his later life: let's just say that the Jesuits weren't casual about their selection of Indian heroes.

The truism that history is written by the winners has been especially relevant to a good part of the last five hundred years of North American history, in which unthinking racism against the American Indian has been rampant, in which massacres of Native women and children have euphemistically been called "battles" in the history books, in which the Native American has long been a cardboard stereotype in John Wayne movies, and Disney movies, and even in twenty-first-century sitcoms. The traditional-white-history appeal of referring to massacres of Indian women and children as battles bleeds over even in contemporary scholarship sympathetic to Native Americans: the premier expert on Black Elk, Raymond J. DeMallie, can "misspeak," I suppose, in speaking of the 1890 "Wounded Knee Battle." Ojibwe scholar Gerald Vizenor has pointed out that "a massacre of tribal woman and children"—i.e., Wounded Knee—is still defined as the "last major battle of the Indian Wars" in the *American Heritage Dictionary*.[3]

One day after the massacre at Wounded Knee, Black Elk—still one of the Oglala Lakota "hostiles"—was involved in a skirmish near Drexel Mission, "about four miles north of Pine Ridge Agency." DeMallie glosses this as (the later) Holy Rosary Mission. Black Elk says, pretty much in passing, but with a certain degree of pride: "there are many bullets in the Mission yet."[4] My reminiscences here are intended to put a few more bullet holes in that Mission.

I kept going, into the cold. I mostly remember the lisping Tree Sparrows, those hardy native sparrows who descend in good numbers into the US every winter, but who might be said to distinguish themselves largely by *not* being House Sparrows, those ubiquitous black-bearded interlopers from Europe. This was also long before I kept Big Day lists, and long, long before I obsessively recorded my lengthy checklists into eBird. I only kept a running list of life birds at the time, scribbled on a blank page in the back of my big ornithological tome, *Birds of America*. The only reason that I'm certain that I saw my first goldeneye on this crazy walk was that I have "Rapid Creek" scribbled vertically beside the bird's text description in my first Robbins, Bruun, and Zim field guide. And every time I thumbed across that page in my early birding years, I felt that flash of recognition: "Oh, yeah, that day and that bird I remember. The WALK." And I remember how really, really cold I felt. But I have kept going.

Yes, these were the Jesuits—the "black robes"—in many ways the preeminent proselytizing order of Catholicism in the era of Euro-colonialism. In fact, boarding schools based on the "monastic model," as Foucault reminds us, became, by the nineteenth century, the "most perfect [. . .] educational regime" for a discourse of power bent upon discipline and punishment.[5] The Jesuitical methods of brainwashing were physically imposing, psychologically comprehensive. To this day, I'm still a recovering Catholic *par excellence,* in that I still haven't recovered much at all from those Jesuitical ways. I still usually dress in black—like an inverted trickster Jesuit, as it were. I still succumb to untoward thoughts such as "My last Confession was seventeen years ago."

And after all, isn't keeping a detailed checklist of birds at the local lake during May migration rather like ticking off the beads of a rosary? There's nothing worse than an obsessive-compulsive raised as a Catholic.

As a second-year tenure-track PhD teaching at the University of Nebraska–Lincoln, I eagerly agreed when a non-Native TA asked me to speak to his Native American Lit. class, in the wake of their reading of Standing Bear's experiences at Carlisle Indian School. He knew that I had attended a latter-day version thereof, and he felt that some first-hand contemporary testimony would be beneficial to their assignment. But the night before, I had a strange premonitory dream: as I began my talk to the class, people in black robes entered the back of the room and promptly took over, showing an old film on an old-fashioned projector, to futile and fading remonstrances from me.

I initiated my actual talk the next day by recounting this dream, as a segue to the "black robes," to the Jesuit priests and brothers at Holy Rosary Mission who ruled my life for one year in the mid-1960s. I was silent, however, about what I myself took as the ultimate import of the dream: that my own talk would likely be ruled, unconsciously, by my internalization of their dictates—that, in sum, they had still won. And the fact that one of the students in the front row was a Catholic nun actually bore this out—especially when she subsequently brought a formal complaint against me to the English Department Chair for my dastardly "apostasy." The nun/student expressed "anger and outrage" at my presentation, to which she had every right. But was I, then, supposed to repress my own anger and outrage at being physically and psychologically abused by the appointed/anointed servants of the Lord? And hasn't such suppression been the fate of minorities throughout the history of Western Christian imperialism—to be silenced? I could—I can—no longer hold my tongue.

Five, ten, fifteen, twenty. Canyon Lake is really just a dammed-up part of Rapid Creek, which continues its flow from west to east, through the breadth of Rapid City, and so the last mile or so of my walk to the lake was along this creek. It was the nice part of town. North Rapid was for the poor and people of color; West Rapid was where the rich white folks lived: I knew this from listening to my mom talk but also just by looking at the houses and cars and people. After work, before Christmas, Mom would even pathetically drive us across town to West Rapid to look at the houses with "real" Christmas lights. I don't know if this was any part of the pull Canyon Lake had on me that day or not. Besides, by then I was pretty much frozen, so I didn't have time for class envy.

Western colonization was spearheaded not only by the military forces of the Custers and Sheridans of the US Army and Cavalry, but by their complicit confreres of religious proselytizing, the Christian missionaries. Together, in what I would dub a "Christo-Custer colonialism," they performed a two-fisted attack upon the Plains Indian tribes, and must have seemed a very strange Janus-faced figure, with a Winchester rifle in one hand and a King James Bible in the other—the "bad cop" brute force of avaricious gold-and-land-grabbing conquest justified by "good cop" ideological rationalizations and sanctimoniousness. As Ojibwe author Gerald Vizenor more cleverly puts it, the colonial enterprise combined the "bilingual signs of calvary and cavalry."[6] There is a certain terrible symmetry in the zeal of the Colonel Custers of the late nineteenth century and the Christian missionaries from first contact on in treating both the Plains environment and its Native people as *tabula rasas,* empty containers in need of being filled with good ol' civilization. Both conquest and Christianization were driven by the same ideology that not only framed my Indian boarding school experience, but also transformed the northern Great Plains into a paean to the glories of US colonialism and capitalism—and an accompanying closet theocracy. Vine Deloria's joke in *Custer Died for Your Sins* retains its black, sardonic humor to this day: "It has been said of the missionaries that when they arrived they had only the Book and we had the land; now we have the Book and they have the land."[7]

In general, the Western colonization of the Native, short of a total holocaust, has entailed a forceful internalization of the imperialist *Weltanschauung* on the part of the colonized, to the point that the result has been a veritable near-destruction of Indigenous cultures and psyches. Holy Rosary Mission was on a mission of culture-slaughter, of social genocide and deicide; it *was* a colonial act. By the mid-1960s, when I was there, sure, there was no doubt a good majority of Lakota parents who had already been "successfully" proselytized, who did think that raising their kids as Catholics or Episcopalians was a laudable—or at least necessary—thing. (Five, ten, fifteen, twenty.) My own Indian mom was already Christianized—and also desperate—enough to think that an Indian Catholic boarding school would be fine for my brother and me. Even my old French-Indian Mnikoju granny had been at least a nominal Catholic, in spite of suffering the slings and arrows of blatant racism in Fort Pierre, South Dakota. But that didn't make it right. What they and their kids suffered was a wholesale erasure of anything Indigenous, an onslaught upon the Lakota way of life and language. Above all, it was a brainwashing into Western theology, which says there is only one (very-human-like) god, and that therefore the eagle (*wanbli*) and the bison (*tatanka*) and the Western Meadowlark (*tašiyagnunpa*)—and yes, the Common Goldeneye—have no part in deity, are no longer *wakan*. Even from a (non-Indian) ecological point of view, that's complete anathema, or should be.

Diné writer Berenice Levchuk's call to memory regarding the more famous Carlisle Indian school also applies to Holy Rosary:

> We must especially remember those who died at Carlisle and never returned home. [. . .] Cruel and unconscionable policy and practices forever robbed the students of their natural childhood and youth. [. . .] There must be a healing of all generations of Native Americans who, as children and youth, have become stunted and crippled physically, emotionally, and spiritually by the boarding-school system. The boarding-school experience must be remembered and told in its true reality. [. . .] Those of us who have been scarred by the boarding-school system should unashamedly tell the whole story of this phase of our Native American holocaust.[8]

To reinforce the brainwashing of the Mission, we were forced to attend Mass seven days a week. As a member of the choir, I learned to sing an ecclesiastical chant that haunts me to this day. In E Phrygian minor, the tune runs e-f-d-e. The absence of a major or minor third gives this particular snippet of melody an especially creepy, alien sound, and before 1980s death metal, the Phrygian mode automatically evoked for me rope-cinctured monks in a European monastery of the Middle Ages, perhaps performing self-flagellation or some other perversion of the Lord. Then there is the irony of the words I was actually singing: "*LORD, HAVE MER-CY.*" It only occurred to me years later, as I pondered a Church complicit in the butchering at Wounded Knee, to ask—how bloody merciful *was* all that? (There are many bullets in the Mission yet.)

And then there was dormitory life. Every Friday and Saturday night, the attending Jesuit Brother would play a recording of Edvard Grieg's *Peer Gynt Suite,* highlighted by the tune "In the Hall of the Mountain King." I'm pretty sure that that melody was meant for our edification and dismay, a replication of the terrors of Hell that kept all little Indian boys awake, fearfully conscious of their sins, and thankfully conscious of the rewards of Christian salvation. No officially sanctioned Catholic hymn could have been more effective. But there was little room for protest: a good old unGodly Anglo-Saxon swear word on my part drove Sister Bonaventure to feed me a bar of soap. The same fate, or worse, awaited any boy who ventured to speak Lakota. My younger brother was an even worse miscreant, a spawn from some lower level of Dante's Inferno, apparently, and he became the Brothers' favorite whipping boy—quite literally. I saw him beaten interminably by the Brothers, by a paddle at least an inch thick. They greeted each peccadillo on our part with a swift series of swats to the buttocks, to the point that I once watched my brother slam his head into the concrete wall several feet away after a particularly vicious blow. It is no surprise that Foucault points to the ecclesiastical origin of the paddle when he describes "that little apparatus used by the Brothers of the Christian Schools," where it was simply called the "Signal"—that is, a brute signifier of pain and punishment.[9]

Mary Crow Dog, author of *Lakota Woman,* attended the Catholic boarding school one reservation over from Pine Ridge—Rosebud—about the same time, noting similar physical abuse: "When I was there [at St. Francis], during the 1960s, it was still run by the Church. The Jesuit fathers ran the boys' wing and the Sisters of the Sacred Heart ran us—with the help of the strap. Nothing had changed since my grandmother's days. I have been told recently that even in the 70s they were still beating children at that school."[10] (There are many bullets in the Mission yet.)

So there it was, a Common Goldeneye, swimming on the still open, snow-banked creek—paddling really hard in place, I guessed, against the mad rush of the water. This relatively neophyte birder was surprised, being mostly used to the summer puddle-duck Mallards. And it looked kind of like a Mallard at first, with its green head. But the green was more neon, and there was a large, white inverted teardrop behind its bill, below its eye, the color of the snowbanks beside it. Of course I had my bird guide, and I quickly thumbed through the pages of ducks: "New species!," I mentally exclaimed, blowing on my fingers for warmth. I had at the time only a faint knowledge that many species of ducks, thanks to their thermal feather structure, actually summered and bred in the far north, and only came south in the winter for the nearest open water. My main emotional impression at the time: what a lone, brave "sonsabitch." My other main emotional impression of that day was getting yelled out royally by Mom when I finally got my frozen cheeks home, for going on yet another insanely long winter walk.

We decided to run away from Holy Rosary once, my brother and me. (If there's any common thread to Indian boarding school narratives, it is this running away.) Not from any consciousness of fleeing the tyranny of colonialist ideology; no—we were just so fucking tired of being physically and psychologically beaten to a pulp. But we were also too young and stupid to realize that home—Rapid City—was almost a hundred miles away. We only got about two or three miles, I figure, through the cactus-ridden semi-desert terrain before we gave up—after just too many "five, ten, fifteen, twenties," I guess—and lay down on the side of the highway, waiting for the Jesuit van to find us and take us back, whipped as we were by both the natural forces of a cactus-ridden habitat and a good deal of Catholic guilt. They picked us up in a van, right along the highway, to our willing return—to the greatest swats on the ass we had ever received. Since most of their boys were from the immediate Pine Ridge area, the Jesuits were little used to such flights from God's true justice. Ergo, God's true justice smote us mightily.

"Make no mistake: a holocaust happened here in our lands and it continues here and elsewhere." So writes Dakota poet and scholar Elizabeth Cook-Lynn—in 2007. She continues: "Anti-Indianism is a concept in American Christian life, just as Islamophobia and anti-Semitism are concepts in Christian Europe." Cook-Lynn sees this Western monomania for cultural and religious imperialism as still controlling US foreign policy, in a quite sinister way.[11] Indeed, it was pretty symptomatic that, immediately after the events of 9/11, the US Administration immediately appealed to the old tried-and-true binary of "civilization" versus "barbarism." Given the brutal history of nineteenth-century US expansionism, there is a certain irony in the congratulatory self-appellation of "civilization" here. Ironic, too, was the too-common sentiment, in the wake of 9/11, that those against the Administration's war-monger policies were dubbed unfit Americans who should leave the country, who should "go back where they came from." As someone part Native American, that left me in something of a quandary.

What seemed to anger the Jesuits even more than running away was the game we played at Holy Rosary Mission called Heaven or Hell. We were hardly conscious of the sacrilege involved, but the game's implications were certainly against the best tenets of the Papacy. We would retreat to a dirt hill behind the Mission cafeteria with a few marbles, and we etched a fine downward line in the loose dirt on the side of the hill, branching the line off into two directions: the left took you to Hell, the right, to Heaven. Thus with each roll of a marble, we parodically played out our own definitions of predestination and/or of good works, playing mock-Saint Peters in our own self-condemnations or self-ascensions. A pathetic reinscription of the dominant religion, no doubt, but it at least allowed us some feeling of compensatory self-agency in a Great White Theological Universe that seemed way too all-powerful and way beyond our ken.

D'Arcy McNickle's novel *The Surrounded* includes the protagonist Archilde's experience at an Indian boarding school, where, at one point, a cloud appears in the shape of a huge crucifix. The Indian boys are ordered by a Jesuit—who reads the cloudy cross as the "Sign!" of the Second Coming—to "Kneel and pray!" Archilde, on his way to his own apostasy and return to "paganism," is relieved when the shape dissolves:

It was not the disappearance of the threatening symbol which freed him from the priest's dark mood, but something else. At the very instant that the cross seemed to burn most brightly, *a bird* flew across it. [. . .] It flew past and returned several times before finally disappearing—and what seized Archilde's imagination was *the bird's unconcernedness. It recognized no "Sign."* His spirit lightened. He felt himself fly with the bird.

When Archilde later learns that his nephew is also struggling with his own rejection of Christianity via a "return to the Native," he says, "'Tell him it's all lies, what the priests say. It's all lies about the devil. Tell him to look at the birds. They fly around, and they don't know nothing about the devil. Look at them fly!'"[12]

Maybe I knew all this already: after all, I've always been looking at the birds. And as a boy, one winter morning close to Christmas, I saw my first Common Goldeneye.

When Catholic missionaries arrived in the Dakotas in the late nineteenth century, they were even then perceived as exotic interlopers, as evident in the following description from that era: Catholics "huddle together in the dark, shut off from modern thought, cherishing dear but exploded theories and legends, reviving antiquated customs, and seeking to impose them as laws upon others, thus binding living men to-day in the cerements of the dead past." These aren't the words of some freethinking atheist, a Nietzsche or a Madalyn Murray O'Hair. It was Episcopalian Bishop William Hobart Hare, one of the leading Protestant churchmen and missionaries of the late nineteenth century, himself later dubbed the "Apostle to the Sioux." Jon K. Lauck's recent history of the Dakota Territory makes much, in fact, of the importance of religion among the Dakota pioneers, although his main evidence brings up the unpleasant realities of Christian sectarian intolerance: "The friction between Catholics and Protestants demonstrates the passionate commitment to religion in Dakota Territory and in the rural Midwest in general." However, Lauck pretty much ignores the presence of Native peoples in the Dakotas, and the untidy fact that the criminalization of traditional Lakota ceremonial practices like the Sun Dance attested to an even greater religious friction at work at that time. Even when he speaks of intermarriage, this author can't seem to imagine that my Irish dad would want to marry a French-Lakota woman: "Religious and ethnic differences in Dakota Territory affected social life and such basic rituals as marriage. [. . .] Ethnic or religious intermarriage was discouraged"; such "ethnic and religious solidarity explains the origin of the old saw holding that a mixed marriage in the Dakotas was a union of a Catholic and a Lutheran."[13] Oh, but it got *so* much worse than that, Mr. Lauck.

Like my Irish dad, my uncle also married a Lakota woman, so I guess she was my aunt. Loud and opinionated, she was the prototypical harridan who kept her meek and sullen husband on the straight and narrow. She was obviously Indian-looking, like my mom, so I was always semi-shocked when we visited her house: on the living-room wall was a huge framed copy of maybe the most famous painting of the Little Bighorn battle, the one with Custer in the center, surrounded, but with his long blond hair flowing and his pistol blazing, ready to meet his heroic end. I finally asked her why she had hung that particular painting so prominently. She said, "Don't you know, Tommy? I'm a *descendant* of General *George Armstrong Custer!*" My mind curdled just a bit. Even this dark-skinned woman considered it a matter of pride to be related to such a splendid Indian killer.

My year at Holy Rosary Mission was not unmitigated torture, however. The Sisters and Brothers did foster my intellectual bent, to the point that I may have been one of the few third-graders in history to have memorized all the US presidents, all fifty state capitals, and—what I'm still most proud of—all fifty state birds. I had become—driven. I was a fourth-grader by year's end, having been untowardly advanced from the third to the fourth grade at the semester break because the sisters weren't exactly sure what to do with me. I also remember proudly watching the Holy Rosary Mission varsity basketball team cream St. Francis 93–37 in basketball. I never forgot the score.

I also recall one Jesuit Brother who was unusual in his kindness towards me, especially when we were occasionally away from the confines of the Mission. On those outdoor weekend excursions, he pointed out to me the newts and suckers in a narrow stream, and he showed me how to peel a prairie cactus for its fruit. In such ways he fostered my budding naturism. If, like the other Jesuits, he truly believed that his mission was the saving of heathen Indian souls, it never came across as his main agenda in our interactions. For that, at least, I am thankful. Of course, the irony was that, at the time, I had been a lifelong Catholic, anyway. Who were they saving me *from*: the Benedictines? The Franciscans?

Upon my return to the Rapid City school system, it took my white teachers a good year to get me to stop ending every other sentence with *en'eh* (rez dialect for "ain't it?"). I earnestly kept up my church-going ways, but only for a while, and I can only think now that my treatment at Holy Rosary Mission had something to do with both this monomaniacal drive for theological meaning— *and* my giving up on it, from some intuition of its cultural insufficiency. As for Holy Rosary Mission itself, a lot more forgetting had to take place: if my year there has been the matrix of a story ostensibly about a Common Goldeneye, it is also still the great aporia and black hole of my life, the still mostly silenced and haunting center of a maelstrom, a complex of repressed memories of a time and place best characterized by my constant fear of both corporal punishment and eternal damnation. For a long while in the backroom of my psyche, it felt as if an age of innocence that included a glorious Great Horned Owl had been woefully exchanged for a bitter worldview of guilt and sin and low ethnic and cultural self-esteem. I felt very cold. But had to go on. Five, ten, fifteen, twenty. . . . Sometimes I still hear the strains of "In the Hall of the Mountain King" as I fall asleep. And I dream of black robes, and of white minds.

✳ JUNE 1969, I-90: *Western Meadowlark*

I love bird songs. Nowadays I identify probably 90 percent of birds by ear before I see them—if I ever do see them. In this regard, *birder* is the much preferable term to the older *birdwatcher* because I have been more of a bird-*listener* for most of my life. That the term *birdwatcher* has also traditionally connoted some little old lady in tennis shoes haunting the city park is another huge strike against it.

Since I am a child of the Great Plains, the bird song that first really made me aware of the languages of birds was that of the Western Meadowlark. It is no accident that the Western Mead-owlark is without doubt *the* iconic bird of the Plains, from web-site banners to conference posters to state license plates.

But then the problem of anthropomorphism, the human-all-too-human, intervenes when one asks, why the meadowlark? Why not the Lark Bunting, or the Vesper Sparrow, or the Upland Sandpiper? Aside from its sheer volubility, I think it has some-thing to do with the extraverted optimism of the song. I might even claim that the adjective *ebullient* should be part of any bird guide's textual description of this species' vocal stylings. One of my old journal entries even hyperbolically refers to the bird's "Dionysian flute." An even older journal entry:

> 4/28/88: Meadowlarks & Mourning Doves singing out-side [in Belle Fourche, SD]: Joy & Sorrow incarnate. The Mourning Dove: "Oh, no-o-o more woe"! The male W. Meadowlark exclaims his flute-like warble, and is inevita-bly answered by a long chatter-rattle from the female. . . .

This is pretty much thoroughly human projective bullshit, of course, an erasure of the real bird via a longtime human bipolar discourse of tragedy versus comedy, of depression versus manic bliss. And it is straight from the nineteenth-century Roman-tic-poet playbook in which various birds became master tropes for both melancholia and mania, a script that Thoreau is simply rehearsing when he claims that the Eastern Screech-Owl says, "*Oh-o-o-o-o that I had never been bor-or-or-or-orn.*"[14]

How do you truly talk about the non-human animal other?: Above all, it was necessary to avoid fables. We know the history of fabulization and how it remains an anthropo-morphic taming, a moralizing subjection, a domestication. Always a discourse *of* man, on man, indeed on the animal-ity of man, but for and as man.[15]

Samuel Taylor Coleridge got it half-right when he slammed centuries of British poetry for forcing "The Nightingale" into the "melancholy" compartment of human affects:

'Most musical, most melancholy' Bird!
A melancholy Bird? Oh! idle thought!
In nature there is nothing melancholy.

Bravo. But characteristically, the poet can combat this cultural cli-ché only by forcing this other species towards the other (human) emotional extreme: "'Tis the *merry* Nightingale," after all, whose "fast thick warble" is a veritable "*love*-chant."[16] It may seem like hard-heartedness on my part to say that, in nature, there is also nothing mirthful and merry-making, in a specifically human sense. Songbirds may well take great "joy" in their vocal effusive-ness, but my point is that there's a danger—of eco-colonialism, if you will—in applying human attributes and emotions to other species, a colonialism not unrelated to the racialized primitivist discourse about Native Americans.

So the Western Meadowlark is pretty much mania incarnate, with all the human baggage that entails. However, its rapid-fire whistled song of great melodic leaps and a final descending trill belies its genetics, for the meadowlark is really an icterid, a mem-ber of the American blackbird family, close kin to those kings of croak, redwings and grackles. But the icterids also include the Baltimore Oriole, that singer of near-human melodic whistling, one of North America's most beloved songbirds. For some reason, I really like that the grackle's *check* and "rusty-swing" *schleenk* calls issue from the same avian ancestor as the oriole's pure, anthemic whistles of major thirds and perfect fourths, and the meadowlark's effervescent warble, and I recall Wallace Stevens's attempt to tie his high modernist aesthetics to the mundane: "Crow is realist. But, then, / Oriole, also, may be realist." Stevens's more usual blackbird/grackle works like the crow in this binary, epitomized in his blackbird of "Thirteen Ways," who "Walks around the feet / Of the women" among a group of religious aesthetes, the "thin men of Haddam," who prefer to "imagine golden birds."[17] The *check*-ing blackbird is one of Stevens's greatest manifestations of the sheer anti-metaphysical mundanity of existence. But at last, those "golden" singers, the orioles and meadowlarks, are also part and parcel of the wonderful avian *real* that surrounds us.

According to Collins's ancient field guide (1959), the Western Meadowlark says, "*Hip! Hip! Hurrah! boys; three cheers!*" You could ask ten thousand people to transcribe a meadowlark's song into human words, and I'd bet not one would match this earnest fratboy huzzah. There is a certain New Historicist pleasure in looking at such old phonetic transcriptions and seeing the bundle of ideologies that ruled the US in the first half of the twentieth century. Thumbing through these crinkled pages, I see a whitestream society that is saccharinely positive about its self-identity: its very birds, after all, are in general so damned sweet, so damned cheerful, so damned social—and so damned morally pure, of course—though they *do* like their beer. The Olive-sided Flycatcher gives sports-obsessed Americans the pleasure of a "collegiate whistle of *hip,* THREE CHEERS"; this is "also written *quick THREE BEERS*"—the latter brew no doubt augmenting the cheering mightily. And, oh, the sweetness of our birds (and thus ourselves): the Barn Swallow calls "*sweeter-sweet sweeter-sweet*"; the Yellow Warbler sings "*sweet, sweet, sweet, I'm so sweet*"; the Black-capped Chickadee has "a sweet whistled *FEE bee*"; and the Rose-breasted Grosbeak sings "a beautiful rolling sugary warble, like a Robin that has had singing lessons!" The Carolina Wren's trisyllabic whistle is either "*sweet William, sweet William, sweet William*" or "*tea-kettle, tea-kettle, tea-kettle*," as if these wild American songbirds are also paragons of middle-class tea-party domesticity. And so, too, the Eastern Towhee's wonderful trill-song has traditionally been heard as "*drink your tea-e-e-e.*" In sum, a whole lot of these transliterations smack of a certain smug bourgeois (and feminized) kitchen-table comfortability.

All of this is enough to make one sing a Mourning Dove's "mournful *coo-ah, coo coo*"—and brings me back to my main point, and to Thoreau's screech-owl and Coleridge's nightingale. Consider that "Mourning" and "mournful" are human projections of what is, after all, a bird's *mating* call: how could such an utterance be mournful in any veritable way, outside of the projections of a melancholy civilization? For it is ultimately the most melancholy civilizations whose superficial discourse is largely one of compensatory sweetness and light.

For many, the meadowlark on the Great Plains evokes a nostalgia for the frontier—for an American West and Midwest where cowboy and settler (still) meet the human Native and the non-human "wild." But nostalgia issues from the consciousness that one is now beyond that past, a belated modernist point of view that includes both an implicit hubris in having transcended such things and a yearning for and an ongoing mourning for the loss of said past. This specific nostalgia for the "primitive" West, from the Euro-colonizers' stance, also necessarily involves the liminality of borders, the fear of and fascination with the sheer difference between "us" and "them": of the Western Self versus the Indigenous Other, of the "civilized" human versus the incredible alterity of the American land itself. And the Others that the settlers encountered in this new land were both human and non-human, those feather-wearing Indians and those even more alien beings, like the Western Meadowlark, born with feathers.

Imagine for a moment, if you will, Lewis and Clark's, or even Willa Cather's, first encounter with the meadowlark's primordial prairie song (I doubt very much that it sang—to their minds— "*Hip! Hip! Hurrah! boys; three cheers!*"). We have to re-imagine, between that pure sound and the subsequent cognition, the truck-load of cultural overlay that these "pioneers" brought to bear upon the song of a bird. I would prefer to view indigenous bird species as unconquered Native tribes that have escaped the imposed borders of Western colonization, and that serve as seminal and liminal reminders of our "frontier"—or "earthier"—heritage, as it were. However, we are "always a little too eager to hear the cultural mutterings of" our "own well-stocked mind[s]," as Scott Russell Sanders has said of Emerson.[18] The calls we hear from the high sky tonight of migrating Snow Geese or Sandhill Cranes *should* evoke from us a jolt of electricity up our spines that speaks through the Kristevan *sémiotique,* perhaps—the pre-linguistic hum of life and the womb itself, if you will—or of a time before Western rationalism turned us into cogitating primates out of touch with our animal selves. But let it be and remain forever just that jolt, that *élan,* even that *jouissance*—for, as soon as the avian is translated into phonetic transliterations and Romantic poems—and books like this—the "other" has already been ruined, translated into the human same.

My own eco-philosophy argues that other species partake of a radical alterity that needs to be granted its due, largely through a removal of the reins (and reign) of human ideology—as much as this is possible. But then, I find myself of two minds, like a fence-line with two meadowlarks. There is an alternative tradition and worldview in which the Western Meadowlark is interpellated into the human "family," and I can't say, from my jaundiced postmodern point of view, that this reading of the bird is any less valid. For my Lakota ancestors, the meadowlark—*tašiyagnunpa*—was the bird closest to the people: "Meadowlarks spoke so often and so helpfully that they were recognized as 'the birds that spoke Lakota.'" This close relationship even expressed itself in the very *melodies* of Lakota songs, usually quoted out of their musical context. Examining Frances Densmore's transcription of one of Sitting Bull's songs, Kenneth Lincoln notes that, with its "descending fourth and two cascading thirds," it is "something like a prophetic meadowlark's song, a recurring pattern in plains chants." Sitting Bull was a lifelong interlocutor with the birds, including the flicker and the meadowlark; he was thus an "interspecies *wicasa wakán* or visionary, beginning when a yellowhammer [flicker] warned the boy of a threatening bear." It was a meadowlark that warned him of his imminent murder just before the Wounded Knee massacre.[19]

I apologize for putting this discussion of Lakota beliefs in the past tense, but the reality is that the "bird who speaks Lakota" has been speaking less and less. One of Julian Rice's Lakota interviewees tellingly complains of a latter-day "alienation from nature which *wasicu* [Euro-American] polarities have brought about": now we no longer understand the meadowlarks. Standing Bear's similar account of this fall from animal grace, as it were, is even more poignant in its naïveté: "The larks in our State

[South Dakota], at that time, talked the Sioux language—at least, we inferred that they did; but in California, where I now live, it is impossible to understand them. Perhaps they are getting too civilized."[20] Ultimately, this reflects Standing Bear's own "devolution," if you will, in which, through acculturation, he loses his connection with meadowlark language. It is really the human author here who is "getting too civilized." Readers can make what they will of the traditional Lakota worldview—of close kinship with other Plains animals—and it probably should remain an alien cultural otherness unto itself, free of New Age interlopers. But the perceived distancing from the language of birds is symptomatic of a general degeneration of trans-species connectedness brought on by Western acculturation—and by a thoroughgoing anthropocentric Western worldview in general.

Her mother and I divorced, my daughter Emma came for a visit the summer she was ten years old, and I took her birding with me one early morning. To keep her entertained, I had her keep "our" bird list: she would write down the birds "we" identified as I rattled off their names. By 10 a.m., parked at a riverside stop, I saw that she was already asleep in the passenger seat. Smiling—oh, the poor little pooped-out darling!—I picked up the pocket notebook from her lap and saw scribbled, as species #12, "Western Metal Lark." Now *that's* a human projection I can live with.

Two years later, another bird trip and list. This time she spelled "oriole" as "oreo." But then, I suppose that Oreo, too, may be realist.

That most renowned of all Nebraska writers, Willa Cather, titled her third novel *The Song of the Lark*. According to *A Reader's Companion* to her fiction, the Western Meadowlark, "common in Nebraska and the West," is "mentioned in several of Willa Cather's novels," including in the preface of this novel.[21] But a quick check reveals the bird to be the European Skylark, an unrelated species and also a bookish, artsy reference of the first order. Even the book's very title does not issue from her home-state songster of fields and fenceposts, but rather from a French painting—itself called *The Song of the Lark*—which Thea, the protagonist, sees in a Chicago museum. There is only one direct reference to the meadowlark in the entire novel, when Thea returns to Nebraska: "It was over flat lands like this [. . .] that the larks sang—and one's heart sang there, too." Even here, the lark's song immediately becomes that of a human "heart" that, as the passage clarifies, is drunk on the ideology of "immigration," on the attraction to a "young and fresh"—because empty—land that was hardly empty at all.[22]

This symptomatic erasure of the real bird is part and parcel of Cather's general erasure of the Great Plains life that preceded Euro-American colonialism. In *My Ántonia*, the narrator Jim Burden experiences an ontological crisis upon his first view of the Plains, as if he were face-to-face with a geographical vacuum: "There seemed to be *nothing* to see; no fences, no creeks or trees, no hills or fields. If there was a road, I could not make it out in the faint starlight. There was *nothing but land*: not a country at all, but the material out of which countries are made."[23] Of course this land was actually teeming with the "countries" of other species—and the tribes of other humans—as already recorded in the nineteenth-century journals of Lewis and Clark, and John James Audubon, and George A. Custer. If the dominant large mammal, the American Bison, had already had its numbers decimated by hunting and outright slaughter, the songs of the meadowlark and the flights of the crane still attested, in Cather's day, to a native bioregion very much vibrant and alive. Cather also conveniently (and characteristically) ignored other human cultures and nations who had peopled these plains for millennia, and whose own myths, folklore, and songs revealed a longtime close co-evolution with both the bison and the birds of this region. It's pretty lamentable, then, that this very quotation from *My Ántonia*—about the Plains as *nothingness*—is inscribed on the first wall that visitors see upon entering Lincoln's Great Plains Art Museum. And so the discourse of colonialism marches on.

> Maybe it was a good thing that they would not let us Indians keep that land. Think of what would have been missed: the motels with their neon signs, the pawn shops, [. . .] the Genuine Indian Crafts Center with beadwork from Taiwan and Hong Kong, the Sitting Bull Cave—electrically lighted for your convenience—the Shrine of Democracy Souvenir Shop. [. . .] Just think: if that land belonged to us there would be nothing here, only trees, grass and some animals running free. All that *real estate* would be going to waste![24]

Again, in contrast to John Lame Deer's "let-be" Lakota attitude towards the natural realm expressed above, Anglo-American explorers, military people, and writers—including Cather—have notoriously found the "New World" to be an anxiety-producing, fearsome emptiness and void, in need of being filled up with things. But there has never been anything empty about the Plains.

To signal the end of a short in-class exam one day, I selected a

Western Meadowlark song on my iPhone. As the timer sounded with the bird's effusion at exam's end, I got a crazy idea: "One bonus point if you write down the correct name of that singing bird." They looked at me puzzled, perplexed, as if I had lost my mind. "For crying out loud," I said, "it's the state bird of Nebraska!"—as I played the song again. They looked at me puzzled, perplexed, as if I had lost my freaking mind. Oh, Nature Deficit Disorder: I gave another timed exam in a second class and, among about sixty students that fine April morning, not one got the bonus question right. But I admit that "Yellow-throated Warbler" was a pretty good guess.

✳ APRIL 1970, FORT PIERRE / MISSOURI RIVER: *Sandhill Crane*

> There is a bird in the heart of North America that is perhaps even older than the river. [. . .] It is as gray as the clouds of winter, as softly beautiful and graceful as the flower heads of Indian grass and big bluestem, and its penetrating bugle-like notes are as distinctive and memorable as the barking of a coyote or the song of a western meadowlark. This bird is the sandhill crane.
>
> —Paul A. Johnsgard[25]

R-r-r-r-r-r-r. *R-r-r-r-r-r-r.* *R-r-r-r-r-r-r.* When as a boy I first heard the cranes migrating up the Missouri River at Fort Pierre, South Dakota, I immediately re-imagined their sound as this long, drawn-out rolling French *r*: *r-r-r-r-r-r-r-r-r-r-r-r.* (That I took French from the fourth grade on is no doubt largely responsible for this thoroughly objective and scientific observation.) I remember these Fort Pierre summer evenings because Grandma Mollie would walk my brothers and me down to the mouth of the Bad River, where it met the Missouri. The white-fluff "cotton" from the cottonwood trees would float into our mouths against our will, and the humidity of the small river town was intense, but we were with our grandma, Mollie Hackett, probably the kindest woman in the world, who was a fry cook in the mornings, a motel maid in the afternoons, and whom the whole town loved, we were certain. Only now does it occur to me how exhausted that poor little Indian woman—already close to sixty at the time—must have been, taking us fishing after working two jobs all day. We boys had our cheap Zebco 77 fishing rods and reels, and Grandma had her little silver-tweed-faced transistor radio with a telescoping antenna. We threw our lines in, hoping for a big catfish but ready to be fully satisfied by a small walleye, and Grandma set her radio carefully down on the rip-rap and turned on the Minnesota Twins game. The voice of the legendary play-by-play man Herb Carneal tried its best to speak across the Missouri, as the mighty Harmon Killebrew came to the plate. Flies gathered about us, but they were as harmlessly lazy as we were in the evening heat. Lazy we were, and happy. I closed my eyes and heard *r–r–r–r–r–r–r–r, r–r–r–r–r–r–r–r, r–r–r–r–r–r–r–r.*

Nebraska's most famous ornithologist, Paul Johnsgard, describes going to see the cranes in Nebraska as a religious pilgrimage:

> The splendor of several thousand cranes flying up and down the river as nightfall approaches [. . .] with the juvenile birds calling constantly in their distinctive baby voices [. . .] touches one's soul at so many levels that it is hard not to weep from the utter magic and power of it all. After every such experience I am as emotionally drained as I am

after hearing a perfect performance of a Beethoven symphony. [. . .] The word "religion" comes from the Latin word *religio,* meaning a bond between humans and the gods, and [. . .] cranes provide that connection perfectly. Often appearing miraculously from incredible heights like celestial seraphim [. . .] our Sandhill Cranes are every bit as wondrous as the angels painted on the ceiling of the Sistine Chapel. [. . .]

All wonderful and rare things in this world carry a significant price tag. [. . .] The price tag on our cranes is simply this: we must be willing to protect from destruction the wonderful river that crosses Nebraska like a beautiful quicksilver necklace, the Platte River. [. . .] It is a river that millions of bison once drank from, and one along which tens of thousands of immigrants once passed on their way to building a complete America. Wading in that graceful river is like wading into history. [. . .] Yet these are also rich gifts that we must be willing to protect, cherish, and finally pass on to our children as if they were our collective family's greatest treasures, which in fact they are.[26]

The passage above might be considered required content for every Nebraska tourism brochure, if it weren't so well-written—from the young cranes' "baby voices" and the Platte River as a "quicksilver necklace," to the final plea for ecological sanity. It is unfortunate, though, that Johnsgard believes these native birds need the analogical support of an Old World classical music and an Old World religion: the birds themselves, in their sheer living materiality, are the true wonders and our greatest treasures, after all, not some specific historical manifestations of human aesthetics and theology. The advent of European ideologies and peoples

to the continent—hellbent on "building a complete America" out
of the habitat of the Sandhill Crane—is exactly why the ornithologist must now call for conservation. And it is because of the
"tens of thousands of immigrants"—including Buffalo Bill and
his ilk—that "millions of bison" no longer drink from *any* river.

✳ JUNE 1970, A FORT PIERRE SLOUGH:
Wood Duck

We called him Pissy Percy. Or Uncle Percy, more usually,
although he was really our great-uncle, our Grandma Mollie's
brother. The "Pissy" part came after he awoke from a drunken
stupor one night to take a piss, and decided to take that piss from
the top of the stairs at Grandma's house, and then proceeded to
break his hip by slipping on his own urine when he tried to walk
down those stairs. So it was Pissy Percy—with a cane—those last
few years of his life.

Grandma Mollie's old, square two-story wood-frame house
in Fort Pierre was the annual month-or-so summer vacation
spot for us Gannon boys—a welcome respite, no doubt, for our
frazzled working mom, and our own heaven-on-earth of sorts,
living with a non-frazzled old Indian woman who seemed almost
always in a good mood and who almost never said no. In sum,
a grandmother. For me, this life on the Missouri was a wonder-
land of fishing and birding; besides the big river itself and Oahe
Dam, there was a black water slough on the south side of Fort
Pierre that began only a half block away from Grandma's—a
paradise for waterbirds that I had little chance to encounter in
my native Black Hills. Prehistoric-looking Great Blue Herons,
Green Herons, even an elusive Virginia Rail, flew onto my life

Percy Frenier in the US Army, 1940?

list, with their short flights and low squawks and awkward wing beats.

Already the inveterate introvert, I found this slough to be a ready escape from Grandma's house, which was the center of social activity for all of our *tiošpaye* (extended family) in Pierre and Ft. Pierre. Every morning, several of my aunts and/or uncles and/or cousins stood or circled around the kitchen table with coffee cups in hand, the late arrivers looking in from the screen door, everyone telling stories—maybe about peculiar nephews wandering about with binoculars—and laughing endlessly, Grandma Mollie's laughter ringing loud above the others.

The morning I was off to see my first Wood Duck, Percy would have still been upstairs, sleeping off another night of bourbon and poker, while the rest of the *tiošpaye* were keeping the oral tradition and home fires going. We Gannon boys watched and wondered about Percy, half in awe—he was a WWII vet who had swum the Missouri as a younger man, by God!—and half in anxious consternation, because of his drinking. It wasn't unlike the mixed feelings I felt later as a young man, drinking a beer, or three, myself and listening to the song about another drunken Indian hero, Ira Hayes—and wondering if I should be proud or heartbroken: it seemed so easy to be too much or not enough of either.

The Percy story most often recounted around Grandma Mollie's table was about the time he'd won all that money at the Stanley County Fairgrounds. I had been a major player in this epic tale, since I had picked the horse he'd bet on and won with. Already well into his cups, Percy had followed the hunch of a wide-eyed eight-year-old (me) who knew even less about horses than he did about human sociality. But—as far as anyone knows—the horse won. And then Percy got even drunker, and supposedly, on an inebriated lark, he buried his winnings of several hundred dollars outside the concession stand. I must have wandered off, since the kitchen-table retellings often included the question, "Tommy, why didn't you follow him?" Or the admonition: "Tommy, you should have followed him!" To which I could only shrug. Well, the whole *tiošpaye* dug around for that money for days, circling the place where Percy swore he thought he (might have) buried it.

The male Wood Duck appeared several summers later, swimming like a mute clown prince in the slough just a block down the road from Grandma's house. Its face was a hallucinatory kaleidoscope, a gawd-awfully gaudy tapestry of green and white and red-orange and black, and its head was crested in the back like a bad toupée, but more gracefully. It was a glorious sighting, but . . . I've got myself thinking about Percy again right now.

Whenever I teach Mohawk poet Maurice Kenny's "Reading Poems in Public," I think of Percy. The Native poet is reading poems to a non-Native audience, "poems of boys broken on the road," poems about "old chiefs swindled of their daughters, / young braves robbed of painted shields." But what does the audience want to know? They "ask if Indians shave." And I sometimes even share my memory with my class, that I had this great-uncle Percy who, like a lot of Lakota men, only had these two or three long chin hairs. I told them that I was just a boy then, who had very badly wanted to ask him, "Is that supposed to be your *beard*, Uncle Percy? Or are you just too lazy to shave? I mean, it's just, like, three whiskers, right, so you're thinking, to hell with it?" But I had always been too afraid to ask.

Towards Percy's end, that last summer, I remember falling asleep one night to Grandma crying downstairs, telling Percy, just home from another drunken night out, "If you don't stop drinking, Percy, it's gonna kill me!" Well, it killed Percy first, and not long afterwards. Like Ira Hayes in a ditch, I suppose, he was found shivering, dying in the snow, walking home from another drunken poker game. The last Percy story for the kitchen-table *tiošpaye* involved his last words: "They said he kept repeating the number *nine* over and over as he lay dying in the snow. Tommy, do you think he was talking about a poker hand?" To which I could only shrug. There was something in the mythopoeic child in me that wanted to remember him as something more than a drunken loser at cards, as, above all, "Great-uncle Percy"—even if my own mythopoetics tended towards the maudlin:

As a young man, Percy Frenier, of French
And Lakota blood, swam all the way across
The Missouri River, at Ft. Pierre, South Dakota—
Or so he told us, my two brothers and me,
As we lay all elbows, chins in palms, before this
Grown Buck Warrior that was our grandma's brother.
And then there was the War, the Second one
Between taut Arian nations, but Percy knew
No awkwardness of allegiance, jumped out of planes
Over that sea-skewed square on the map called France
As if on some dream-time moonlit raid for horses
From the next camp: new quest, in a painted box.
But then there were other times, after these first
Awed impressions—late nights home, and later
Harangues and sobs, and once my grandma saying,
"If anything happens to you, then I'll die, too."
Happen? To Percy? A few drinks on the town,
Fit for a war hero, a Hector just a bit
Beyond his time—yet we kids looked inside
And saw a spider smirking on the walls
Of our whole race, and feared, and walked more slowly

To the town's swimming pool, and—dread night—
For then there was that time we were still up,
Watching the Carson show, or something, and Percy came
Down the steep steps from upstairs, stopping halfway,
And taking a piss right on the stairs, step-slipping
Onto his own urine, falling then,
And breaking his hip. And we laughed, later,
Dubbing him "Pissy Percy" at the swimming pool—
"Old Pissy Percy!" Well, six months later,
Percy resumed his drinking—with a cane,
And slower gait, and slower voice, and slower
Smile on our grandma's face, and I saw, too,
The waters of the Missouri grow less wide,
And the air over France less high, and even God
Assumed a Power less ample, Good less good.
Then all gods died the night Percy came home
Drunk from a poker game—or rather, never
Came home at all—found trembling, in a ditch,
Chanting a number: "Nine . . . Nine . . . Nine. . . ."
And Grandma later guessed it was the card
He'd needed in a poker hand, but I
Balked at such closure, unless "Nine" could be
The number of times he'd jumped on Mother France,
Or times that he swam, proud, the Great Missouri,
Or the number of horses he'd brought home that Great
        Night
In a dream I have—that maybe Percy had.

One last thing: as the poem says, Percy's—and Grandma's
maiden—French-Indian last name was Frenier. As someone
who took French more semesters than I want to remember, I can

assert that I never heard it pronounced the French way (*fren-yay*) during my Fort Pierre summers, but I did hear it pronounced at least *two* Anglicized ways instead, adding to the mythos—or confusion—regarding good Uncle Percy. When I interviewed my mother a few years ago for another book project, she said that, when she was a child, the other kids and townspeople—and the elder Freniers themselves?—pronounced it *FREN-yer*. Percy and his brother Louis (pronounced *Lewie*) were then young men just starting out in their own business and—apparently putting on some uppity Frenchified airs—they interjected, "No, it's pronounced *fruh-NEER!*" Still rather a faux/near-French. My translation: "We may be half-breed Indians, but we're not your *ordinary* half-breed Indians, damn it!" Life is pretty much a series of such small—and usually pretty laughable—compensations and self-reinscriptions, I suppose. Maybe I should just be happy that we all pronounced "Louis" without the *s*.

✳ AUGUST 1971, SASKATCHEWAN:
Western Grebe

> Thirty miles to the north lay Canada. It occurred to him that he had never been to Canada. Once in high school they had scheduled a game with a Canadian town. [. . .] but they didn't get to make the trip. The road north out of Harlem had been drifted shut. As Loney looked at the prairies he thought of the name of that town—Val Marie. It still sounded so foreign that he couldn't help wishing, even now, that they had made the trip.
>
> —James Welch[27]

Marie is my mom's name. Or rather it's Genevieve, but no one ever called her that, as far as I know. "Marie" is her middle name.

A divorcée who re-entered the workforce by the time I was in fourth grade in order to get us off welfare, she worked at Job Service of South Dakota until retirement, while pretty much raising us four devil-spawn sons on her own. In September 1985, she was named Indian Employee of the Month by an entity called the Indian/White Relations Committee. As the certificate states, the award was for "serving as a role model for both Indian and White communities." I kidded her at the time that she probably didn't have a lot of competition. But I guess it's really not that funny.

One might ask why they even needed an Indian/White Relations Committee. Well, western South Dakota was, and still is, a pretty racist place. And with, historically, very few Black or LatinX folks to be racist towards, it's all about the Indian here, as the sons and daughters of Scandinavian, German, and Irish rancher-settlers moved to the nearest urban center (Rapid City) and maintained much of their traditional deep enmity towards the local Natives, an ethnic/culture war that may have peaked with Custer vs. Crazy Horse but that continues to this day. Speaking about the very decades of my mom's racial travails, Mary Crow Dog has testified, "In South Dakota white kids learn to be racists almost before they learn to walk." Likewise, in Susan Power's *Roofwalker,* one of her Native characters asserts, "Whites in Rapid City feel about Ind'ins the way the KKK in Mississippi feels about blacks."[28]

In an official Rapid City press release about the award, mom's supervisor is quoted: "Gannon is an extremely conscientious and dedicated employee"; furthermore, she's "totally dependable and reliable." *Ouch.* Of course, any comparable (white) man of the month would need no such emphasis on dependability and reliability. Translation: "We found an Indian who shows up for work!" Her supervisor continued: "Gannon is a single parent and raised four boys. While no easy task this has given her a work ethic we all could use."[29] The subtle condescension still rankles.

Mom herself put on a brave face about it. In her own words quoted in the release: "You can't be a quitter. Otherwise, you're always running away from yourself. Twenty years ago there weren't the opportunities for Indians that we have today." And yet, I remember several times my mom coming home, sobbing, because her workmates (including supervisors) had called her "squaw." Up there with the N-word, it's probably the worst word one can call a Native: it roughly means "you no-good savage/animalistic whore of a woman of color." So yes, my mom used to come home from work bawling. There are no tears heavier than that. This racist job harassment happened well into the 1980s, and it was done by good-old-boy white males who, I know, actually considered Marie to be their friend. She couldn't even tell them how much that awful, wretched name hurt, and so she held her tears until she got home. Indian/White Relations Committee, indeed.

Worst of all, I remember my own white dad calling my mom "squaw" many times during the few preschool years I was "lucky" enough to have them together. For better or worse, I've repressed most of the specifics of these dreaded racist primal scenes.

Mom was driven, from the beginning, to make a decent life for us kids. And she did her best in this regard, despite the many cards stacked against her. She took great care that we boys maintained a strong connection with the older generation, especially with Grandma Mollie and her brother Percy. And that's how we all ended up in Canada.

I don't remember much about that weeklong trip. I vaguely remember how uneventful it was crossing the border into Canada,

G. Marie Gannon, high school graduation photo, Fort Pierre, SD, 1955

something like stopping at the front gate of a state park. And the wheat fields and grasslands of Saskatchewan looked a hell of a lot like those of North and South Dakota, as far as I could see. I also remember being irritated by the many stops that Grandma and/or Uncle Percy required. But then, I was just barely a teenager, with little patience for anyone else's needs and desires; perhaps the *main* feeling I had throughout the trip was how out of place and alien I felt, even among close family members. I do remember going to a museum in Regina, where I heard a couple speaking very rapid Canadian French. I couldn't make out much, but I didn't feel too deflated, since my French teacher from the south of France had warned me about the difficulty of understanding a Québécois accent. Most of all, I remember camping out at a big lake north of Regina and seeing on the lake a floating Common Loon and a bobbing Western Grebe, the latter being a lifer. I could wax euphoric for a paragraph or two about how cool and interesting these two eerie long-necked waterfowl are, but I won't. I'm more into feeling pissed off that I don't even know the name of the lake, and I never will. But really I'm pissed, right now, again, about Mom being called a "squaw."

James Welch's *The Death of Jim Loney* may be the most underrated Native novel ever. My favorite part of the book involves Jim Loney's various hallucinations of a "large bird and dark," which serves as an evolving objective correlative for his descent into schizophrenia. But I've always been interested, too, in his sudden infatuation with Canada, as he makes his drunken way back to the reservation to commit suicide-by-cop. He's never been there, but almost made it there once, for a high school basketball game: "He thought of the name of that town—Val Marie. It still sounded so foreign that he couldn't help wishing, even now, that they had made the trip." "Val Marie" becomes one of those many wonderful recurring images, metaphors, even sounds that populate Welch's work—like the "dark bird"—that connect him to the Poe and Faulkner tradition of American literature, that mark him as a great novelist, no matter what his ethnicity. The name of the town, "Val Marie," invokes both a maternal valley and the mother of God, as Loney's final journey—along Milk River!—then on to Mission Canyon—takes him back, as he sees it, to his Native heritage, and to death, and to (as I see it) his mother's womb and to a uterine heartbeat: "Val Ma-rie, Val Ma-rie, Val Ma-rie, Val Ma-rie."[30]

Squaw. Yes, Mom knew what it was to feel Indian in the latter half of the twentieth century. Because of this near-self-loathing, she therefore also felt—like many Natives of her generation—a deep allegiance, even obeisance, to the values of the dominant culture. Indeed, the slang term "apple"—red on the outside, white on the inside—may well have been coined to describe my dear old mom. She told me once when I was in junior high, "Tommy, never be late, or people will blame you for living on Indian time." So all my life I've tried to be twenty minutes early for everything; as a result, I have also spent much of my life just waiting, waiting for those more comfortable in their full whiteness to show up— on time, or fashionably late.

In my junior year of high school, AIM leaders Russell Means and Dennis Banks—on their way, as the world would soon learn, to occupying Wounded Knee—showed up to speak at our Rapid

City Central High auditorium. After just a few sharp spiels from these AIMsters about racist white colonizers and land theft, the white students began booing loudly. When the booing continued unabated, the Indian students—who made up 10–15 percent of the student body, or so—got up and walked out en masse, in protest of their classmates' reaction to our guests. I sat there in a veritable crisis of identity—then finally got up, sheepishly, and walked out towards the exit . . . finally sitting down in one of the last few rows in the upper shadows of the auditorium. Alone. Wishing that I had never been born. Wondering who the fuck I was or to whom belonged. I knew I could pass as a white kid. I also knew at least some of the history of my own mother's painful battles with racism. I needn't mention here that one might well read that liminal seat in the back of the auditorium as a too obvious metaphor for the rest of my life. So I won't.

My mom made my first and only trip to another country—and my first Western Grebe—possible. She worked her ass off most of her life, for us kids. It's true that she was often short-tempered and in a foul mood, probably from having to work so damned hard just to barely make ends meet. And then to come home crying from being called a "squaw," after all her efforts.

Oh, I almost forgot. In her teens, Mom lost four of her fingers to a grease fire. One of her hands is just a thumb. I can't tell you which hand it is because I've repressed it. Because Mom repressed it. It is the Great Unsaid in our family. We never ever really *see* the hand, consciously, except on those rare occasions when Mom has had to pose for a photograph—with her thumb-of-a-hand politely hidden behind her, its very pointed absence reminding us, for once, of its presence. But her resulting inferiority complex likely explains in large part her great drive to succeed, her need to compensate for her physical wounding by making something of her life, and her kids' lives. Right now I'm seeing a brown hand with only a thumb in my mind's eye. And wondering where Mom ever found the goddamned gumption. Because right now I feel pretty fucking amazed. And thankful.

Sometimes it's a good day to die, but more often it's just a good day to go birding. And sometimes it's a good day to suddenly appreciate my mom.

> Loney was on the Old Highway, running hard toward
> Harlem, thinking of Val Marie, his body empty and light.
> He was conscious of nothing those first several miles but
> his shuddering breath and the impatient beat of his heart.
> Val Ma-rie, Val Ma-rie, Val Ma-rie, Val Ma-rie.[31]

In 1974, as a freshman in college in Iowa City, the last thing Tom remembered before he jumped off the Iowa River bridge was a black vortex hovering on the mind's horizon. And a recent dream. . . .

He had been playing pinball in a large gymnasium, stoned on pot. A girl he knew but couldn't place said she had a message for him, forcing him behind a curtain. Reluctant at first, in his paranoid state, he finally accepted the note and read it: "Do not read any more poetry," signed, "Your Eye Doctor." Oh, no, he thought, I'm going blind!—and he went quickly home to bed. His ophthalmologist arrived; his mother burst out: "You're dying of consumption!" As totally shocking as this news was, he realized immediately that she was right. He'd sensed a burning sensation in his lungs for some time: as proof, he promptly spit up some blood. Since they obviously expected him to die at any moment, they left the room. His first consideration was what to do with his poetry. Should he burn it, or give it to his brother, who would burn it later anyway? His left lung was already a huge pinched nerve. He shook violently a few times, and thought, this is it, the end. Somehow he held on, and stumbled out of bed, and stepped out . . . into a dormitory hallway. Another door was open. Some doper friends were scattered around a bare room, watching the pot smoke strike the ceiling. He told them, "I'm *dying*. Consumption." They said, poor fellow, still eyeing the ceiling. He regained consciousness, all of a sudden, in the U of Iowa Memorial Union building. Immediately both his lungs contracted to half their size in a single spasm, and he collapsed onto the floor. So this is finally it, he thought. . . . But he recovered again at last, and got up, like a minor Indian character in a Western novel whose only distinction was to die very slowly, very dramatically, from the hero's well-placed bullet. Tom wandered about the Union—up those stairs, straining his diseased lungs—in search of a girl he'd met in his humanities class. If only he could talk with her for a while, he reasoned wildly, the end might be less bitter, or by some miracle, might be avoided entirely. . . .

When he woke up in a hospital, a pair of psychiatrists came every day, to ask him how he felt. He wasn't sure: he was in a fugue and remembered very little of that first month or two. He did remember telling these people in white that he kept imagining his mom driving to Pine Ridge and back, that year or so when she commuted there for Job Service—and he imagined her just *thinking*, and *thinking*, during that drive. Years later, he would look back on this last sentence and could only imagine what he imagined her thinking about.

✳ MAY 1977, A RAPID CITY MARSH:
Red-Winged Blackbird

I've only been pecked on the head, hard, by two birds in my life: by an Eastern Kingbird as I was walking to high school—its scientific name isn't *Tyrannus tyrannus* for nothing—and by a Red-winged Blackbird as I was birding, slogging my soaked tennis shoes through a cattail marsh one spring. To recite the refrain of many a nature text, the redwing—with its frog-croak song and its badge-of-blood shoulder patch—is one of the signature harbingers of spring on Midwest wetlands, etc., etc., blah, blah, blah. But this mean little bastard made the top of my head bleed, and I was wearing a baseball cap, mind you. All avian "spots of time" can't be winners. I'm being stupid, of course: a birder enters any bird's nesting ground at his/her own risk.

One of my greatest *bêtes noires* is our human—and specifically Western literary—propensity to see and use birds as mere symbols. And one of my guilty pleasures is to listen to conservative hate-talk radio, out of sheer masochism—and to keep up on what the other side is thinking. So I was listening to Michael Savage about a decade ago, when his rant about the Senator Craig scandal had somehow wandered to the bird calling in the background of the Senator's "I am not gay" press conference. Yes, it was a Red-winged Blackbird's *conk-a-ree* song, as a subsequent caller informed him; but Savage's immediate reaction was so typically Western, and by the way, so typically traditionally "literary": he asked himself aloud, "What does the blackbird symbolize in literature?" Yikes! This was the very subject, really, of my book manuscript at the time. I couldn't handle the conceptual torture, and so I fled to sports talk radio.

But I continued "listening" to Savage in my imagination: I could well imagine that at least one caller fed Savage the standard college-freshman answer—"the blackbird stands for death"—and that our good doctor (he has a PhD in nutrition) then applied it cleverly to the good Senator's doomed career. But again, how symptomatic of mainstream anthropocentric culture to see other species as "all about us," as if some God had put other animals here to remind humans of our own mortality. Likewise, when my daughter Emma was taking a college-prep literature course one summer, I asked her what kind of questions she had on her exams. "Oh, you know, Dad. Like, what does the marlin *symbolize* in *The Old Man and the Sea*?" Well, there was a *real, individual* blackbird singing during that press conference, with as much reason and worth to do so as the human fellow frantically trying to save his political ass. A deconstructive reversal of foreground and background might be instructive here: "What's that stupid primate sputtering about while that magnificent bird croaks his wonderful tune?"

The death equation hardly works with the redwing, anyway. The black birds traditionally demonized in Western folklore are the crow and raven, not even loosely related to the blackbird family. Much closer, taxonomically, are Wallace Steven's grackles, sometimes also read by critics as symbols of death—though reading them as emblems of sheer mundanity, of reality itself, works better for me in the context of Stevens's corpus. In contrast, though—if I *have* to talk symbolism—the redwing has always suggested to me the *jouissance* of the new spring, a powerfully ebullient paean to and the epitome of nature's general rejuvenative powers. But this, too, is sheer anthropocentric projection.

One old nature guide phonetically transcribes the redwing's spring song as "a pleasing *conk-er-EEE* or *oolong TEA*."[32] As for the latter, I resent the association of an imported drink of the leisure class with such a gritty, in-your-face, bad-ass bird. But it is no worse than my own old transcription, really: I'd long heard it as *cong-er-EE,* and so I soon developed my own inner ditty that plays like a bad tape loop whenever I hear the redwing's song, to the tune of the chorus of that classic campfire song "The Happy Wanderer": "Cong-er-ee, Cong-er-ah, / Cong-er-ee, Cong-er-ah-ha-ha-ha-ha-ha-ha-ha." No, it's no worse at all.

Having such a ditty on the mental Muzak soundtrack keeps down other memories, perhaps, as in this "Flashback":

I remember it now for the first time, I guess:
pond-side dragonflies as long as popsicle sticks,
and redwings as loud as a thousand carnival rides—
and dad sprawled out drunk in the grass by the car,
and mom bent over, bawling, in the front seat.

✳ JUNE 1978, SPEARFISH CANYON:
American Dipper

The American Dipper is a most unbirdlike bird, an odd duck out of water, a border animal that deconstructs our smug discursive categories of fish, flesh, and fowl. For starters, it is a passerine—a perching bird or songbird—that gave up its arboreal ways in its evolutionary journey just so that it could stand on a wet, mossy rock in a mountain stream and play at being a seabird of sorts, diving and walking under water in search of aquatic bugs and fish eggs.

I first saw a dipper while attending college at Black Hills State, in Spearfish, South Dakota. Because of my studies and my hippy-wanna-be stoner ways, this wasn't one of the more earnest birding eras of my life, and I was no doubt driving or riding down Spearfish Canyon in 1978 for reasons other than ornithic edification. My friends and I must have stopped to check out the magnificently high granite cliffs of the Canyon and maybe smoke a bowl, but I do remember seeing a small, chunky, mouse-gray bird standing on a rock in the middle of Spearfish Creek and wondering how the bird didn't just fall off the rock and be swept downstream immediately.

I call the dipper a border creature in deference to two of my favorite nature writers, Linda Hogan and Paul Shepard. Hogan's essay on bats claims that these animals "live in double worlds of many kinds. They are two animals merged into one," a "milk-producing" mammal and a "flying bird. They are creatures of the dusk, which is the time between times, people of the threshold."[33] Many of Hogan's favorite animals are just such double-world dwellers, and I often tell my students that there is a certain wonderful appropriateness for a mixed-blood human to cherish such an alter-species kinship. And it is also no small significance that, for Hogan, these other animals are also "people," at last.

Shepard's border animal is more of an epistemological conception, a being "at the edges of categories"—and therefore cognitively disturbing. "Marginal animals" like these are "psychologically provocative"; their existence is a disturbance in our need for an orderly cosmos, "producing taxonomic crisis and cognitive dissonance." Hogan's bats and my dipper have themselves undergone no radical change in their ontology; it's we who find some intellectual angst in this taxonomic provocation. And so, in regarding the dipper "an exception and offense to our typology, a wild denial of the ordering of the world in which Adam, Orpheus, and Linnaeus [. . .] named the animals,"[34] I feel a certain Dionysian liberation.

My undergraduate college years first brought my own divided identity to something of a crisis of consciousness. Half my time was spent among Skin (Native) friends, mostly from the Pine Ridge and Rosebud reservations; the other half was made up of Anglo buddies. These latter, when they found out that I was part Skin myself—my mom had come to pick me up for a long weekend or something, and then the cat was out of the bag—started calling me *GANjun* (as in *IN-jun*) instead of Gannon. When they later found out that I was studying French, the name became *GanJON*—which they pronounced *GahnJO*", in a long, mocking nasal drawl. Meanwhile, my Rez friends sometimes called me *iyeska* (Lakota for, roughly, "dirty half-breed"). And with them, my French again came back to haunt me: "Eez, Tom, you speak Indi'n [Lakota] with a French accent," they once told me.

Through my twenties, the pattern continued. My white friends continued their condescending attitude regarding my Native/"mutt" status, while a good number of my Skin friends also considered me a near-second-rate human, as an impure, all-mixed-up iyeska. Both prejudices resulted in a series of specific, painful denials of my very status as a human being. I eventually made the private resolution to erase race entirely from my conscious identity. I was beginning to think of myself as a nobody in a nowhere land, and that was fine with me. Perhaps this explains, in part, my eventual academic championing of other animals: at least here there weren't humans bitching about identity, and who was who, and why that made them better. So, if a bit of Edward-Abbey-esque misanthropy came to color my worldview, it was understandable.

What makes a land bird take to the water? What makes it choose to live between worlds, on the edges of water, rock, and air? Why would the son of a "squaw" go to college, and study French, and psychology, and Wordsworth? I was a border creature: part white, part Indian, a fucked-up and anxious young fellow of both rock and air. Pictures of me from those college years reveal the eyes of an anxious bird in an alien habitat, eternally ready to fly away to a place deep inside. However, the bird analogy always ultimately fails, in that I imagine that the American Dipper is comfortable in its liminal status. But I doubt that I will ever be.

✳ JUNE 1979, A PENNINGTON COUNTY DIRT ROAD: *Common Nighthawk*

My best home-from-college summer drinking buddy Jerry and I had just redeemed hundreds of crushed aluminum beer cans for some four dollars and change, enough to get another cheap twelve-pack of skunky beer. As we slammed down can after can to partly forget that we were mute pawns in whatever was really happening in the late twentieth century, Jerry turned onto a dirt road southeast of Rapid City, just past the airport, one of those bumpy gravel roads that only a tire salesman could love.

"You might be in for a treat," Jerry hoped out loud, knowing that I was something of a bird nut. After another mile or so, he pulled over, turned the car off, rolled down the window, and took another pull on his third Old Milwaukee. Then, my own window rolled down, I heard a loud *burr-urt* or—I can't really do any better than to describe it as a FART. Loud human flatulence, coming from the shortgrass prairie to the north.

Jerry laughed and laughed, and I remembered reading that male nighthawks make such sounds as a courtship display, diving straight down from on high and swerving abruptly just before hitting the ground, creating a minor sonic boom in the air. Ah, romance. If an ancient off-color nickname for the kestrel is the "windfucker"—for its habit of bucking (or "fucking") the wind as it hovers in place—then I guess the nighthawk could just as well be called the "windbreaker." Jerry took another chug of beer and laughed.

I first became familiar with nighthawks during one of my grade-school summers spent at my Grandma Mollie's in Fort Pierre. It may have been the same summer that my brothers and I learned about another means of redemption. After we cashed in our empty pop bottles for a nickel at the mom-and-pop butcher's shop downtown, our boyish curiosity led to the discovery that these empties soon re-appeared out behind the store—accessible by an alley—and were easily retrievable through an ill-crafted chicken-wire fence, if a boy's hands were small and curious enough. Yes, Grandma wondered on several occasions how the Gannon boys got so sugared up on the one quarter she gave us for spending money that day.

A block south of the store, across the street from the Fort

Pierre National Bank clock that read two minutes after eleven for probably as long as even Grandma could remember, was a laundromat—a modernist marvel in a remote 1960s small town— and there we young and curious entrepreneurs discovered that chewed-up gum on the end of a long stick could retrieve the quarters that patrons had fumbled and dropped behind the parallel rows of washing machines. I suspect that we were that mom-and-pop store's most frequent customers that summer.

The laundromat was a flat-roofed building, and so this is where the nighthawks come in, since they'd learned in the last century or so of evolution that sun-soaked flat roofs hatched their eggs just as agreeably as the bare ground did. Above the laundromat, then, were four or five nighthawks, fly-catching in an almost lolling fashion, spitting their nasal-metallic *peent* calls, all the slow summer long.

There is something iconic, even prototypically Great Plainsian, about a nighthawk in erratic, seemingly haphazard, flight overhead—not unlike a mutant Chimney Swift. And the wings: long and thin and bent at the elbows, with a discrete white stripe towards the end of each wing. I have seen them weaving and heard them peenting through Fourth of July small-town fireworks, as the people ignored the true glory of their absolute birdness. However, I never did hear the farting courtship flight during those young summers in Fort Pierre—I suspect now that they did that on the bluffs to the west of town—and I'm glad I didn't. What a distraction that would have been to a pack of young, curious—and yes, giggly—boys. That memory remains relatively untainted. Nostalgic. Romanticized. Of another warm and lazy Fort Pierre summer at Grandma's. Of empty pop bottles twice redeemed. Of nighthawks over the laundromat.

✳ AUGUST 1981, OLD FAITHFUL: *Common Raven*

After a fine undergraduate education in the humanities, I found that my majors in English and psychology and minors in French and Native American studies had rendered me virtually unemployable. So I took a job as a counselor at Sky Ranch for Boys, in the far northwest and most godforsaken corner of South Dakota, flattering myself that I'd at least be putting my psych degree to use, even though I knew that the position required no college at all. The job was really glorified babysitting, and never mind that fancy-ass psychology: as far as I could see, the more brawn you had to keep a group of troubled teens in line, the better.

But one of the perks of the job was the occasional road trip, and so in the summer of 1981, I found myself driving one of the ranch's three vans full of wayward youth to Yellowstone National Park. Driving the last hundred miles or so to Yellowstone was my first experience with the sublime—such beautiful heights that nonetheless scared the living hell out of me. I could *almost* imagine myself steering the whole vanload off the cliff. And the next cliff. And the next. It became a poker game of survival.

But there were also birds. I hadn't returned to my childhood hobby yet with fervor, or it would have been a lifer heaven, no doubt. But I did mark my first Clark's Nutcracker in my bird guide when I got home. Who could forget those odd long-tailed jays hanging tamely around the picnic tables, eager to live up to their nickname of "camp robber"? I also recorded my first Common Raven, at Old Faithful, of all places. I hardly paid any attention to the famous geyser since the huge raven standing nearby was so much more impressive—obviously a bigger chunk of bird than your standard American Crow, with a gnarly dark scar of beak and a squared wedge of tail that defined the term "fearful symmetry." I didn't hear its squawk, but I have since, and its deep "throat-singing" is quite different from a crow's *caw*. You'd think the makers of *The Lone Ranger* (2013) would have given this difference its due, but the movie is one long confusion of crow with raven, of *caw* with *squawk*. (Indeed, movie-going in general is often a painful experience for the experienced birder.)

One of the sub-themes of my academic writing has been that birds are very often aligned along a Western-Civilization binary of good vs. evil, heaven vs. hell. On one side of this bipolar spectrum are larks and bluebirds and orioles—indeed, songbirds in general, those "ethereal sprites" of flight and song. On the "dark" side are the vultures, the owls, the crows and ravens: morbid, even infernal, creatures of the chthonic and nocturnal.

This metaphoric use of the avian is rampant in literature, of course. My favorite literary raven isn't Edgar Allan Poe's, but rather the wolf-companion raven of Chickasaw writer Linda Hogan's prose and poetry. In her essay "Deify the Wolf," she notes "the psychological fact that wolves carry much of the human shadow," and she also describes the wolves she is watching as accompanied by a group of "gypsy ravens," who are "thought to direct the wolves to their prey," to partake in the leftovers; and sometimes "a person happens across a coal black raven standing inside the wide arch of those ribs like a soul in a body."[35] This dark avian spirit of death is acknowledged as a shadow image in Hogan's essay, although, as a Native champion of eco-awareness, Hogan refuses to vilify either wolf or raven: they are simply there, fulfilling their roles in nature, and what is truly fearful are humankind's untoward projections regarding them. It is fitting, too, that a Native writer would defend and resignify these alter-species shadows: like the wolf, raven, and the dark human of Fanon's *Black Skin, White Masks,* the Native American has long been an unwilling bearer of the Western collective shadow. The Western bipolar psyche strikes again.

And so Hogan's positive re-signification, from a different, Indigenous worldview must play against the backdrop of the Western demonization of such species as the raven and the wolf—and of the human primitive, the Indigenous Native, wild savages all. And if not ostracized as animal, both Native and bird are conversely idealized as spiritual, as abundantly evidenced in the imagery and metaphors of the Western literary canon. If the bird, then, is incorrigibly either some etherealized skylark or oriole, or some chthonic owl or raven, so, too, is the Indian—as seen through the Western imagination—a heathen-savage id, a Jungian shadow figure—or, in typical bipolar fashion, a nostalgically redemptive Noble Savage or Spiritual Indian.

Derrida's poststructuralist take on the "animal" as concept is very much in agreement, including its indictment of Western theology: "I was dreaming of inventing an unheard-of grammar and music in order to create a scene that was neither human, nor divine, nor animal, with a view to denouncing all discourses of the so-called animal, all the anthropo-theomorphic or anthropo-theocentric logics and axiomatics, philosophy, religion, politics, law, and ethics."[36] To this day, such a liberational way of thinking and being about the animal Other remains a dream.

The Lone Ranger of 2013 isn't worth an earnest film review, or even a concerted critique of the Native hooey, since it's really just Johnny Depp playing Jack Sparrow again. But one wonders, for instance, how a Comanche like Tonto is familiar with the Ojibwe notion of the Windigo, or with the Lakota expression "It's a good day to die"? The US Army captain is also an ahistorical knock-off of Custer, and the Comanches' final charge has echoes of the Little Bighorn. All further evidence that mainstream America can't really see the Indian without a few prototypical Plains Indian signifiers.

But I gave up on the film when a raven flew over a desert canyon, accompanied by the *caws* of an American Crow. Ouch. Indeed, whether Tonto's crown-of-a-bird on his head is a raven or crow seems a point of confusion throughout. (When the young Tonto first encounters the bird in a flashback, it is clearly a raven.) Worse yet, however, are the African White-headed Vultures in the movie, serving as mood props for the early burial scene. In the US desert Southwest.

About thirty years later, I finally got farther west than Yellowstone, driving out to California for my daughter's high school graduation. Ah, in the deep, wild, high-desert canyons of Utah—ravens! Ah, the mountain roads of Nevada—ravens! And more—ravens! By the time I got to the California border and hit the first rest stop—well, frankly, I had almost been ravened out. Standing stolidly on the picnic tables at the rest stop were more ravens, mere scavengers, even beggars, welfare opportunists in an oh-so-human world. Not one was the dark, mystic bird of Poe or the black-priest death attendant of Hogan; these seemed more like some new near-domesticated pigeons of the West. Yes, colonization, even assimilation, is a bitch, even for this noble and numinous archetypal bird of death and night.

✳ JUNE 1983, A PENNINGTON COUNTY DIRT ROAD: *Long-Billed Curlew*

> What is most audible when one is paddling the river is
> the sound of [. . .] an occasional Long-billed Curlew
> screaming its annoyance over our intrusion. [. . .] What
> is absent are ringing telephones, traffic noises, sports
> broadcasters excitedly blaring out inane comments on
> [. . .] the Cornhuskers' most recent touchdown over
> yet another obscure, mismatched opponent, and all
> the other noise pollution that we increasingly take for
> granted as a partial price of modern living.
>
> —Paul A. Johnsgard[37]

Johnsgard is writing about the Niobrara River, which runs through northern Nebraska on its way to the Missouri. Niobrara is the Ponca word for "running water": so this is a river named by a people who—having been forcibly displaced—no longer run with it anymore. Even in the river's very name lie the dark shadows of colonialism. The passage is ultimately interesting in its contrast between raw nature and a techno-urban setting, including the humorous dig at his home state's iconic pastime. As this book perhaps too dogmatically demonstrates, it is impossible to write about birds and nature without being political. Even our trained ornithologist breaks into cultural critique, evoking a pristine environment unspoiled by the noise pollution of "modern living." And I couldn't resist finding in the river's very name the dark shadows of colonialism.

The bird that Johnsgard describes, the Long-billed Curlew, is pretty rare now. I'm lucky if I record this giant sandpiper once or twice a year on my manic summer drives through the Nebraska panhandle. Thankfully, the bird's name is onomatopoeic, a ready

mnemonic device for its call; and I do often settle for identifying it solely by this long, high, drawn-out slur-of-a-whistle, *cur-
LEEEE, cur-LEEEE*. Actually seeing one on a fencepost, with
its unbelievably long, thin, curved beak, is a wonderful bonus.

They're a little more common just north, in southwestern
SoDak. I first saw the bird, amazingly enough, only a few feet
away from me, as I birded a dirt road east of Rapid City, the car
windows down in my beat-up blue Plymouth Volare. It was flying
right beside me, its flight parallel to the car's, going nearly as fast.
Size-wise, this huge species seems more a fowl than a shorebird,
and I freaked out for a second, wondering, what Great Bird-God
is this? I stopped the car, still amazed, and the curlew's flight continued, slowly veering off into the distance. If I can never again
expect a curlew to fly alongside my open-windowed claptrap of
a station wagon, I can still complain that there are now too few
curlews running with the Niobrara.

I first saw Paul Johnsgard in Vermillion, South Dakota, in 2003,
where he gave a talk called "Birds of the Prairie." He drew his
first bird when he was five, he said, by way of introduction, and
then provided his slideshow expertise on the rapidly vanishing
birds of the Great Plains, such as the various prairie chicken species, the Burrowing Owl and, yes, the Long-billed Curlew. But I
was mostly captivated by the fact that he *looked* like a bird: with
his unkempt wavy hair that seemed to end in a crest in the back
and his beaked nose, I readily imagined a very tall albino cardinal.

A decade later, I gave a reading to promote my own bird
book, a critical study of the birds in British Romantic and Native
American poetry. An audience member emailed me afterwards,
"Thanks for your book, and for such an entertaining presentation.

Do you know just how bird-like you are, pacing back and forth like that?"[38]

❋ JUNE 1985, SKYLINE DRIVE: *Field Sparrow*

William Wordsworth has a small poem titled "To the Small Celandine." I have no idea what the small celandine is, beyond the fact that it's a flowering plant, but the central point of the poem is that this "modest" flower is not the long-vaunted rose or lily or tulip. Sure, these latter blooms will always "have their glory" in human discourse, but Wordsworth, in contrast—and so characteristic of his corpus—would rather praise the small and neglected, who—like his human Lucy—"dwelt among the untrodden ways."[39]

I heard my first Field Sparrow hiking up Skyline Drive, a pine outcrop of the Black Hills that cuts off South Rapid City from West Rapid. I must have seen this rather nondescript species, too, to even identify it (in those primitive days before iPhones and birdsong apps), but it is the song that has always made this bird for me, made it one of my own small celandines. The song is a high series of whistles that begins with a few distinguishable individual notes but then accelerates to a rapid trill. To complicate matters, the song also usually either ascends or descends in pitch during its crescendo. In my last decade or so of eBird reports, I have often noted which song variant the bird sang—or if there were several birds, I'd record the number of those that ascended and descended. I'm sure that this has been more a fulfillment of my OCD nature than a valuable contribution to ornithological knowledge.

Bird-guide writers often refer to the song as having a minor tonality, although the tones are so amazingly microtonal that assigning the tune to some human musical scale—and thus, analogically, to a human emotion of sadness—seems absurd. This is surely human projection at work again. As Coleridge tells us, "In nature there is nothing melancholy"[40]—except (as far as we know) the modern moping Western human psyche.

Non-birding friends sometimes ask me, "Tom, what's your favorite bird song?" I usually answer, since there's really never one right answer, "Oh, either the Field Sparrow or the Warbling Vireo." No deep, hidden, and poetic thrush for me: in fact, I consciously answer this way because both birds are relatively small, nondescript members of an order that includes many more obvious choices, more renowned singers, but these two still make me smile whenever I hear them. The vireo's song is also a speedy song, from beginning to end; it sounds like a series of loop-de-loop slurred whistles that impress by seemingly ceaseless repetition. As I once remarked to a grad student on an outing to Branched Oak Lake, "It's like a never-ending song. Except that it ends." In the summer on the Great Plains, they can be heard from nearly every cottonwood tree, their favorite nesting site. Due to their relative commonness, in fact, I suspect that many other birders find them to be an earworm they'd rather be rid of than not; but I still get off on them, wondering how many millennia it took to come up with that particular wonderful set of melodies, such a fine example of avian artsong.

Indeed, my attempts to hear the music in rapid bird songs leaves me speechless before an aural sublime. The Field Sparrow's whistled trill and the Warbling Vireo's almost never-ending warble involve an incredible amount of sonic data—packed into a compressed time frame—an avian microchip, as it were, sounding at supersonic speed. Don Stap asks how one can even "register the song of a hermit thrush," for instance, "which lasts less than two seconds, but [. . .] may contain forty-five to a hundred or more notes, and as many as fifty changes in pitch." Songbirds' much faster metabolism leads them to a different perceptual world-time, in which a single several-second song may well contain the complexity of a classical sonata. This accelerated time frame also applies to their sense of hearing: "Why would birds produce intricately structured sounds if they couldn't hear the details?" According to Rosemary Jellis, this explains "why even the most extensive bird songs seem so brief to us. The bird with its speeded up time sense must feel as if it had sung an operatic aria."[41]

It's sad to see one of my old favorite bird books writing off a whole species for having an insignificant song. The bird is the Henslow's Sparrow; its song is no less significant than any other human or non-human calling to its significant other, or partaking in phatic conversation with its universe. But here is ornithologist C. M. Jones's 1881 description:

> The musical performance of this bird has very little to commend it. When the muse inspires his breast he mounts to the top of a weed. [. . .] There he sits demurely until the spirit moves, when he suddenly throws up his head and with an appearance of much effort, jerks out his monosyllabic "tsip," apparently with great satisfaction. Then, having relieved himself he drops his head and waits patiently for his little cup to fill again. Somehow I cannot watch him [. . .] without a feeling of pity for a

creature so constituted that he can be satisfied with such a performance.[42]

And even the great Roger Tory Peterson, in the twentieth century, denigrates the bird via a small attempt at humor, describing this bird's utterance as

> one of the poorest vocal efforts of any bird: throwing back its head, it ejects a hiccoughing *tsi-lick*. As if to practice this 'song,' so that it might not always remain at the bottom of the list, it frequently hiccoughs all night long.

But I find this bird's insect-like song to be tonally rich and more interesting than many birds' vocal efforts: the House Sparrow's *schleep*, for instance, is much less musical to my ears. But I see that I'm falling into their trap. Any bird's discourse should be given its due, whatever our human aesthetic projections. And so: apologies to all House Sparrows, who do in fact have their own share of art and culture; the male's little ritual courtship, in which it hops around the parking lot dirt for its plain-Jane mate, is a masterpiece of machismo in miniature.

And yet the standard bird guides have written such birds into inconsequence, in the high, dry tones of what passes as scientific observation and categorization. I can imagine coming upon an aliens' *Guide to the Life Forms of Planet Earth* and stumbling upon humankind's description: "Very aggressive towards other individuals of its own species when under the duress of overpopulation, especially when combined with bogus religious ideologies. Recently extinct." (But their artful songs were oh-so-*not*-insignificant!)

❋ JUNE 1985, FORT MORGAN, CO: *House Finch*

Occasional road trips to Colorado to visit my crazy aunt in Fort Morgan were one of my first exposures to non-South Dakota birds. At Annie Marie's house, a new species was quite close at hand: there were all these little red-stained finches chittering and nesting in the flowerpots hanging on her very porch.

Flash forward from 1985 to a decade or so later, and House Finches had made their way to Rapid City, where they are now fairly abundant. In fact, there is a story here, of avian and Native decline and return, not unlike the Native American experience of the last few centuries. Many Native bird species have also had their ranges and populations radically altered by the incursions of Christo-Custer colonialism; and the European propensity to introduce Old World birds into North America is a sad corollary of Western colonization itself.

The fate of the House Finch has ties to that of the House Sparrow, that "English Sparrow" brought to the New World and intentionally set free in the wild by a New York museum in the 1850s. By 1884, famed naturalist John Burroughs can already note their "rapidly increasing" numbers and foresees the need to "wage serious war[!] upon" this species. But Burroughs admires them nonetheless, for their "Old World hardiness and prolificness"—much like his own European colonial forebears, of course. And the poor native birds being driven out by the House Sparrow? He believes they are "less shrewd," "less quick-witted," and "less sophisticated"[43]—like their human Native cohabitants, no doubt.

But yes, even a century ago, the English Sparrow was very much scorned—even though, ironically, its advent to the Western hemisphere had been the direct result of purposeful human importation. Thus a 1915 editorial in the *Omaha Sunday World-Herald*—titled "An Abused Family"—complains, "Anybody who inhabits a house with beamed eaves will cheerfully admit that the English sparrow is an abomination." Why? They build "nests that look like so many dengenerate [*sic*] haystacks and" they increase "their own population faster than could be tabulated by the swiftest of all adding machines": in sum, they are "utterly impossible pests." *(Hmmm.)*

The essay's rather odd raison d'être, however, is to defend sparrow-kind in general: "But this much is certain—his family [i.e., sparrows in general] is of the most gentle and beautiful and interesting of all birddom. Be he ever so obnoxious, the English sparrow is the only blot on the 'scutcheon of the ancient and honorable line of sparrows—long may they live!" So there is a second irony in the editorial: the *other* sparrows our Nebraska journalist goes on to describe as more "honorable" members of an "ancient" family line are native (American) sparrows, which are, in fact, not at all closely related to the House Sparrow, which is an Old World weaver finch. This conflation of a European bird with Native sparrows makes the latter an "Abused Family" indeed.

Then there is the editorialist's peculiar conclusion: "So don't let yourself get the idea that the only good sparrow is a dead sparrow, for they're different from Indians[?!]. Go out this afternoon with your old opera glasses and take a look." What a shame that an apparently well-intentioned nature writer makes a reprehensible allusion to the expression "the only good Indian is a dead Indian," a scurrility clearly evident today to anyone forced to "take a look" at such a racialized discourse, with archaic opera glasses or not.

Moreover, the demonizing of any other particular animal—

or other animals in general—seems to issue from a specifically Western way of thinking. Luther Standing Bear describes the parallel between Native Americans and other species in terms of the European settlers' hostile attitude towards both: "Only to the white man was nature a 'wilderness' and only to him was the land 'infested' with 'wild' animals and 'savage' people." And such infestations—such "pests"—needed to be removed:

> I know of no species of plant, bird, or animal that were [*sic*] exterminated until the coming of the white man. [. . .] The white man considered natural animal life upon this continent, as 'pests.' Plants which the Indian found beneficial were also 'pests.' There is no word in the Lakota vocabulary with the English meaning of this word.[44]

The immediate result of the Old World House Sparrow's rapid adaptation to US urbanization, not surprisingly, was a drastic population reduction and range redistribution of native sparrows and finches—including the House Finch—to the widespread laments of ornithologists. (And of course, Native Americans suffered an even more severe reduction and forced redistribution of their population.) However, in the latter part of the twentieth century, due to the vagaries of natural selection and changes in urbanization, the House Sparrow has actually declined in urban areas, being largely replaced, once again, by the native House Finch.[45] I have witnessed this species displacement myself, in the expansion of the House Finch's range both from the western US, into Rapid City, South Dakota, and from the eastern US, into Vermillion, South Dakota, with a concurrent decline in the previously ubiquitous House Sparrows. Just as—if I can be indulged a wayward fancy—has the dominance of the Euro-American worldview, in roughly this same time span, met with some new and firm contestation from human Indigenous ways of knowing.

✳ SEPTEMBER 1987, NORTHERN BLACK HILLS: *Mourning Dove*

> A man and a woman and a blackbird
> Are one.
> A man and a woman and a pulp novel
> Are nothing but trouble.

In 1987, my future wife was living in Belle Fourche, and I would drive up from Rapid constantly because she and I were deep in steep love, and the very birds were magnified in their birdy import. She noticed a pair of Mourning Doves in her front yard and immediately identified them with us. *As* us. Not long after, she would claim that they had been *white* doves and that our love was fated, and all that good romantic rot.

But in my memories, too, the courtship was inextricably bound to birds. My fiancée became my birding acolyte for a feather of time. We went on bird outings, to Orman Dam and the like, and I kept our day list, and I helped her start her own life list, and I gave her my old childhood field guide as a present, and life was good. The real thrill for the rather calloused bird-lister that I had become was to experience another's new-found appreciation for the *bird* per se. I imagined it to be like watching a small child watching her first bird. It took me back to my own first few bird hikes in the fourth grade—up at dawn, and up Piss Hill, in search of that Great Horned Owl. . . . This return-via-a-neophyte pattern was repeated several times later, including with my daughter Emma, when it actually *was* a small child watching her first bird: by the time my daughter Em was fourteen months old, she was able to look at a picture of a Mourning Dove and say, "WHOO-whoo-whoo." My own jaded, time-weary self melted away through the eyes of another.

My journal from 1988 reveals my wife and me in the semi-bliss of birding. One April afternoon brought four new species for her, including a Mallard. The duck was in flight, its green head glistening in the sun, an image she described as "just like a duck stamp!" I might have retorted, "How symptomatic that signifiers (i.e., photos) have replaced signifieds (i.e., real birds) in this postmodern age," but I held my enamored tongue. In May that same year, she described the Violet-green Swallows at Canyon Lake as "fat little wind-up toys." I soon began to fancy her as a Dorothy Wordsworth to my William.

Some journal entries were less Wordsworthian, as when I noted that she now "grinds her teeth, asleep, like a House Sparrow: *schleep . . . schleep.*" And there was the time that we were out birding in the Black Hills and she mistook her own nose-hair-whistling for a bird: "Shshshsh," she said, and looked around in slow anticipation, until realizing where the sound was actually coming from. We both had a good laugh at that one.

More precious memories involve—oh, the chickadees at Wind Cave National Park, which, according to her, were whistling, *STE-ven; STE-ven.* In love, I could but only be charmed by such a cute anthropomorphism. Another morning, she made an untowardly denigrating remark about grackles. So I made her read Wallace Stevens's "Thirteen Ways of Looking at a Blackbird," which I was teaching at the time. She told me that she'd never look at them the same way again, and I think that she meant it. Finally, when we moved to eastern South Dakota, to Vermillion for my master's degree, I took her for a walk around campus one evening to show her her first Northern Cardinal. It was our last chance of the day, right before sunset, and there he was, singing loud to beat hell, sitting in a tree for a long time so she could get a good look and listen: "That was just for me," she finally said, patting her chest, tears in her eyes.

Yes, I gave her my old childhood field guide as a present, when life was good. I later took it back when things went to smash—a wretched thing to do, I knew even then. But what really hurt was that she didn't even care enough to want it back. The heart is a lonely birder.

✳ DECEMBER 1987, BELLE FOURCHE, SD: *[Species Unknown]*

> Now the fifth Grandfather spoke, the oldest of them all, the Spirit of the Sky. [. . .] "My power you shall see!" He stretched his arms and turned into a spotted eagle hovering. "Behold," he said, "all the wings of the air shall come to you, and they [. . .] shall be like relatives. [. . .]" Then the eagle soared above my head and fluttered there; and suddenly the sky was full of friendly wings all coming toward me.
>
> —Nicholas Black Elk[46]

I'm dreaming, in bed, in our trailer house outside Belle Fourche, South Dakota. I've just had a series of out-of-body flying dreams—always intense—which I frequently experienced from my late teens well into middle age. I'm still flying, in the next dream, as I enter this college student union game room, full of ancient pinball machines and those Pac-Man and Galaxian arcade games of the 1980s. When I alight, a partridge-like bird runs up to me and says, in a high metallic voice, "Buy me some games! Buy me some games!" I say okay, and go to get some quarters. . . .

The best flying dream in years, and it's also a lucid dream: I know I'm dreaming and feel in control of my flight. This time, rather than the laborious breast or butterfly strokes that usually propel me absurdly through the air in these dreams, I'm actually flying with real *feathered* wings! I'm way above Ft. Pierre, my emotional womb away from the womb, the site of my childhood bliss of Grandma and fishing and nighthawks over the laundromat.

Many of the flying dreams I remember have a numinous quality, with an accompanying shining, electric feel and ambiance. They often include not only flying birds, but birds that talk to me:

> I'm walking by a UNL building and see two migrating warblers, and I stick my hand out and—catch one! It starts talking to me. It's a drab warbler, with a little faint orange around its beak. I ask it what species it is, what humans call it. It says, "They've called me so many names in other countries that I don't remember what they call me here." The bird turns into a human boy and follows me to school.

My lover and I go for a walk. I tell her, "I can fly," and I start flapping. She turns into a crow and flies much higher than I can imagine. . . .

In another dream, I'm taking a quiz in school. Q: What are humans made of? A: Birds. Yes, in the dream, it turns out that "birds" is the right answer.

I am awed by the vision of a great bird, half-heron and half-eagle. . . .

Steep cliffs: suddenly I am in a shallow impression in the rock, among—and apparently one of—a nest of eaglets. Yet they seem to be at the same time human people, Native Americans in the Old West, and their fear of falling off the cliff reflects their trials and tribulations.

I'm outside in the pre-dawn darkness, on my way to bird somewhere, and the clouds and stars are beautiful. I decide to fly just a little bit—the breaststroke is always easiest—and though I only get a few feet off the ground this time, the sky looks wonderfuller and wonderfuller.

A small flock of cute little Violet-green Swallows are migrating though eastern Nebraska?! Unheard of. I see them on a dirt road just northeast of Lincoln. As they dive close to the ground for insects, I reach out and catch one in my hand through total luck. Its little heart is beating fast in my cradled palms as I quickly note the white crescent moons on each side of its upper tail. eBird will have to believe me now!

At Grandma's house: a golden owl.

Sherman Alexie points out a Winter Wren on the UNL campus, a new species for me! As I write down the details in my little notebook, he says, "I should buy me a pen like that, too." I quip, "I think you can afford it."

At a lake, a resort area. A female House Sparrow flies down and starts talking to me. I forget what I say, but the House Sparrow replies, "The diabetes." And I'm pretty sure she means me. I shrug as if to say, yeah, what can yu' do? The House Sparrow says, "Well, I just want to go to a place where there's peace. But I do know where we can get lasagna."

Yes, birds have spoken to me a lot in my dreams, but usually their wise words are a far cry from Black Elk's visionary Spotted Eagle or Standing Bear's meadowlarks that speak Lakota, one of whom warned Sitting Bull of his imminent murder. A century of assimilation is a bitch. By the way, I've never been diagnosed as diabetic, but—especially given family history—I strongly suspect that I'm at least borderline Type 2. But I can't tell anyone that I was first diagnosed by a bird.

✳ JANUARY 1989, RAPID CITY, SD:
European Starling

This section could have been called "Killdeer," or "Northern Bobwhite," or "Blue Jay." I'm pretty sure that I've reported on eBird at least once an odd overwintering Killdeer or a singing-too-early-in-the-season bobwhite that was really a starling, that bastard of a mime. Unlike a mockingbird, whose imitations of several other species often follow one another in rapid-fire fashion, so that there is no doubt that it is the Great God Mockingbird showing off his chops, the starling will imitate the same bird for a good while, as if earnestly practicing a new song on its ventriloquist set list. Most commonly, the imitation occurs intermittently among the starling's own—more *starling*-like—dissonant hisses and whistles: the human aesthete little wonders that such a bird might well want to add a few more pleasing songs to its repertoire.

My first old journal note of such imitations is from Rapid City in January 1989: a starling imitating a killdeer—and I've heard many a "killdeer" in my suburban backyard and the middle of the city ever since. Subsequent notable imitations include a Blue Jay's *too-weedle* flute-whistle, a goldfinch's *per-chik-er-ee,* a bobwhite, a bobolink, an Eastern Meadowlark, a Clay-colored Sparrow's *buzz* song, a junco, a Baltimore Oriole, and even a Red-tailed Hawk's scream. I even suspect that the local starlings are getting better at imitating the calls of our native American bird species—or am I just getting better at identifying the calls of the species that they're imitating? I have also heard a starling sound like a jackhammer, believe it or not: the thought of birds acculturating to the industrial/machine era is almost too jarring to contemplate.

Again, this is the *European* Starling, and the irony struck me early on, of an immigrant bird mimicking the avian natives of the continent: maybe the starling's co-optive gestures really are akin to Walt Whitman's barbaric yawp, some desperate urge by an alien interloper to sound Indigenous. I might conclude, from a Native point of view, "Yes! The colonizers won! The cowboys always win!" But at least the starlings are learning the language of the natives—a little bit of bobwhite, a smattering of meadowlark. . . .

Is it sad that two of our most common and well-known birds, the European Starling and House (aka English) Sparrow, are foreigners, both brought here intentionally by Euro-human-kind? The old story goes that the starling was introduced in New York City in 1892, thanks to the efforts of an eccentric who was "determined to introduce into America all the birds mentioned in Shakespeare"; romantic fiction or not, the result has been such that "North American birds and people have been suffering ever since." Its arrival to the Great Plains came only a few decades later, and it was first recorded in Nebraska in 1932. In that same year, Nebraskan ornithologist Myron Swenk predicted that "they will increase in abundance rapidly, and soon the obnoxious traits of the species will be revealed," adding that the starling "nicely combines all the detestable features of the English sparrow [. . .] and adds a few of its own for good measure." Pearson et al.'s venerable *Birds of America* likewise expresses a fear of the ecological results of this "interloper in the new land" as early as 1917, even suggesting that the bird's "undesirable qualities" may be "accentuated when [. . .] introduced into a new country": these fears led to a good deal of ornithological angst and "apprehension," for the interlopers were already the "persistent enemy of many native birds."[47] But note that not once do these natural scientists make the analogical leap to *human* immigrants overrunning the Native populations, or having their "undesirable qualities" worsened in their exposure to a "brave new world."

I was surprised to come across a poem by Native poet Sherman Alexie in which nesting starlings are described as "Rats with wings." But the narrator's view changes, empathy-wise, and the crux of the poem is that both humans and starlings are irrational animals just trying to raise their kids, come hell or high water:

> What is the difference between
>
> Birds and us, between their pain and our pain?
> We build monuments; they rebuild their nests.
> They lay other eggs; we conceive again.
> Dumb birds, dumb women, dumb starlings, dumb men.

So I have had a pretty much lifelong love/hate relationship with the starling, this bird who is both an unsympathetic colonial interloper and a sympathetic-because-demonized feathered rat of an underdog. My lack of sympathy most often arises when I'm birding by car, driving though small towns of the Great Plains, so often lauded as nostalgic beacons of some real America (that began dying already in the 1950s), where too many of the inhabitants no doubt recently voted for a closet-racist conservative. Why am I supposed to join fellow Nebraskans in celebrating these near-ghost-town manifestations of Manifest Destiny? Think of all the xenophobic ideology tucked away in one main street soda fountain drugstore. (Indeed, Nebraska's longtime tourist buzz-phrase "The Good Life" was as racially coded as a certain politician's recent inane campaign slogan "Make America Great Again.") And when I bird these places, *en passant*, they're full of nothing but immigrant House Sparrows, Euro Starlings, and Euro Collared-Doves: in sum, even these towns' avians are revelatory of a particularly problematic worldview.

And yet the starling does have an amazing plumage when seen in the right light and season (I speak both literally and metaphorically): an iridescence of purples and greens that rivals the grackle. When the bird molts in the fall, its new feathers look as if small white stars were flashing on its entire body. I have answered many emails and Facebook queries from non-birding friends around Christmas time: *What are those beautiful birds on my lawn with all these stars on their feathers?! . . . What? Starlings? Come on, Tommy! You liar!*

And as for all that colonization stuff? Hey, it wasn't *their* fault. And at least they *are* learning some of the natives' language—they're just trying to get along, one might say.

And yet, and yet—to conclude where I began: starlings are among the best mimics in the bird world. As pets, they "develop a striking repertoire that mixes human sounds with typical starling vocalizations." Also common is the "tendency to sing off-key and to fracture the phrasing of the music at unexpected points"—as if satirists or postmodernist masters of juxtapositional pastiche:

> One bird sang "a fragment of 'The Star-Spangled Banner' with frequent interpolations of squeaking noises," and another "routinely linked the energetically paced *William Tell* Overture to 'Rockaby Baby.'" The birds also sometimes repeated phrases in odd situations. One bird repeated "'basic research' as he struggled frantically with his head caught in a string; another screeched, 'I have a question!' as she squirmed while being held to have her feet treated for an infection."[48]

I can't resist reading some of these utterances as satires or protests against their human scientific observers. How many birds and other non-human animals have lost their lives to "basic research"? How many could have wished their final utterance to be "Wait! I have a last question! *Why?*"

✳ JANUARY 1991, GAVINS POINT DAM: *Long-Tailed Duck*

The Long-tailed Duck used to be called the Oldsquaw.

That was its longtime official name in all the bird guides and ornithological tomes. The ornithologists recently changed the name for obvious reasons: "squaw" is perhaps the most pejorative word-arrow applied to Indians, the closest thing to the N-word in its intentionally hurtful racist and sexist vitriol, and science can't be involved in such things, obviously, as an "objective" discourse above and beyond such paltry matters as the politics of ethnic epithets.

The truth is that I'm lying in even claiming this bird in my table of contents and in the title above. I *still* have never seen an Oldsquaw. I mean, a Long-tailed Duck. Oh, I've shown up at nearby big lakes during winter on the rare occasion when the bird has been reported—and rare they are, here in the middle of the US. They're "sea ducks," after all. But I never had a decent spotting scope to span the usually several hundred yards to the middle of these big lakes where such deep-water diving ducks like to float. My binoculars have always failed me, and the bird has remained one of a handful of rarities that occur in my spot of ground once or twice a year as a huge tease, but forever remain as mysterious as a unicorn, or a god.

The Long-tailed Duck used to be called the Oldsquaw.

And the name—the older, oh-so-"poetic" one—has always haunted me, too, as I thumb through my old bird guides—as an odd, painful reminder of *human* racial politics. You see, my Irish father used to come home shit-faced drunk and proceed to beat the hell out of my Indian mother as we small kids watched in howling agony. One of my first memories was of dear old Dad beating my mom down this set of outside stairs that ran along the side of our tenement-apartment building. During these beatings, "squaw" was his favorite term of endearment for her. Restraining orders and divorce would follow. As a witness to such batterings, I may have already unconsciously longed to be somewhere else, away from all that human crap. Oh, maybe birding or something. . . .

The Long-tailed Duck used to be called the Oldsquaw.

✳ APRIL 2001, U OF IOWA ENGLISH-PHILOSOPHY BUILDING: *Common Grackle*

> O thin men of Haddam,
> Why do you imagine golden birds?
> Do you not see how the blackbird
> Walks around the feet

Of the women about you?

—Wallace Stevens[49]

Walking out of the English-Philosophy Building at the University of Iowa, I took a sharp turn around a cedar and stumbled upon a grackle in an old elm. (The Common Grackle is that big, purple-headed, *check*-smacking blackbird who frequents US lawns.) For several seconds, we stared at each other from a two-feet distance. And for at least one of those seconds, I was struck at how utterly *alien* this two-winged iridescence really was, and how incredible it would be to see such a creature if I were a visitor from another planet, or even just a homo sapiens who had not been habituated to the ubiquitous shapes and sounds of such beings from my first days of consciousness. Then, as I returned to the mundane, I wondered at how little of the actual bird I was still really seeing, overlaid as my raw perception was with all the cultural accoutrements that had also been donned at a relatively early age, from nursery rhymes of four and twenty blackbirds baked into pies to critical readings of Wallace Stevens's thirteen different, apparently esoteric—though thankfully non-culinary—ways of looking at such a bird.

When we can get beyond such cultural projections and aesthetic baggage—if only momentarily—birds become veritable agents of defamiliarization, in their radical suddenness of movement, their existential extremes of sound and color. Of course, this can only be true for those humans who still spend a modicum of time out of doors. For the rest, there are pictures in books, words in poems, and a hundred ideologies of "golden birds"—for the better or (usually) worse. Stevens's poem is at least a wonderful attempt to get us to re-see the real grackles around our feet.

I'm dreaming that I'm birding. I don't even know what season it is, but there are lots of species, so I start a Big Day list. I then come upon a little Lakota boy, who shows me some grackles, all oil-slicked and dying. I say, way too sanctimoniously, "Humankind's fall—or original sin—was thinkin' we were better than everyone else."

A week or so after that dream, I awakened to a backyard scene of grackles frozen in the snow, having succumbed to an early South Dakota blizzard:

LOOKING AT THIRTEEN BLACKBIRDS
        CONFUSED BY CLIMATE CHANGE AND
        CAUGHT IN A SNOWSTORM IN
        VERMILLION, SD, 27 NOVEMBER 2001
dead.
froze. dead.

        dead.

    dead.

  dead.

  dead.

    dead.

    dead.

 dead.

dead.

dead.

still moving? no. dead.
dead.

✳ FEBRUARY 2003, KIRK FUNERAL HOME:
Prairie Falcon

> Tommy recalled a car trip west at an early age, to the
> Black Hills: great pine mountains raised their ponderous
> hulks towards him in greeting. His mother sang to the
> radio as she drove, and his father would arrive later, to
> their rented trailer house, with gravel-truck dust on his
> clothes, like every night, and two fifty-dollar bills in his
> hand, like every Friday.
>
> —from my unfinished adolescent novel,
> *Intimations of a Dope-Crazed Seer:*
> *The Short Life of Thomas Abercrombie*

I was in the middle of teaching *Death of a Salesman* at the U of
South Dakota when the call came that Dad was near death and
that I should come quickly. It couldn't have been coincidence—in
fact, a made-for-TV movie couldn't have timed it better: Dad *was*
Willy Loman, working himself into the grave and forever asking,
"But is there any *money* in it?" Willingly or not, I had played Biff:
my withdrawal from the dog-eat-dog world of money-equals-
success into an English-major career may have initially been an
unconscious swerve on my part, but by the year of the phone
call—and with some small thanks to Arthur Miller—I was now
inordinately conscious of my Biff-ian status. I even saw my choice

of an academic career in the humanities as a reaction against the father, despite my lifelong affinity for natural science. Ironically, I'd just received word that I'd been hired for a tenure-track position at a Division I institution, to begin the next fall. When I tried to tell Dad about it, he assumed that it was yet another pathetic job that only the bookishly unambitious would undertake, a position something akin to a clerk in a nineteenth-century Russian novel.

He would die in February 2003. That first call came the December before, and so I picked up Emma in Denver, to see her grandpa—for the last time?—over Christmas break. We went into Dad's bedroom when we arrived: "I got spots on my lungs—cancer . . . not much longer to live." For some reason, probably delirium, he started calling me "honey," and it turned into my job, the week or so I was there, to fix him breakfast in the morning: two eggs over easy and two pieces of toast, in one of Mom's ancient black cast-iron pans. The smallest pan: it was perfect for two eggs, over easy.

After Christmas, we checked Dad into the veterans hospital up in Sturgis. The hospital was called Fort Meade, of all names, near the Lakotas' sacred Bear Butte, of all places. When we went to see him there, the first thing he did was claim that a slanting chrome pipe under the sink was a snake. (I hadn't heard him mention snakes since I'd come home after grade school one day, and he had stopped in from a bender, suffering from delirium tremens, and he grabbed me tight and said, "Get the snakes off of me, Tommy! Get the snakes off!")

A few more lucid minutes later, he complained about what he perceived to be a shoddy job of connecting the IV to his arm: "I wouldn't hook up my truck to a trailer like this! The D.O.T. wouldn't stand for it!" This struck me as actually pretty funny and astute. Cable news was on the television, and the day's big head-line was a report of the first clone being born. Dad immediately turned to us and asked, "Now why can't I get cloned?" I couldn't tell whether this was another one of his jokes, or a truly plain-tive cry against mortality. As we were leaving, he yelled at me, "Get that big-payin' job, so I don't have to keep supportin' yu'!" I felt hurt and insulted, especially since he hadn't supported me for many years, but I wrote it off as more delirium. Oh, by the way, Dad, what about all that court-ordered child support that you never paid Mom?—when we kids really needed your damned money? But now I'm only growing bitter.

When he came home from the hospital to die, our final con-versations were brief, his words often cryptic. One regret of his was clear: "I want to spend some money now, Tommy—but it's too late!" Then came his last words to me, from his literal death-bed: "Tommy . . . Tommy?" Pain-killing drugs and at least two terminal diseases had rendered him incoherent. "Tommy. Listen to me." And he pulled me close by the front of my shirt: "*Don't use cruise control on icy roads.* Do you hear me?" Yes, I did. And I immediately felt cruelly cheated. Surely even this Willy Loman of South Dakota truck stops, this magnificently extraverted huck-ster and shyster of tractor-trailer horse-trading, had accrued *some* wisdom to impart to his oldest son, especially if it were some final regret regarding, some renunciation of, his Willy-Loman-esque life choices. Biff the English major deserved at least that much. And yes, I have read his words metaphorically—over and over, and up, down, and sideways—as only an English major can. And my readings are all either too shallow and Hallmark-ish, or too deep and close to home, to share on the written page. *(Insert your own reading here.)*

Visitation, the evening before the funeral, took place at the

Kirk Funeral Home, on the southern outskirts of Rapid City. The man in Dad's casket was unrecognizable, either from a mortician's lack of talent or from that eternal estrangement between the living and the dead. Some of Dad's trucker friends were there, and I felt the momentary irreverent suspicion, from the looks on their faces, that some of them must have owed Dad money, and this was their easy way of paying him back, or maybe of dancing on his grave, since they were now debt-free. One of my brothers and I eventually walked outside for a cigarette, and a Prairie Falcon appeared in the undeveloped field to the south and flew in our direction, zipping by us like a bird on a personal mission, as is this species' wont. I'd never seen a Prairie Falcon this close to town, and my first thought was—"Dad's spirit?"—a thought that I immediately suppressed. My second thought was, what kind of human hubris allowed people to believe such nonsense, rendering another life form a mere tool for the human spiritual? My third thought: but wasn't it really kind of grand to believe such a thing? Yes, my mind was a tree with three blackbirds—as I now render even blackbirds human, all too human.

Later that night, my three brothers and I had a few beers as I probed them for anecdotes about Dad for my eulogy the next morning. It ended up being pretty impromptu and somewhat bookish, but mostly a series of attempts at humor, because Dad *was* a character, straight out of Dickens, a ceaseless deliverer of punch lines who was a punch line himself in his inveterate parsimonious ways. Those there in that Catholic church who didn't know him very well—knew him for that. Of course, there was so much I didn't say, so much that couldn't be said: no doubt this was why I was blubbering through the second half of the eulogy. Yes, some of the tears may have issued from authentic sorrow for the old bastard, but some of them flowed, I believe, from a great cognitive dissonance, from the realization that I was taking part in a discourse of bad faith. At last, I was *so* angry at myself for crying, although I wasn't even sure why I was angry. It may have been because I knew that I was performing, that tears were expected, and that I had merely unconsciously fallen into the social role of demonstrative mourner. Or it may have been that the wisdom I carry to my grave is not to use cruise control on icy roads.

✳ APRIL 2003, U OF IOWA ENGLISH-PHILOSOPHY BUILDING: *Northern Cardinal*

There is a photo of my brothers and me from 1968, we three oldest on our knees, gathered around our three-month-old youngest brother in his baby walker. I'm holding an amateurish drawing of a cardinal in front of me, and my best birder-acolyte brother, Terry, is holding up an even more amateurish chickadee. How bad was it, growing up on commodities and food stamps and Salvation-Army-gift Christmases with a single Indian mom—and a heavy-drinking dad who might show up at any time to beat on us—that we resorted to crayon drawings of other animals to hide behind, to salve our daily suffering? The human animals in this photo look desperate.

As if in retribution for my bad art, I wouldn't see an actual Northern Cardinal until more than a decade later, when I went away to college in the southeastern corner of the state. But those were darker years at the University of South Dakota, when I courted darker birds, when the bright red of a cardinal in the sun would have made me avert my gaze. Add a little LSD to too much William Blake, and I was stalking the oldest buildings on campus after midnight, peering into dark windows for a glimpse of my darker shadow-self. During that era of my psychic (d)evolution, that bright red bird of daylight song had little place.

I dreamed the other night that I walked down into this dark basement, and I found myself on this cement floor with a low ceiling, surrounded by birds. Cranes, crows, cardinals, etc., were all casually walking around, all the approximate size of humans, and all of them were talking. Or was I only reading their minds?— I couldn't tell. A huge robin walked right by me and said or thought, "What is this fellow doing here? He is an apostate!" A huge starling was screaming, "And what about the women and children? We have no bandages to cope with such carnage!" Suddenly, I was surrounded by four huge crows. They said, "We are here to take you to the Bird-God. You have nothing to lose but your brains."

By the time I returned to the University of Iowa for my PhD, the cardinal's ascendency was now a given; I now felt completely at home with this rock-star vocalist of the US Northeast and Midwest. Oh, I never fell for Collins's transliteration of the bird's loud, clear two-syllable whistle as "*what-cheer what-cheer what-cheer*," but in my lighter moments, I conceded that it was pretty damned close. My dissertation was an over-four-hundred-page tome, a too-detailed examination of the representation of birds in British Romantic and Native American literatures. By the end of the book, I was calling for a cross-species semiotic communication based upon *listening* to birds' sounds—at the same time realizing that my argument was beyond the pale of respectable humanist-rationalist critical discourse.

And so I awoke the day of my dissertation defense with a sense of dread: would I be called to task for my apostasy? My whitestream committee members might good-humoredly accept Black Elk's talking kingbirds, but such talk from a PhD candidate at the turn of the twenty-first century? I stood outside the English building smoking a hurried cigarette ten minutes before my defense would begin. A cardinal began singing loudly from the tree beside me, *fitCHEW fitCHEW fitCHEW fitCHEW fitCHEW.* That's what it sounded like on one level. On another, it was saying—I swear—"Don't worry, Tom. It'll be fine. You've been speaking up for us birds for years, and we're here for you." Unlike many of the avian events in this book, I offer this without the slightest suggestion of irony or postlapsarian nostalgia. And I walked into the defense room buoyed by a bird, utterly self-confident.

I dedicated the published book version of my dissertation— edited down to nearly half its original length, of course!—to the usual family and friends and academic mentors, "who have tolerated my avian eco-eccentricities these last several years; and to the Northern Cardinal in Iowa City who assured me that they would."

✳ MAY 2003, CLAY COUNTY PARK: *Bald Eagle*

> He will appear, may you behold him!
> An eagle for the eagle nation will appear.
> May you behold!
> —Nicholas Black Elk[50]

I went on a "Big Day" in the spring of 2003. That's when you run yourself ragged from sunrise to sunset, through as many habitats as possible, to identify as many species as possible. My no-longer-nimble body hadn't come close to my record of fifty-six birds in years, but on that day, I had fifty-five species by—my Lord, it was only 3:00 p.m.! This would be a piece of cake, I thought. But no, the late-afternoon doldrums set in over Avian Land (more commonly known as the southeast corner of South Dakota), and by 5:30, I was about to admit defeat. Then, after practically wading through the dense underbrush of a riverside park of cottonwoods and birches, I looked up through a hole in the trees and saw a pair of Bald Eagles—species number 56!—doing a dalliance high above the Missouri River, performing contrapuntal flips and loops around each other. . . . Well, Walt Whitman has already described it better over a hundred years ago in "The Dalliance of the Eagles":

> The rushing amorous contact high in space together,
> The clinching interlocking claws, a living, fierce, gyrating wheel,
> Four beating wings, two beaks, a swirling mass tight grappling,
> In tumbling turning clustering loops, straight downward falling,
>
> . . . .

One might well smile at the quaint word *amorous* in the context of the energy and vigor of ritual flight, of a natural act presumably free of any Hallmark sentiments, of life and nature in action and flux, presented here as a quickening vibrant string of present participles. I even wondered that moment, in fact, how much I was seeing a pair of eagles in actual flight, and to what extent that vision had been conditioned by this century-old verbal flight of Whitmanic effusion.

Whatever the case, my master birder knowledge did intuit that one of the eagles had certainly said to the mate, "Not today, honey, I have a headache." But the other had remonstrated, "But, dear, Tom Gannon needs to tie his Big Day record, and you know how much he has done for our cause. I mean, nearly five people have read at least several paragraphs of his book!" Despite the hint of sarcasm that I discerned in this eagle's voice, I was flattered by this nonetheless, as I watched their thousand-feet-high courtship flight disappear quickly downwind and downriver; and as I sauntered out of the deeper woods nearly drunk with elation, I derived from that vision the courage to carry on, to continue my Big Day to nightfall, shattering my old record by two species.

But in "our dejection do we sink as low," as Wordsworth wrote.[51] I soon rediscovered that feeling of never-again nostalgia that I had first felt when I reread a particular edition of Keats's selected poems. "I'll never read this (whole) book again," I had thought—still in my twenties—and a warm, electric swell of self-pity arose from my gut and spine, establishing a prototype for many a later response to "final" things. I'll probably never break this record again, either: indeed, I had almost wished, when stuck on species number 55, not to break the old one, as sort of a tribute to my youth. And now I scarce even believe in the "game" anymore, this rather vacuous intellectual exercise of listing birds, and in the very process, othering them, rendering them dead names and numbers on a taxonomic list. It was as if the synchronicity of the eagles dancing their way into number 56 on my Big Day list was a necessary epiphany, a scolding from "nature" that the number meant nothing, and the bird was all.

As with my own dallying eagles and Whitman's poem, my lifelong interest in both words and birds has created many inevitable associations of specific bird sightings and literary analogues. Thus I cannot watch a grackle strutting across the lawn without thinking of Wallace Stevens's blackbird poem. Nor could I appreciate my first Hermit Thrush without interminable lyrical eruptions into consciousness from Whitman's "When Lilacs Last in the Dooryard Bloom'd." A more synchronistic words and birds pairing occurred while I was writing my dissertation—and reading Gary Snyder. "It Pleases" offers one of Snyder's better meldings of politics and aesthetics, a scene of an eagle or a hawk—or heaven forbid, a vulture—soaring above the Capitol in Washington, DC: "Far above the dome / Of the capitol . . . A large bird soars," its "Wings arced, / Sailing easy" in the wind. A "dark-suited policeman / watches tourist cars"—but the police and politicians have no inkling of the true strength of flight—of the true power of nature—*above* them: alas, the true "center of power is nothing! / Nothing here," inside the granite walls of human legislation and ideology. But the raptor and the real world of "Earth-sky-bird patterns" go on, and the natural "world does what it pleases"—above and beyond a human society of smug, blind anthropocentrism—and at last to the vast detriment of that realm.

And just so did I watch in wonder a Bald Eagle above the University of Iowa's golden dome, at the very time I was deliberating upon this poem—and then regarded in greater wonder the scores of students and faculty aiming their empty eyes at the narrow strip of sidewalk in front of them, as the bird flew overhead. Truly, the center of power is nothing here, too, in a Midwestern academic setting well aware of Ecology with a capital *E,* all too ready to read and laud Aldo Leopold and other nature writers as kindred spirits—but still largely blithely unconscious of a natural world squawking and flapping outside the windows of their cloistered, bookish lives.

"If It Flies, It Dies." So runs the mantra of a local group of good ol' boys, who recently boasted of their motto to me in a South Dakota bar. They speak with pride of shooting Red-tailed Hawks on a regular basis, because there are "too damned many of 'em." They also sheepishly recoil from their initial boast of also shooting Bald Eagles, possibly from some vague recollection of the patriotic iconography in the aftermath of 9/11. But their attitude towards other species is clear, and indeed, this attitude is much more common—no doubt *the* attitude of the vast majority of Americans—than some of us in cloistered academia might want to acknowledge. But perhaps our own eyes-on-the-sidewalk dissociation from actual birds is just as lamentable a symptom of a general loss of relationship to the wild, to the earth, and ultimately to reality.

In contrast, the climactic epiphany of Lame Deer's vision quest offers a Lakota worldview that today's ecologically minded might quote fondly and yet still consider quaintly antiquated: a voice says to him, "We are the fowl people, the winged ones, the eagles and the owls. We are a nation and you shall be our brother. You will never kill or harm any of us."[52] Again, the contemporary animal-rights advocate might facilely embrace Lame Deer's vision as a *metaphorical* truth; but to imagine the avian-human relationship as a viable speaking kinship, to envision other species as *oyate*—or "peoples"—on a level equal to humankind: so far, in whitestream ecological and ecocritical writing, this has been but a cognitive truth, not an intuitive one. Perhaps it is time for a new worldview that synthesizes the theoretical dictums of Deep Ecology, etc., with the practical—and emotional—attitude that might conceive of an "eagle nation" as a veritable race and people worthy of reciprocal conversation.

Anthropologist Shepard Krech III can ask, "Were [. . .] Indians ecologists or conservationists?"—and assume the answer to be *no*, because, for one thing, he can't seem to get beyond his own Western conceptual box in describing the Lakota view of the American Bison as "animated other-than-human persons."[53] But the bison is, after all, like the eagle and the meadowlark, another *oyate*—that is, a different people or tribe. In Krech's view, such an animistic attitude precludes the Native American worldview from any rightful inclusion in a spectrum of viable contemporary theories regarding ecology, environmentalism, and animal rights. Which may finally be a good thing, in the end: I'm more and more convinced that even the most radical attempts to get beyond the human in Western thought still end up in the human-all-too-human.

Deep ecologist Paul Shepard tells us that the "loss of numen or spirit in animals is the great modern defeat," and this includes our "loss of sensitivity to birds."[54] As a cultural example, one need only point to the devolution of the eagle from a Native spirit mediating earth and sky to a two-dimensional iconic signifier of US nationalism. Indeed, we Americans view the wild Bald Eagle, almost by necessity, through a culturally colored lens, as an icon of (a however bedraggled) national pride, as an emblem of rugged individualism, and, perhaps today, as an untoward reminder of our fear and shame regarding the possibility of our own environmental suicide. The new re-*vision* of other species that I would call for must necessarily fight against such anthropocentric associations. Above all, we must try to see the eagle for her/himself, not for what we want the bird to represent to us, in the service of our own oh-so-human needs.

One is almost amused, then, to note the totemic aspect of various professional sports-team names in the US, as if the combatants were in need of the spirits of Bear, Lion, Falcon, and Eagle: totemic figures, all, of brute force and mindless courage. Furthermore, amid the human motives of patriotism and commercialism, the icon of the eagle in the US has become a veritable travesty. In Shoshone/Chippewa poet nila northSun's poem "moving camp too far," the irony is poignant, in the image of "an eagle / almost extinct / on slurpee plastic cups."[55] And especially for those who have reservations regarding the US's recent foreign military excursions, the blatant flying of eagle iconography is all the more painful.

It is no surprise, then, that in recent Native American literature, the "noble" raptor itself has become an emblem of ontological insecurity. In James Welch's *The Death of Jim Loney,* the mysterious "large bird and dark" that is the dominant hallucinatory image of doom in the half-breed protagonist's descent into madness can be read as a negative, ironic version of the eagle as divine intermediary, of the being closest to *Wakan Tanka.* The bird is intentionally unidentifiable, but seems very much a raptor, with connotations, no doubt, of the death-boding owl, but also of the diurnal raptors of the sky, of, ultimately, a (failed) connection to the realm of Native visions. "Sometimes I think it is a vision sent by my mother's people," Loney says, but that "vision" is never consummated. However well-intended his final suicidal "quest" is, Loney remains ultimately detached from his Native heritage—

like the lone bird itself, whose flight is often "out of tune"; and the novel's finale is an ironic avian ascent of failure and darkness: "the last thing he saw were the beating wings of a dark bird as it climbed to a distant place." The bird's literal flight is upwards, but the novel's tone and theme has me hearing Wallace Stevens's coda to "Sunday Morning" behind this flight, of birds sinking "Downward to darkness, on extended wings."[56]

Vine Deloria's writings are a re-affirmation of a Native counter-attitude towards the earth and other species, a view that is—to quote one of Deloria's book titles—*For This Land*: "The traditional Indian stood in the center of a circle and brought everything together in that circle. Today we stand at the end of a line, discarding or avoiding everything on either side of us."[57] This "line," for Deloria, is Western linear history, a "line" that has become *not* the ascending slant of modern progress, but the descending-into-darkness of a postmodern angst—of Stevens's and Welch's birds—the story of endings, of so-called Western civilization itself.

Lame Deer, who heard the voice of the eagle, was a *wičaša wakan* ("man of power") whose main power, spurred by his early vision, was derived from birds: "As for me, the birds have something to tell me," especially the eagle. When he prepared for a "big ceremony," an observer need only "look up at the sky and watch. Most of the time you'll see an eagle circling up there, just a tiny black spot going round and round. The eagle power is always there."[58] But we know now that, in ecological terms, this "always" is no certitude, and that the eagle and thousands of other species of birds may go the way of the Passenger Pigeon. Then the "power" will be gone. I think again of the flight of Jim Loney's "dark bird" which flew up and became a speck, too, and then disappeared, leaving Loney dead, and us alone.

✳ JUNE 2004, ARDMORE, OK:
Northern Mockingbird

The year 2004 was something of an annus mirabilis for me, the only time in my life that I spent any length of time—about two weeks—away from the northern Great Plains. A visit to my brother in southern Texas—a pure vacation besides—allowed me to get plenty of new species (twenty-three), including the Golden-fronted Woodpecker, White-winged Dove, Yellow-crowned Night-Heron, Common Poorwill, Bewick's Wren, Inca Dove, Red-shouldered Hawk, Black-crested Titmouse, and the now ubiquitous—even on the northern Great Plains—Eurasian Collared-Dove.

The fact that it was a car trip helped. Since Rapid City, South Dakota, to southern Texas is a two-day drive—hell, driving through Texas itself is half the trip—we stopped the first night in a motel in Ardmore, Oklahoma. Lord knows, I needed the break, between my mother constantly telling me how to drive and my preteen daughter and niece in the back seat calling each other "chunky monkeys" the whole drive there—and *laugh*ing, and *laugh*ing. . . .

My first lifer of the trip was a White-eyed Vireo singing its *snap-sputter* of a song before dusk along the small stream behind the motel. Then the next morning, I heard him, my first mockingbird, at 6 a.m., atop a streetlamp, awakening the gates of hell with a continuing series of inchoate chucks, whistles, and warbles. Just showing off, obviously, with several rounds of *chee-chee-choo* and *aah-aah-eeh* and a variety of low buzzes transcending transcription. This began my fifteen-day encounter with this species, the alpha songbird of these here parts, where the robin and even the cardinal play a distant second fiddle. (Although, I swear, the farther south you drive, the sweeter the very cardinals seem to sing?) When I virtually ran out of the motel room, binoculars in hand, I also saw my first-ever Scissor-tailed Flycatcher behind the motel, with its compulsive rising calls that matched its short flights into the air in pursuit of insects, its two-pronged tail longer than its mere kingbird of a body.

If this was the American South, I liked it. I had never been south of Nebraska, Iowa, or Colorado before this, a lifelong child of the Great Plains and its prairie birds: the songs of the Dickcissel and Western Meadowlark; the Eastern Kingbirds and Redwinged Blackbirds pecking my head as I vied for other species. Then this summer trip to Texas. The "robins"?—are mockingbirds! And there are wrens whose first names aren't "House"— and cowbirds with *red* eyes—and grackles with tails the size of your arm: "Oh, brave new world that has such species in it!" It was like some exotic country in Wallace Steven's sensual South, full of colorful avian wonders. Yes, the grackles in the nearest town had these humongous tails—Great-tailed Grackle is their apt name—who looked, and even sounded, mutant, as if the Common Grackles around Los Alamos had spent a few generations evolving. I would also see my first Greater Roadrunner, in an alley just a mile or so north of my brother's house in Canyon Lake, Texas.

Later, my brother tells me, he had something of a "pet" roadrunner, who followed him around outside the library in the nearby town of San Marcos. I don't know if this is the truth or not. It is *Texas,* after all.

"Why do some birds mimic the sounds of other species?" According to the Cornell Laboratory's response to this question, mockingbirds

> continue adding to their repertoire as they grow older. Northern Mockingbirds can learn as many as 200 songs, and often mimic sounds in their environment including other birds, car alarms, and creaky gates. One theory is that if a female prefers males who sing more songs, a male can top his rivals by quickly adding to his repertoire some of the sounds around him.

Unfortunately, I read this passage as human allegory as soon as I encountered it. I initially flattered myself that I, too, had evolved into a skillful and experienced mimic, with a fine repertoire of voices. Then it gradually occurred to me that I was really just a mockingbird (or worse yet, a starling) who had learned one lone plaintive song early on—oh, say, a Baltimore Oriole's descending sad slur of a whistle in late August—and that fetching but plaintive snippet of a motif has really limited the direction, the melody, of the rest of my life.

If this was the American South, I liked it. The birds, that is. The human people and discourse of Texas were another thing. Apparently, lots of public tax money is funneled into signs that one encounters along nearly every road and byway: CHURCH. So much for the separation of church and state. Let's just say I'm pretty sure that none of them signify a synagogue, or a mosque, or a Native American peyote ritual site. I was also struck at the apparent absence of any signs to Native American reservations, until it became clear to me that these were not the type of colonizing people who would put much stock in that: "Texas was home to several hundred groups of American Indians," but before Texas even became a state, "most of the populations of Native Americans were either eradicated or removed." And so, "despite the state's enormous size, only three reservations exist in Texas today."[59]

I was frankly surprised that the number was as high as three.

There has been a meme circulating on Facebook for many years now, in which a cat is holding open Harper Lee's *To Kill a Mockingbird* and complaining about the apparently misleading title: "There isn't anything in here on how to kill a mockingbird!" Even some of my English-professor colleagues have shared it, thinking it a real knee-slapper. But I've never understood the humor because the joke is based upon a falsehood. The book does indeed offer information on how to kill birds—you use a *gun*: "Shoot all the bluejays you want, if you can hit 'em, but remember it's a sin to kill a mockingbird."[60]

I love Texas highways. Everybody's going 85, sure of their God and their white privilege. If they knew my mind, they'd probably just shoot my liberal mixed-blood ass.

Was that a Chihuahuan Raven? Fuck. I *could* slow down.

Long birding trips mostly involve syncing your three basic needs: gas, a piss, and your next Diet Coke.

Another small southern plains town, another shitload of

Great-tailed Grackles and Eurasian Collared-Doves acting as if they owned the place because they do. And one near-obligatory Mississippi Kite in desultory flopping flight on the edge of town by the water tower. Did I just count nine House Sparrows? Let's just round it up to ten. It's TEXas.

Rush Limbaugh or country music or Bible talk. Christ. Choices in a democracy. Might as well listen to the Spanish station because I don't understand it well enough to get pissed off enough to want to turn my Subaru into an oncoming semi.

Yep, that's a goddamn Cattle Egret. Write it down. 7:35, TX Hwy 15, uh—DAMN. Five map apps on my iPhone and not one can tell me what county I'm in.

This is the worst gas-station beef jerky I've ever had.

If you forget about the song and erase the yellow, meadowlarks are pretty goofy-looking birds.

If I lived here, I'd be home by now. (How many times do I tell myself that same old joke? I gotta get me a hobby.) What was THAT? A bird. Order Aves. What the world needs now is a little Avian Order. Shut your mind the fuck up. I swear, Tom, I'll stop this car.

There's something about a two-lane highway that can make you regret your entire life.

Then—oh!—a Scissor-tailed Flycatcher on a barbed-wire fence and something warm wells up inside and you want to bless or save the world or not even care that it will never be blessed or saved.

Hawk. Not a good enough look to tell—? Red-tailed Hawk, then. Yep. Sure. That's the ticket. Write it down.

I could turn all these random thoughts into a poem, but that would just be stupid.

I love Texas highways. Everybody going 85, smug in their God and their white privilege. If they knew my mind, they'd probably just blow away my commie mixed-blood ass.

✳ JUNE 2005, FOLSOM CHILDREN'S ZOO:
White Stork

The Folsom Children's Zoo in Lincoln, Nebraska, served as one of the avian highlights of the too-little time I spent with my daughter as she was growing up. In town for a week to visit her dear old dad, she enjoyed the zoo visit for two main reasons. The first: she loved those tiny monkeys, the Pygmy Marmosets. I recall her exclaiming, "Oh, they're *so* cute!" over and over, holding her palms over her mouth in pure pre-teen glee: and this was just as I expected, from a girl raised into the social norm of a Disneyfied oohing and aahing over tiny mammals with large, near-baby-human eyes. The same little girl who, when I once said offhandedly during a walk, "Hush up, sparrow," exclaimed, "But Daddy, they can't help it—they're *birds!*"

The second was when Emma's initial feelings of shock and dismay were replaced by a squeal of ever-increasing delight as she watched a European White Stork "playing" with a ground squirrel. Almost nonchalantly, the large white bird caught the rodent in its bill as it ran by, and then speared at it for a minute or so, and then swished it around in a conveniently located water dish, and then—well, then the bird rather agonizingly repeated the spearing and swishing cycle several times, as if performing the long-tried-and-true routine of some jaded old washerwoman.

Then this proverbial winged deliverer of Euro-babies, with a rapid back-thrust of the head, gulped the Chip 'n Dale meal down in a flash. Touching my arm but not taking her eyes of the bird, Emma said in a low, slow, reverent voice, "Daddy. that's. the. coolest. thing. I've. ever. seen." Now this was *not* what I had expected from a young adorer of cuddly little marmosets. And it seemed that there was a strange and new dark twinkle in Emma's eye, indicative of an incipient awareness and acceptance of a Darwinian stork-eat-chipmunk world, of some sadomasochistic cosmos in which the animals of Disney are unveiled as wretchedly misleading, all-too-human simulations. This is the same girl who had written me a year or so earlier:

> Everything is going fine around here. [. . .] Well, I guess it hasn't been that good, because a few days ago, I found a baby bird, and [her dog] Buddy got it and, well—you know the rest. For the rest of that day, I felt disturbed and shaky.

The little girl who was once disturbed and shaky at the thought of another animal's death now had this strange new dark sparkle in her eye. That she later began writing morbid horror stories in high school may thus have been partly my fault, my own fault, my own *grievous* fault.

I'd forgotten that these places are sometimes allowed to keep native birds, and not just endangered ones—e.g., Snowy Egrets, and Black-necked Stilts, and a pair of pathetic Bald Eagles, who were obviously utterly miserable and bedraggled in the hundred-degree heat of a southern Nebraska summer day. It cannot be denied, in this twenty-first century, that even the best-run, best-funded, most "humane" zoos have their share of such outrages. And it's the large mammals—the primates and jungle cats—who seem to suffer the most. The native eagles, hawks, and owls one often sees in zoos and nature-conservation sites are usually there because of wing injuries (often caused by humankind, of course), so there is some rationale for their confinement. But the human privilege of watching a gorilla, a scarce yard away, staring back through a thick pane of glass in obvious existential despair, has little rationale at all, it seems to me; that, ironically, we're saving them from other murderous members of our own species just doesn't seem excuse enough.

> Nonhumans are born free, and everywhere they are in chains.
>
> —Bruno Latour[61]

"A Robin Red breast in a Cage / Puts all Heaven in a Rage," Blake famously wrote,[62] and enraged I was when I visited an art exhibit of John James Audubon paintings in Iowa City when I was in grad school. This ostensible tribute to birds and one of their greatest artists also included the strangest of sights: European goldfinches in a cage. Yes, they're even more brilliant than American Goldfinches, with their boldly patterned red, white, and black faces, but that doesn't justify the still common European practice of making them caged pets. (In fact, displaying *American* Goldfinches in such a fashion is against US federal law, and this is no doubt one of the reasons that the European birds were here.) Beryl Rowland claims that "no bird has been more cruelly treated than the goldfinch. Even today it is caged and sold in European street markets." As for European finches in general, one should probably also lament the traditional "practice of blinding the bird to improve its song."[63] Excuse me, but no one needs to be reminded of this history of cruelty at a John James Audubon exhibit, a supposed sacred site for lovers of birds.

✳ JUNE 2006, CRAZY HORSE MEMORIAL:
Turkey Vulture

> Crazy Horse never let a white man take his picture.
> [. . .] He was buried the way he wanted it, with nobody
> knowing his grave. The whole idea of making a beautiful
> wild mountain into a statue of him is a pollution of the
> landscape. It is against the spirit of Crazy Horse.
>
> —John Lame Deer[64]

"Is that a Golden Eagle?!"—I thought, I wondered, I hoped. My daughter Emma and I were on a ramshackle tourist bus taking us to the base of the Crazy Horse Memorial, in the beautiful southern Black Hills of South Dakota. But no, it was just a Turkey Vulture. (Yes, I've spent my birding life saying stuff like "Oh, it's *just* a robin" or "just another damned Dickcissel," and this behavior has been a most grievous sin, but that's another story.)

According to the official tourist-trap literature and lore of the monument, Crazy Horse's outstretched arm is pointing towards the western SoDak landscape itself so that we can imagine him uttering his famous (but likely apocryphal) words, "My lands are where my dead lie buried." (Less sublimely, Lame Deer describes the arm as "pointing ahead like 'this way to the men's room.'"[65]) By the end of the bus ride to the base of the construction site, the arm has become pretty well defined. I ask Emma, "You know what he's saying, Em?" *Huh*-uh. I exclaim triumphantly, "Get off our fucking land!" I've subsequently told this story to my undergraduate students so many times that I'm no longer sure of my exact words. I suspect that I added "fucking" after the fact for the benefit of a classroom full of twenty-year-olds. I confess to telling my students a lot of questionable, even tasteless, things. During the first week or so of my Native American Lit classes, many of my students still think that all Indians are lazy drunks who are close to the earth. So I tell them, "Hey, I'm not that close to the earth."

But I have been to the Crazy Horse Monument a good number of times before and since the trip with Emma, so I have been immersed in the troubled politics of the whole monolithic enterprise. For instance, there have been moments when I have imagined some veritable face of the Other peering out from the interstices of this commercialized and appropriative white man sculpture. But according to Lame Deer, "He [the sculptor Ziolkowski] might have good intentions, but he doesn't see that all that gigantic carving up of our sacred mountains is just another form of racism."[66] So I also conversely imagine that it is indubitably saying, "Fuck you." Or maybe this man who seemed forever in motion on horseback when alive is saying, "Free me from this static prison. Here I am, petrified, mortified in stone. Didn't you try to capture me, to kill me, enough when I was alive?" But much more often I despair at the irony of it all, this celebration of a Native warrior in the cause, finally, of a Western grubbing capitalism that this particular warrior had vehemently despised. And of course these tributes to dead Natives are always also implicit/unconscious celebrations that the "Injuns" *are* good'n'dead, that *we* have conquered them. (Note that the motto reiterated all over the Memorial—"My lands are where my dead lie buried"—has as its most crucial words, *dead* and *buried*.) This consummate capitalist tourist-trap site, this *monumental* place, continues to be a center of ideological conflict, an ongoing battle of worldviews, fraught with the all the ironies noted above. Lakota poet Tiffany Midge ends her poem "Mt. Rushmore & the Arm of Crazy Horse" with the hope that the sculpture itself will remain unfinished, that it will remain "just an arm—attached to a hand pointed toward / battle. Just an unfinished tribute to an unfinished war."

Midge's poetic fancy may well be rewarded. At least it's the running joke among Black Hills locals that we'll never see the work finished in our lifetime—or our children's lifetime, or their children's. . . . At last, the Monument is and will be a long, long work-in-progress. Kind of like colonization.

Also at the Crazy Horse Monument is the Visitor Center's book (and assorted kitsch) store. There's even a coloring book for sale for the kiddos, the *Crazy Horse Memorial Coloring Book,* with a picture of the great white sculptor—the real hero—on the cover. Hey, it's not just a face on—and a defacing of—a mountain: it's a total franchise.

In a Facebook entry a few years ago, I noted that *Tašunka Witko,* our greatest Lakota cultural hero, "died today" in 1877. He refused to become Christianized, and they killed him. Ironically enough, Neihardt's version of Crazy Horse in *Black Elk Speaks* baldly portrays him as a Christ figure. Ironically enough, Neihardt wrote that chapter himself, without Black Elk.[67] The extent of this and other appropriative editorializations on Neihardt's part—including transforming (the already closet-Catholic) Black Elk's Lakota ceremonialism into a more Western-sounding, ultimately monotheistic discourse—didn't become known to the general reader until over half a century later. Nor, in the popular mind, has this discovery by any means got in the way of a good (white) story. Neihardt's literary colonialism—inscribed and circumscribing—

still circles around Black Elk's story, and Crazy Horse's story, like a vulture.

Of course, it is Mount Rushmore, a few miles north of Crazy Horse, that has received more criticism from Natives; for Lame Deer, it meant

> that these big white faces are telling us [. . .] "we have made your sacred Black Hills into one vast Disneyland. And after we did all this we carved up this mountain, the dwelling place of your spirits, and put our four gleaming white faces here. We are the conquerors."
>
> And a million or more tourists every year look up at those faces and feel good [. . .] because they make them feel big and powerful, because their own kind of people made these faces and the tourists are thinking: "We are white, and we made this, what we want we get, and nothing can stop us." [. . .] They could just as well have carved this mountain into a huge cavalry boot standing on a dead Indian.[68]

Surely the project of Crazy Horse can't be as bad as this? And yet on one level, it may be even worse, an insidious *sort*-of tribute to a hero on the losing side—yet another self-congratulatory act on the part of the winners. Such recuperative uses of other, more "primitive" cultures by Western civilization—including monuments to Natives—are acts of both liberal penance and an ongoing conservative self-justification for a guilty past: whatever the case, it's always the colonized others "who end up losing"—again.[69]

Then there's the terrible marketing idea known as Crazy Horse Malt Liquor, created by Hornell Brewing Co. in 1992 (and eventually distributed by Stroh's Brewing). Their incredibly bad taste in choosing an Indigenous name for cheap booze is compounded by their (self-alleged) ignorance. A lawsuit resulted in an apology from Stroh's, in 2001; as an attorney for the Crazy Horse estate explained, "Hornell didn't know Crazy Horse was a real person or that there were any Sioux Indians alive"![70]

In 2011, my eBird report for Fort Robinson State Park—in the Nebraska panhandle—includes the following comment on seeing some Turkey Vultures: "of course!!!!—what a tribute to vulpine colonialism, this place." The historical markers about the former Red Cloud Agency and the faux rebuilt jailhouse near where Crazy Horse was murdered are ham-handed and heartless epitaphs to a people presumably doomed to extinction. The real raison d'être for the state park isn't that different from that of its original status as a military fort, a colonialism now masquerading as a benign tourist trap.

On one of my returns to Crazy Horse a few years later, I saw another vulture—this one circling the monument's huge head in slow flight—and I thought again, "How fitting. Scavenger colonialism in a nutshell." In principle, I hate when birds are used as tropes for human politics; but even I couldn't help myself this time.

Yes, another *using* of the avian, Tom, for your own anthropocentric concerns, a blatantly anthropomorphic metaphor. But I remain of two minds. Like a tree with two vultures. Sometimes that tree is a painful cognitive dissonance. Sometimes it's a more comfortable, even liberating, consideration of two wildly different

Turkey Vulture, Crazy Horse Memorial, SD, 24 June 2011

possibilities. And then there are times when it's just two fucking vultures being vultures. Those are the best times.

✳ JULY 2008, KOUNTZE LAKE: *Snowy Egret*

What am I doing here, not far from downtown Denver, at a city park lake in Lakewood, Colorado, taking a picture of a Snowy Egret resplendent at dawn?

I blame it on my first wife's restless soul, bless her wandering heart. As soon as we were married, we moved from Belle Fourche back to my hometown of Rapid City, in pursuit of better jobs. These two jobs turned out to be in a flower shop and a donut shop. So we moved to Vermillion, South Dakota, where I would qualify myself for an even better job by earning a master's degree. Both of these moves—and all subsequent ones—were her idea: hell, we moved about five times in Vermillion in the space of two years before I got the notion that her seemingly inveterate need to move was something of a character trait, even perhaps a "flaw." We were both rabid Jungians at the time, and she saw my reluctance to move every three or four months as a refusal to grow psychologically; I saw her ceaseless moving as symptomatic of an ego consciousness forever trying to flee itself. I joked after one of our moves, "Nope. I don't think it worked. You're still you."

In short, we had already been moving away from each other even as our daughter Emma was born. (Her first word was "da-da." Well, actually it was "dih-puh" [diaper]. But "da-da" was second, I swear.) We divorced when Emma was two, and even though I had joint custody and full visitation rights, I "refused" to move with my ex-wife to Riverton, Wyoming, and then eventually to Lakewood, Colorado. Instead, psychically stunted as I am, I remarried, moved to Iowa City to pursue my PhD, and took plane and car trips to Wyoming and Colorado to see my beloved daughter Em when I could.

When Emma and her mom moved to Lakewood, my yearly visits inevitably included a stay at a Motel 6, just off US Highway 6. It was only a few blocks from Emma's house, I could get there without too much big-city driving, and the price was right. It was also a short drive to Belmar Park, next to the public library and home to Kountze Lake, a small body of water by South Dakota and Nebraska standards, but redeemed by the fact that several species of herons and egrets were present there even during the summer months. So before Emma even dreamed of rousting her teenage body out of bed, I would bird the lake for an hour or two before picking her up and having her talk me through downtown Denver—"Look, Daddy! That's a prostitute!"—or taking her to Denver's pathetic excuse for a zoo.

So here I am, looking at a Snowy Egret standing in Kountze Lake at dawn, as the orange-red sun rises behind the dark silhouette of the bird and throws its rippling orange and gold crescents all around. Resplendent. And I ultimately have my first wife to thank for all this.

✳ AUGUST 2008, FONTENELLE FOREST:
House Wren

The worst day of my life—yesterday—began with an uneventful drive through Lincoln's Pioneers Park at dawn, to check off a few early-rising species, as a fine start to my Big Day. Success: I had twenty-two species, including both species of meadowlark, by the time I got to my second scheduled stop, Wilderness Park. But there the trouble began. I was so intent on identifying those dark-winged shadows in the underbrush that my directional gestalt got turned around, and I ended up walking out at the Old Cheney Road exit, several miles south of my parked car. At least I was alert enough to turn directly back on the trail and finagle my way, after a few detours, back to the proper exit. "Damn, I've lost a good half-hour of the morning," I thought, driven to get in as many habitats as possible during those first few golden hours of birds at their most active.

After a second stop at Pioneers Park, for a sojourn through their now-open Nature Center and my first sighting of a Carolina Wren in Nebraska, I drove southwest of Lincoln to the Spring Creek Prairie Audubon Center, plopped down my four bucks, and confidently set out on their walking path. (Or paths: as with Wilderness Park, it's more of a collection of paths that intersect in a willy-nilly fashion.) Nearly at the end of the main path that made a circumambulation of the prairie pond, I took a right turn at the woods, recognizing another fruitful bird habitat. But—yes—I had gotten lost again. My assumption (and apparently mistaken memory) that this trail would meet the main one near the end was mistaken—it was a dead end, so I circled back, cursing once more, and after a few false side trails, I found my way back to the main path. "Damn," I thought, "now I'm a good hour or so behind, at least." It was after high noon already, and so I decided then that I'd have to cut Platte River State Park from my itinerary, to make sure that I'd get to Fontenelle Forest—the golden goal of the day—before its office closed at 5 p.m.

Next it was 30 miles or so east on I-80, to another favorite stop, Schramm Park State Recreational Area. After checking out the Platte River across the highway (Great Blue Heron: *check*), I drove up the park's steep one-way-loop road to its highest altitude, where their nature trail began. I briefly looked at the big sign with a map of the trail on it, but it was so dilapidated that it was pretty illegible, though I could make out that "Nature Trail #1" was only 1.5 miles. "Ha, that's nothing!" By this time, I should have recognized the effaced sign as blatant foreshadowing, but I was still in a hobbyist lather, hell-bent on adding more birds to my list.

So much for a birder's hubris. By this point, I also should have realized that I was playing out my own sick version of a minor

Greek tragedy. And I realize now that—well, I should have taken my Diet Coke with me. Of course, "Trail #1" meant there was a Trail #2, which, towards the end of Trail #1 (or so I'd figured), would intersect the first trail at several points; however, the cute rustic wood-burnt signs distinguishing the two at trailside must have been written, I began to suspect, by Franz Kafka. I told, or asked, myself, "Trail #1 *is* a loop, isn't it? When is it finally going to get me back to my car?" I couldn't believe it: I was lost *again*. Finally, Trail #1 just seemed to end . . . at the back of the Eastern Nebraska 4-H Center, and a stack of canoes, and a big blue blow-up waterslide. This is getting bad, I thought. Out of pure dejection more than anything, I kept walking through the 4-H complex, remembering that I had passed this place on the highway several miles before Schramm Park. I pondered heading out to the highway and making that long walk, but instead I retraced my steps back to the path, past 4-H workers who were wondering, perhaps, what kind of creeper wandered into a teen retreat with binoculars around his neck.

I finally found a sign that read, "Trail #1/To the Ak-Sar-Ben Aquarium." Ah, some certainty. Of course it couldn't mean all the way down to the Aquarium at the Park's entrance. . . . But it did. Now I just had to walk back up the hill I'd driven up originally, a sixty-degree grade of well over a mile. With Virgil, I thought, "*hoc opus, hic labor est*"—and wondered, as usual, whether I had mixed up the *hoc* and the *hic*. The sun was out from behind the clouds in full force, I was thirsty beyond measure, and I could barely lift my legs off the ground. I felt a pain where my left leg joined the hip, as if I had slightly pulled a ligament there. Back in my car, that hot Diet Coke never tasted so good.

This wasn't the Big Day that I had had in mind. But at least there was the Fontenelle Forest Nature Center just south of

Omaha, lauded by every Nebraska birding publication and web-
site, and this would be my first time there. But by now, as I paid
the office lady my fee, I actually wondered what other people
might be thinking of my appearance: completely sweat-soaked,
shirt untucked in an "I-don't-give-a-fuck-anymore" attitude, and
sandaled feet with more dirt and mud evident than flesh. In my
sudden paranoia, it seemed that she pointed out the bathroom to
me as if I were a vagrant in search of a truck-stop shower.

But when she gave me the Center's map, I took it like a long-
lapsed Catholic receiving the Eucharist once again. A map. The
glory! And so detailed, *ooh*: each trail (so what if there were 30
or 40 of them?) glossed with a textual description of its habitat
and—*hmmm*—climbing grade. And so, no, I never got LOST on
this set of trails; but I should have realized that such a riverside
terrain would be full of hills and hollows, and that my strained
leg ligament would only get worse. At least this time I brought a
bottle of water.

By the time I got to the far bottom of the series of trails—to
the Great Swamp, as it is called, in hopes of that rare warbler
or three that the brochures had boasted of—my left leg, after
so many hills and valleys, had become pretty much a useless
appendage dragging behind the other. Worse yet, the trip back
was much more uphill, from the ground-floor level of the Missouri River to the natural levee upon which the Center itself was
built. The water was reassuring, but now I wished I had brought
my cell phone. What if my leg finally stiffened up entirely, and I
had no option but to try crawling out of there? Each trail in the
series I'd chosen to follow back was indicated on the map as 0.9
miles, or 1.3 miles, etc. But each trail also seemed to be taking
close to an hour. I was further delayed by having to interminably
duck the webs of these fat, black spiders that hung across the trail

from almost every overhanging tree; or sometimes I had to brush
the webs away just to continue on the path; or sometimes I didn't
even see them, ending up having to knock a spider off my shoulder or head every now and then. So when one trail intersected a
dirt road, I decided to take the latter instead.

But the dirt road was an uphill hour of pain itself. A car or
two passed, and I almost hoped that someone would stop and
give me a ride: but by now I was sure that I looked like a long-
haired, stumbling drunkard—of uncertain ethnicity, besides. Or
my binoculars were just the ruse of a sociopathic hitchhiker bent
on random murder. And even if I were taken at my face value—as
a mere lover of nature—it's well documented, anyway, that birders have long been deemed by the general public—along with
poets and communists—as people bordering on lunacy.

I only sipped at the bottle of water, vowing not to take the
last swallow until I came into sight of my car. For a new fear had
come to me: they closed at 5 p.m., and it was now after 7 o'clock.
Was there a gate they locked?—I couldn't remember. With all
the time I had on my hands, don't think me silly for working out
a contingency here: I would climb the fence, sleep in my car, and
wait until they opened in the morning. Finally I came to pave-
ment, and an actual city street, which also seemed to go on a lot
longer than the map indicated. A nice bourgeois neighborhood,
and I knew I was an incredible sight by now, and so I kept to the
street as much as possible, certain that my dishevelment deserved
no sidewalk, deserved no closer proximity to real people in this
fine-lawned Omaha suburb. As I turned onto the boulevard that
led to the Center, I asked myself out loud the question that had
only been a muted thought at my previous stops of the day: *What
have I done?* I got into my car at last, wondering if I could even
drive. I could, and did, but upon arriving home in Lincoln, my

legs had tightened up so much that I groaned aloud dragging my
birding stuff up the stairs of my apartment building.

My tragic flaw through all this has been my irrational passion for
birding, and specifically, for the idea of the Big Day itself, as some
manly marathon or quest. But my positive passion had reversed
itself the last several miles of my ordeal, as I silently (and guiltily)
cursed the House Wrens that laughed at me every few yards from
the side of the trail with their snake-rattle chattering. Previously,
their interminable scolding had been one of my favorite, oh-so-
cute birding moments. A few years later, eBird would flag me for
counting fifty of them in Wilderness Park. But the wrens were
then so rampant that I could barely hear any other birds through
their ruckus. In fact, my early May birding reports for—often
forty to fifty—House Wrens now simply include the one-word
comment: "rampant."

"I'll never go on a Big Day again!," I may have said out loud—
or at least, "I'll never go to Fontenelle Forest again!" (A promise I
have broken many times, of course.) I figure that I walked at least
a good forty miles that day, though I think fifty miles is probably
closer to the truth. I usually enjoy the sheer exhaustion and physical strains of my Big Day adventures, and it occurs to me now
that part of the appeal is the suffering itself—a sort of expiation
or sacrifice out of guilt for something I'm not even conscious of.
In sum, it's a specific variety of religious experience, whatever the
motive. Furthermore, I'm not a stupid man in general—though
my wife might argue with that: I don't think I would have consciously refused to print out all the trail maps beforehand unless
some part of me hadn't *wanted* to get lost—and to suffer accord-
ingly. This time I did take it to an extreme that I don't wish to

repeat. Such self-flagellation—metaphorically speaking—is a religious task for younger men.

I was going to go to the University tomorrow to make some handouts, but I'm too sore to walk the two blocks from the parking meter to Andrews Hall. And my right knee actually hurts more than my left hip, probably from the strain of my right leg compensating for its truant brother. I think I'll take some Advil, maybe take it easy for a few days before classes began.

But no—two days later, spurred on by a post in an online birding group, I drove a half-hour out of town to some wetlands, and to four new species. Life's quest for complete meaning via surrogate objects goes on.

✳ MAY 2009, THE LAKE BESIDE LAKESIDE, NE:
Black-Necked Stilt

Nebraska Highway 2 is the most well-known scenic alternative to driving across Nebraska if you want to avoid the soporific experience of Interstate 80. In fact, a Google search just informed me that Highway 2 is now officially called the Sandhills Journey Scenic Byway. Such byways are wonderful for back-road birding: I've driven four hundred miles around north-central Nebraska without hitting a town with more than five hundred people or so. The best part of Highway 2 for birding lies between Hyannis—don't blink—and Alliance; there the sand-dune habitat is pleasantly pock-marked by numerous small, shallow lakes, and in the spring, there are also many stretches of sheet water—temporary standing water from recent rains—along both sides of the road.

So it's ideal for waterbirds. I discovered my favorite spot along Highway 2 pretty much by accident, on my first trip through: one of the larger lakes was right next to a small town, and a convenient backroad behind the town accessed the lake. The town was propitiously named Lakeside. This has got to be good, I thought. And it was: of the nine species I quickly recorded there, four were lifers.

There was the Willet, a large, plain gray sandpiper best known for its call, *pill-will-willet, pill-will-willet.* There was the Ruddy Duck, with its fat, clownish-colored face and bill and its short spike of a tail. There were lots of Eared Grebes, with their golden wisps of "ear" feathers that seemed like psychic emanations in the proper sunlight. And there were Black-necked Stilts, loudly cavorting along the western shore with their usual American Avocet companions, their accomplices in raucousness—two of the largest and most stunning shorebirds of North America. Tall and thin and black and white, the stilt is most notable for its extremely long legs—thus its name—and the fact that these legs transgress the laws of (human) nature, as it were, by bending the wrong way at the "knee": this joint buckles backwards as if the lower half of the leg were one long forward-protruding "foot."

This lake is now an annual, sometimes biannual, stop for me. Several pairs of Ruddy Ducks remain through the summer, as do about forty to fifty Eared Grebes, although eBird keeps questioning my apparently hyperbolic numbers. But the convocation of stilts and avocets has always been the highlight. The last few springs, however, were missing the Black-necked Stilts; I imagined, against all human good sense, that their avocet buddies missed them as much as I did.

My usual reason for finding myself on Nebraska Highway 2 was that I was on my way to visit my family in Rapid City. Mom hadn't been much of a conversationalist since the turn of the twenty-first century, sitting as she usually did at the kitchen counter taking oxygen through a mask for her COPD. But when I arrived this time, I did my best to ask her questions for my next book, about Grandma Mollie, and Great-uncle Percy, and that shadowy Indian father of theirs, a certain John Frenier, who "may have come down from Canada," as Mom remembered. When she asked out of politeness, "Did you see any birds?"—a perfunctory question that always made me want to answer, "No, Mom, not a one"—I told her about the four new species I had seen. I concluded, "The town is called Lakeside, but I can't for the life of me find the name of the lake anywhere." Now laconic from COPD and never much one for humor, she said quite seriously (I assume), "Maybe it's called the Lake Beside?" Later that night, when I was entering my sightings from the day's drive, eBird prompted me to name the location that I'd just designated by clicking on the map. I typed, "Lakeside, NE (the lake beside ~)," and it's been my name for it ever since.

✳ MAY 2009, DEVILS TOWER: *American Goldfinch*

In 2009, I made my first trip to Devils Tower in many, many years. There were lots of American Goldfinches there.

A brochure by the Devils Tower Tourism Association states straightforwardly, "In 1906, President Teddy Roosevelt designated Devils Tower as the nation's first national monument. Devils Tower could be called the nation's first <u>natural</u> monument." Less straightforwardly, regarding the nearby town: "SUNDANCE. Just the name conjures to mind cowboys, outlaws and the wild west." No doubt. Sundance is "in the Black Hills of Wyoming where the Native Americans held their sacred Sun Dance ceremonies." But its name no longer "conjures" that ceremonialism, apparently. Now it conjures the "wild west"—and a hip film festival. Neighboring Moorcroft, too, is "a bustling town, where the culture of the Old West is still evident." (Indeed, these are the same sort of people who are members of local "Friends of Custer" organizations.) And in Hulett, Wyoming, we have plenty of "friendly folks, who, when asked will point out the new golf course, Custer's Trail"—since, again, of course, "the area is rich in the heritage of 'Western Tradition.'" And by the way: "Created in 1875, the county was named for General George Crook, a famous Indian fighter."[71] Of course.

Calling a golf course "Custer's Trail" is tasteless enough, but worse yet is the name of Devils Tower itself. In Lakota, its name is *Mato Tipila*—the Bear's House, or Bear Lodge; in Kiowa, it is *Tsoai* ("Rock Tree"). Via the act of colonization, such eco-therapeutic, nature-connected mythopoeicisms were replaced by Devils Tower, and so a dualistic good vs. evil theology gets projected upon an igneous intrusion; the very landscape gets overed on and demonized. In binary contrast: "The choice of town names such as Faith, Eden, Mission, and Sinai [. . .] reflected Dakota settlers' religious inclinations. In the 1880s southern Dakota settlers even considered naming their future state 'God's Country.'"[72] And yet this new holy land is sprinkled with infernal place names like Devils Tower and the Badlands, as if the Good Christian God cannot get on without His Shadow, often projected upon the local Indigenous and the "bad land" itself.

The Andy Griffith Show has always been a personal favorite of mine, but Mayberry was certainly a Southern enclave of white monoculturalism, with no room for the minority Other. When the mythic West did occasionally appear in a storyline, that's exactly what it was—completely mythic. The following witty repartee, from a 1963 episode called "Aunt Bea's Medicine Man," demonstrates the whitestream ideology regarding the Native American in the early 1960s. Yes, the discourse presents the Native as living a healthier, closer-to-the-earth lifestyle (itself a stereotype), but at the same time, the Indians are "devils." Not accidentally, this last assertion (the "Shawnee—they're devils") has been expunged from the most recent TV version of this sitcom episode—which I just watched the other night. But I'd already transcribed the "devil" line from the original version on VHS, and so I ask—rhetorically—why are they erasing such history, such a happy hunting ground of American discourse?

> COLONEL HARVEY [*hawking his 170-proof "Indian Elixir"*
> *to a Mayberry street crowd*]: Have you ever seen a fat or
> a worried Indian? Have you ever met an Indian with
> ulcers? [. . .] No! Why? Because the Indian's way is
> Nature's way. [. . .] Colonel Harvey's Indian Elixir:
> good for what ails you.

Later in the episode, at Andy's house after supper, the Colonel makes bogus smoke signals with his cigar, performs some ridiculous sign language with his hands, and then pompously utters some "Native" macaronic gibberish. He explains to Opie and Aunt Bea, who are sitting there awe-struck, where he apparently learned these wonders: "Shawnee. I lived among 'em. They're *devils*."

The Colonel's imitation of the Shawnee language via semantic mumbo-jumbo has many forebears. Among the many troublesome Native stereotypes in Disney's animated *Peter Pan* (1953) are those involved in that insipid tune "What Made the Red Man Red?," which begins, "Why does he ask you 'How?'" and facetiously concludes that "the Injun, he sure learn a lot, / And it's all from asking 'How?'" *Hau* is the ubiquitous Lakota word for "Hello" and "you betcha," but it has also become the crux of many an egregious Euro-American movie and cartoon misunderstanding or tasteless pun. Worse yet, the song's chorus, with its nonsense clang-association words, simply reduces Indigenous languages—and meanings—to vacuous phatic signifiers. "*Hana Mana Ganda— / Hana Mana Ganda*" is "translated" by the clever white narrator as follows: "*Hana* means what *mana* means, / And *ganda* means that, too." My translation: this particular tribal language—like all Native languages, no doubt—is either incredibly deep and mystical regarding interrelationships—since everything seems to mean everything else!? Or: It is the pure gibberish of an ethnicity incapable of anything else. Except, perhaps, for being "devils."

In 2009, I made my first trip to Devils Tower in many, many years. There were lots of American Goldfinches there.

❋ MAY 2009, LITTLE BIGHORN BATTLEFIELD: *Eurasian Collared-Dove*

In May 2007, I saw on the news that an Indian Peafowl was loose in Santa Fe, New Mexico, having eluded the authorities for over two days. As one news site so brilliantly informed the non-bird-ing masses, "Peacocks aren't native to New Mexico, so animal control officers assume he's an escaped pet."

In a blog post, I implored these people: "Please catch it! Avian immigration has long been a curse to native bird populations." I was being both serious and tongue-in-cheek here. Where were these animal-control people when other invasive species such as House Sparrows and European Starlings were let loose in New York City in the late nineteenth century? (Contemporaneous to the Indian Wars, by the way.) "We must catch this—thing," I continued, "before its concupiscent ways, as with most over-breeding foreigners, lead to a vast reduction in our native grouse and quail populations. (Oh, wait—we've already taken care of that.)"

I added that, in the last year or two, I'd noticed good numbers of another introduced immigrant, the Eurasian Collared-Dove, in both eastern and western South Dakota, rapidly expanding its range from the southeastern US. It had only just become an established US resident, in Florida, in—1982! Just a few decades later, in 2012, I heard that the bird had made the *Alaskan* Christmas count for the first time that year. Wow, that's some manifest destiny for one species. I'm not sure how native Mourning Doves are going to be affected by this interloping cousin; all I know is that this new bird's wheezy, jay-like *nyah nyah* is just plain creepy, a downright mean-sounding sneer. And if there is a consistent semantic difference between a pigeon and a dove, this bird is much more of a pigeon. For some reason, the sneer and attitude remind me of the then-utterly-alien, ironically incongru-ent strains of "Gary Owen," as played by Custer's men on their way to battle, to Black Kettle's camp at dawn on the Washita, and later to the Lakota, Arapahoe, and Cheyenne encampment on the Little Bighorn. Whether the southern plains of Oklahoma or the northern plains of Montana, the Old World fife and drum corps must have certainly been an earsore to the meadowlarks and other natives of the grasslands.

My first trip to the Little Bighorn since I was a child was a 2009 birding excursion through Montana. Of course you can't just *bird* the Little Bighorn Battleground National Monument, given its political import: it was formerly known as the Custer Battleground National Monument, and many of the local white Custer-worshippers are still angry about the "politically correct" name change. But it remains sacred land—defined as such, Vine Deloria would claim, through the sacrifice of many lives for an ideal, for "a cause we hold dear."[73] And like Gettysburg and other battle sites, it has been deemed sacred ground by both sides. It was already Great-Plains-hot in late May, and the heat seemed almost visible, rising from the asphalt around the visitor's center with the aura of blood, from the elation of illusory victory, of wide-eyed fear, of last-gasp despair.

But there were also birds, thankfully, to take my mind off the dismal human political baggage of the place. The dominant passerine that day seemed to be the Eastern Kingbird. And such an alpha, such a bossy bird, such a sputtery bluster. And then I thought, *that* figures; a certain other contingent had once assumed that they could boss their way onto the Great Plains, too. There were also plenty of European Starlings, and—oh, yes—Eurasian Collared-Doves. Of course. Symptomatic avian signifiers that the colonizers had won. The site might as well have retained the official name of Custer.

That other bossy contingent, of US military and gold-diggers, was initially stymied by the uncomfortable fact that, damn, there were already other people here when they arrived. And so the Great Plains are pockmarked throughout by a plethora of historical markers and place names—and tourist traps—for battles and "massacres." There is a hefty memorial stone among the US Cavalry graves at the Little Bighorn battlefield (and tourist trap). Worn from the Montana weather and sternly archaic in its typography and very discourse, the epitaph must be one of the earliest official markers to still grace this site:

TO THE OFFICERS AND SOLDIERS
KILLED,
OR WHO DIED OF WOUNDS RECEIVED IN
ACTION
IN THE TERRITORY OF MONTANA,
WHILE CLEARING THE DISTRICT OF THE
YELLOWSTONE
OF HOSTILE INDIANS.

The name was changed, as noted above, from the Custer Battlefield National Monument to the Little Bighorn Battlefield National Monument in 1991. (The former name wasn't official until 1946[74]—significantly, right after the patriotic surge of World War II.) There are now headstones scattered along the hillsides of the site marking the fall of several Lakota warriors. However, the many neat rows of Cavalry white headstones in the main cemetery are the park's most salient feature, and the first and main attraction greeting the visitor upon entrance. The rest of the venue largely remains the relatively desolate rolling dry-grass prairie that it was at the time of the famous battle—or massacre—of 1876.

According to the National Park Service's official brochure, *Little Bighorn Battlefield*, the stone tributes to fallen Natives didn't begin until 1999, and they were erected for the sake of balance:

"These unique markers are an important addition to the historic cultural landscape, providing visitors with a balanced interpretive perspective of the fierce fighting that occurred here in 1876." Thus Lame Deer, in the early 1970s, could still complain, "Some of my people died at the Little Bighorn, but only the white soldiers are buried there."[75]

And so visitors to the site are still confronted with this epitaph in stone, which continues to erase the crimes of colonial aggression and land theft by way of the final damning epithet, "hostile Indians." But now, wouldn't *you* have been hostile, too, given the situation? Might not an Indian Shylock have had good reason to say, "If you prick me, do I not become hostile?" I'm reminded of seeing the Crocodile Hunter, the late Steve Irwin, on one of his TV episodes, jabbing at a poisonous snake with a stick and jawing in his rich drawl of an Aussie accent: "When you poke them with a stick, they tend to get irritable and aggressive." Even my seven-year-old daughter had the sense to raise her arms and earnestly exclaim, as we watched that episode together, "Well, stop *poking* it then!"

My first record of a Eurasian Collared-Dove in South Dakota was in Rapid City in June 2006. Three years later, I called a friend in Chamberlain, South Dakota (in the middle of the state), and I heard that now-familiar catbird-on-steroids sneer in the background. My friend was outside—not far from our invasive pigeon.

In my adopted home state of Nebraska, the bird was first reported back in 1997; then, in "the spring of 2000 they moved to the city, appearing in Omaha."[76] But they have remained denizens, mostly, of small-town Nebraska. I saw my first Nebraska collared-dove, in fact, in the tiny hamlet of Elmwood in 2007, but only one of them. Ten years later, I birded—on a lark—the tiny hamlet of Elm Creek, Nebraska, in the middle of the state, and counted fourteen of the sneering feathered bastards (I say this affectionately) in the space of a few blocks. Only their fellow colonials, the House Sparrows, outnumbered them.

I never found out whether the Santa Fe authorities ever found that peacock, though I assume that they did. It probably strutted right up to an animal control truck, too proud, too vain, too stupid, to ever suspect re-capture. Just as I picture Custer strutting onto the Great Plains, on his way to the Little Bighorn.

✳ MAY 2009, BOWDOIN NATIONAL WILDLIFE REFUGE: *Marbled Godwit*

My 2009 spring birding trip was supposed to end up on the west coast. I had spent weeks marking up my bird guides and making lists of potential lifers, mostly seabirds I might readily encounter on the shores of Washington and Oregon. However, something untoward happened on the way to the ocean that radically changed my plans. When I hit the Bighorn Mountains in northeast Wyoming, I started experiencing panic attacks when I drove down the higher mountains' long, steep descents—breathlesswhiteknuckle episodes that were pure anguish, however irrational. By the time I'd driven two-thirds of the way across Montana, I'd decided that, if such ranges were mere foothills of the Rockies, I certainly couldn't handle the real ones. The snow-capped peaks of the next range looming larger and larger in the west were called the Crazy Mountains, which seemed less than auspicious in my neurotic state of mind, so I decided to turn north at Big Timber and—oh—see a little more of Montana's beautiful grasslands, leisurely looping my way back home through the Dakotas. I was left to ponder how I might salvage a trip that had begun with such grand oceanic goals.

I had loved James Welch's novel *The Death of Jim Loney* for years and had just taught it in my Native American Lit class again, so the opportunity to see some of the places in a novel set in north-central Montana was one saving grace of the trip. An old asphalt two-lane called Highway 66 took me to the Fort Belknap Indian Reservation, and so I was already within the pages of the book.

This reservation looks much like the South Dakota Badlands, although you can see the Little Rockies in the distance. And look, there's Hayes, and its run-down government housing: it looks like so many small, poverty-stricken towns on the reservations in South Dakota that I suddenly feel that I've driven many hundreds of miles for nothing: *la plus ça change* and all that. A sign along the two-lane highway tells me that the local high school teams are called the Thunderbirds—a signifier painful to unpack, speaking as it does of a too-rapid transformation from a mythic time, and a time more deeply connected to birds, to a mundane era of cheap wine in alleyways.

On the north end of the Rez is the town of Fort Belknap per se: I drive up and down the town's residential streets to bird a bit, but it's hard to stay in a birding state of mind when every other block, it seems, has an addiction treatment center. My birding trip is now a full-fledged sociology/ethnic studies course, and I don't like it.

Ah, there really is a Milk River—fit ironic accompaniment to

Loney's tragic return to the Death Mother. And there's Harlem, finally, the main setting of the novel, just north of the Rez, across another two-lane highway going east-and-west. I decide to bird the streets of Harlem, too, just because I can. I take a photo of the Entering Harlem sign and yes, there *is* a Kennedy's Bar, just like in the book, and so I take a picture of the gaudy red, white, and yellow sign to prove to my students that it exists and that I've been there. I even think of going in and having a beer or two—it's early afternoon—but no: this is a birding trip, however wayward. And yes, the European Collared-Doves have made it this far north already, as if sinister latter-day reinforcements of Thunderbird wine and everyfuckingotherthing the colonizers brought with them.

Back on the highway, I hear on the radio that another town in Welch's book—Havre—is pronounced like "have her." The Francophile in me never would have guessed. The ocean could wait: these were all invaluable things to know for my pedagogy.

Not far east of Harlem—yes, I was now already driving *away* from the direction of the Pacific, damn it—was Bowdoin National Wildlife Refuge, which I had only learned of the night before, during a frenzied ad hoc web search for decent places to bird, in a motel room with a deer's head on the wall and a sign that said, "Please DO NOT CLEAN Birds or Fish in Rooms." On the short drive to Bowdoin, I got a Canadian radio station broadcasting a live humor skit, and for a moment I wanted, as Jim Loney did during one of his last lucid moments, to be in Canada, maybe even be Canadian. But the far north of Montana would have to be the next best thing.

Bowdoin NWR was damned near perfect: one of those great eco-tourist layouts in which a well-maintained dirt road circles the entire wetlands—a birder's dream. As if to greet me at the beginning of the circuit, a handsome Swainson's Hawk perched as a lookout in a tree near the entrance. Savannah and Baird's Sparrows sang from the fields on the dry side of the road, a welcome cacophony of trills and buzzes, as a Northern Harrier delicately glided low nearby. Waterbirds included copious Eared Grebes, mixed flocks of avocets and stilts, and tons of Wilson's Phalaropes spinning in the water like crazy wind-up toys. *The hell with the ocean,* I thought.

Lifer #1 at Bowdoin was a Cinnamon Teal, the male a burnt red-brown, yet another of those unusually plumaged birds I had stared at in my bird guide for years, salivating. A couple Marbled Godwits—lifer #2—were standing on the field side of the road, large sandpipers rather like curlews, but with long bills that curved up, not down. From these same fields I heard what sounded like the song of a "mini-Western Meadowlark," as if the loud, glorious song were being attempted by a smaller bird; my binoculars revealed that it was a Chestnut-collared Longspur: lifer #3. Then, among the numerous flocks of Northern Pintails and Northern Shovelers and Ruddy Ducks was lifer #4, a Canvasback, which looks vaguely like the more common Redhead, but has its own distinctive, more massive head shape.

Yes, *the hell with the ocean.* For a Great Plains birder still stuck on the Great Plains, this was damned near Utopia. Despite the four lifers, the most memorable part of the Bowdoin circuit was the eternal line of hundreds of Yellow-headed Blackbirds in the cattail reeds on both sides of the dirt road, squawking their butt-ugly, constipated frog-songs at me from just a yard or two away. I kept thinking, such character! Such hutzpah!—as I snapped photo after photo of a species who knew that this was its home, who gave not a damn for the occasional human interloper in a road-worn Toyota sedan, who knew that it was *in its place:* and at that moment, I also knew that I was an utter landlubber, a prairie rube, who had no need for the sea.

✳ JULY 2009, PIONEERS PARK: *Brown-Headed Cowbird*

It was a hot July day in Pioneers Park on the edge of Lincoln, which meant that the birding probably wouldn't be that great. My main reason for the excursion was to serve as mentor to an English graduate student who had suddenly developed an interest in birding. So we drove around the park looking for raptors and then ended with a walk along the trail behind the Nature Center. It was an utterly mundane summer-doldrum outing, with a decent count of thirty-nine species; but on the back of the trail, the unexpected occurred: let's call it the episode of the Unknown Bird.

My birding acolyte had pointed out a bird in a tree, and then she went through the by then perfunctory act of asking me to identify it, with at least a pretense of anticipatory excitement. I raised my binoculars almost smugly and saw a—sparrow? A bit too big for one, I thought. There were faintly darker markings on the head of an otherwise generally monotone tannish bird, but I couldn't for the life of me fit it into my mental avian database. It then gave a loud trill of sorts, and the grad student looked at me again, sure that "Mr. Bird *Listener*," oh, master of bird *songs*, would have his clue now. But nope. I was still completely stumped. And chagrined, embarrassed, and hemming and hawing, and—well, it was no doubt an absolute low point in my birding life.

That evening, it didn't take me more than five minutes with my bird guides to ascertain that the bird was—of course!—a female Brown-headed Cowbird, which—as I later explained to the student—was one of the most utterly nondescript birds on planet Earth. And truth be told, I had almost always seen the females of this species with the much more distinctive males and so probably hadn't ever bothered memorizing the female's appearance, sexist wretch that I was. But the damage had been done. On subsequent walks, my almost always quick identification no longer always struck her as completely satisfactory. The student had begun to silently question her teacher. There was a loss, a falling off, a small death that created a forever gap between us.

"A change in the common name of *Molothrus ater*"—the Brown-headed Cowbird—"tells the history of the Central Great Plains' avifauna. In the 1800s it was called the buffalo bird; in the 1900s it became the cowbird."[77] Moreover, it should be no surprise by this point that, in such other non-human histories, *the very birds still speak of human colonialism.* Before the greed and blood-lust of Buffalo Bill and his murderous ilk, the American "buffalo" dominated the Great Plains in both size and numbers, and thus defined much of the nature of the Great Plains ecosystem. The genocide and near-genocide of many Native tribes had a non-human analogue in the extinction of entire native species, including the Passenger Pigeon and—almost—the American Bison.

Even speaking from the selfish self-interest of a birder, I have much to lament about the bison's near-erasure. However, besides the cowbird's name change, one assumes that this species's numbers have only increased with the replacement of wild bison herds by earnestly capitalist big cattle ranches. I *have* seen them on the backs of cows—and my surprise every time I see them there continues to surprise me.

General Custer's first encounters with cowbirds involved their propensity to fly-catch around large mammals—like bison and, in this case, horses:

> In most localities where these [buffalo] flies are found in troublesome numbers, there are also found flocks of starlings, a species of blackbird. [. . .] I have seen our herds of cavalry horses grazing undisturbed, each horse of the many hundreds having perched upon his back from one to dozens of starlings, standing guard over him while he grazed.

This avian interlude is part of Custer's introductory chapter of his *Life,* in which the Great Plains, or "Great American Desert," is described in some earnest, as geographical backdrop to the grand historical events to follow.[78] This passage is yet another typical Euro-American imposition of Old World ornithology upon New World birds. The Brown-headed Cowbird is a member of the American family of blackbirds (*Icteridae*), but the European Starling is not—and the latter is now an American bird only through human intervention.

Paul Johnsgard also associates the cowbird with the bison, claiming that it should have been called the "Buffalo Bird"[79]—as indeed it was. But other birds had also followed, had co-evolved with the bison before the Great Bovine Displacement (to coin a phrase). Imagine flocks of bold black, white, and blue Black-billed Magpies, their tails as long as their bodies, chattering loudly beside a bison mother and her calf. Unlike the cowbird, the magpie had to withdraw with the herds of bison; in Nebraska, for instance, the species was once common statewide, but now it is pretty much confined to the northwest corner of the state. Another large corvid, the Common Raven, suffered a similar fate:

it "apparently occurred statewide" in Nebraska when the colonizers arrived, "and was fairly common until about 1877, when the
disappearance of the bison led to its rapid decline."[80] Now imagine a European Starling on the back of an American Bison. Yes,
these birds have made that adaptive leap. Now we have a Euro-
colonial bird—here because of humankind—on the back of one
of our enslaved—er, domesticated—walking food sources.

But finally—despite all this—I've developed a certain soft
spot for the cowbird. It has to do with its typical pose on a power
line: the bird's beak is raised in the air, as if it were putting on
airs. A row of a half-dozen cowbirds striking such a pose reminds
me of a group of beautiful women in a fancy bar, so dazzling that
you know better than to even dare ask them to dance.

✳ JUNE 2010, IDYLLWILD, CA: *Steller's Jay*

Daughter Em graduated from Idyllwild Arts Academy on June
4, 2010. She had specialized in creative writing, although she had
already told me matter-of-factly, "Daddy, I don't want to teach."
She must have stored away the untoward memory of me grading
essays all weekend, or the sight of me trying to bird and grade at
the same time, binoculars around my neck and a student essay in
hand.

On this day when Emma became an adult of sorts, I recorded
twelve lifers: awash I was in the glory of the new birding territory
that was California. I rose early, in a Motel 6 in Hemet, California, and drove to a known good-birding venue (thanks, Internet),
James Simpson Park, an area on the southeast edge of town with
a hiking trail and some good scrub-pine/near-desert habitat. Lifers included a California Towhee (perhaps the drabbest sparrow

ever), a Costa's Hummingbird, a flock or two of Bushtits (perhaps the bawdiest bird name ever), a Canyon Wren (now one of my favorite singers ever), a Phainopepla (a name as hard to spell and pronounce as it is to get as a lifer), a Black-Chinned Sparrow or two, and—the beauty of the morning—a gaudy burnt-orange-and-black Hooded Oriole. Wait, my daughter is graduating this afternoon? Better take another shower and put on a suit.

Then my brother and I made the harried drive up the San Jacinto Mountains to the town of Idyllwild. A lifetime of driving in the Black Hills hadn't prepared me for the steepness, the constant razor turns, or especially the fact that everyone behind me was going twenty miles per hour faster than my nerves could manage. Thankfully, there were also frequent pull-offs for redneck tourists like me, so the locals could pass my tardy ass. Arriving in Idyllwild was thus more an emotional relief than a celebration. But at least we had time to drive around for an hour or so before the graduation ceremony.

A large, dark fowl waddling along the side of the road was a Mountain Quail, my first lifer of the afternoon. The mountain conifers were a perfect setting for my first Mountain Chickadee, my first Western Bluebird. When we stopped at an open area to take a short walk, I heard an odd woodpecker call—*ick-a ick-a*—sort of like a flicker with a cold. The oddly patterned red, black, and cream face had "clownish" written all over it, probably because that is the adjective used to describe the Acorn Woodpecker in almost every bird guide I had ever owned.

During the boring commencement address by Sonny Bono's fourth wife, I walked off, just for a minute, into the nearby woods and spied the first Steller's Jay of my life. A few mediocre shots of the female took their place on my SD card among dozens of photos of Emma walking down the aisle, of Emma sitting at miserable attention during the boring commencement address by Sonny Bono's fourth wife, of Emma receiving her diploma. Yes, I did dutifully attend to all of this, and was so proud of Emma that tears came to my eyes. I was mostly proud of what a wonderful human being she had become—so warm, so loving, so empathetic towards both human and non-human. My tears may also have been an unconscious acknowledgment that she probably hadn't learned this interpersonal wonderfulness from me. I knew that she would not likely spend *her* future daughter's graduation mostly concerned about adding to her lifer list. So there I stood on top of Idyllwild mountain, wondering what the hell had happened to *me*.

✳ JUNE 2010, SPIRIT MOUND: *Dickcissel*

The National Park Service web page about Spirit Mound, a small butte (by South Dakota standards) just a few miles northwest of my old undergraduate stomping grounds in Vermillion, South Dakota, reads as follows:

> On August 25, 1804, the two captains [Lewis and Clark] and several other members of the expedition journeyed north from the Missouri River to explore a "mysterious hill," known today as Spirit Mound and *Can O'ti la Paha*. [. . .] they topped the hill and saw, for the first time, a panoramic view of the Great Plains. They "discovered" the Great Plains, the grasslands and relatively treeless prairie inhabited by large herds of bison and elk. Lewis and Clark chose to journey to Spirit Mound so that they might understand why the Indians revered this location.

Besides *Čanotila Paha*, it was also called *Paha Wakan*, which opens up a whole can of translation problems. *Paha* means hill or butte in Lakota—as in *Paha Sapa* (the Black Hills). Simple enough. *Wakan*, however, literally means power, force, energy, and—since such things are invisible—even mystery; but because the first makers of English/Lakota dictionaries were Christo-Custer-colonial men of the cloth, *wakan* has usually been translated as "spiritual," "sacred," or "holy." The problematic translation of this single word epitomizes the cross-cultural misunderstandings regarding the Lakota cognizance of a seemingly impossible—by Euro-colonial standards, anyway—union of the sacred and the secular, the miraculous and the mundane, the physical and the metaphysical—which should mean, via Occam's razor, an erasure of the latter term as an unnecessary conceptual imposition. But *Wakan Tanka*—literally, a quite this-worldly "power big" or "power great"—was predictably rendered by the Jesuits as a metaphysical and monotheist "God."

Čan means simply "wood" or "tree." And so the *čanotila* have been translated as "tree people," "tree spirits," or "tree fairies" (probably most literally, "tree dwellers"). One old translation gives "imps of mischief,"[81] and indeed they are often associated with *Iktomi*, the spider-trickster. As "little" people, too, they seem somewhat structurally related to, say, the leprechaun figure of Irish folklore. Clark's "Field Notes" to Lewis and Clark's visit to Spirit Mound refers to it as "the *Mound* which the Indians Call Mountain of *little people* or Spirits." But even before that explanation, the butte is referred to as simply "this mountain of evel Spirits."[82] As with Devils Tower and the like, the Western binary of Good vs. Evil is immediately projected upon an Indigenous place with much more complex connotations.

My own alternative misreading of Native American relationships to "Nature" and "religion" denies such compartmentalized categories. The central problem in any critical reinscription of a Native way lies in the nearly inevitable imposition of a Western dualism that has inveterately distinguished between spirit and matter. Traditional Native views are, instead, quite *naturalistic*, in the sense that spirit and matter are one, with a preference—semantically and philosophically speaking—for matter, in its best, naturist sense. For one thing, the belief in an individual afterlife seems more the exception than the rule in traditional Native American religions, until the syncretistic meldings with Christianity in the sixteenth through nineteenth centuries. The vast majority of Native conceptions of so-called spiritualism, I would claim, are thoroughly immanent and materialist, even animistic, if you will, without the connotations this last term has as some primitive, outdated way of seeing, and with the implication that an emotional and intuitive—dare I still say spiritual?—communion with other species is a positive thing.

Apparently the "evel spirits" left Lewis and Clark alone, but Clark did see some birds. Because of the large number of insects "involuntaryly driven to the mound" by strong winds,

> the Small Birds whoes food they are, Consequently [. . .] resort in great numbers to this place in Surch of them; Perticularly the Small brown Martin of which we saw a vast number hovering [. . .] in the act of Catching those insects; they were So gentle that they did not quit the place untill we had arrivd. within a fiew feet of them.

The editors gloss this "Martin" as probably either the Bank Swallow or Northern Rough-winged Swallow. Clark also notes the large number of birds on the adjacent plains, including blackbirds, wrens, and a "Prarie burd a kind of larke about the Sise of a Partridge with a Short tail &c." This is our old friend the Western Meadowlark—not recognized as a distinct species until Audubon sojourned west in 1843.[83] Lewis and Clark were among the first Euro-Americans to appreciate it. As a menu item. Yes, if the swallows could be carefree, the meadowlarks could not: "our boys prepared us a Supper of jurked mee[t] and two Prarie Larks (which are about the Size of a Pigeon and Peculier to this country)." If they were really the size of a partridge or a pigeon, those were some pretty good-sized meadowlarks.

Dining on a few meadowlarks hardly presented a great threat to the avian ecosystem of the Plains. But Lewis and Clark represented a grander attitude of disdain for the environment. For instance, on this same day, they "set fire to the Praries in two Places to let the Sous know we were on the river." No telling how many prairie birds' nests, etc., perished in these ad hoc smoke signals. As for the "Sous": Clark's spelling was notoriously bad, as evidenced by the oft-rehearsed joke that he somehow found the talent, in these journals, to spell "Sioux" twenty-seven different ways![84]

> What does god look like? These fish, this water, this land.
> —Linda Hogan[85]

Birds have never been primarily anthropocentric symbols for the Lakota. For instance, if the "spotted eagle" (*wanbli gleška*) is revered as the life-form closest to *Wakan Tanka,* it is still first and foremost a real bird, with actual talents of acute eyesight and great mobility that the Lakota admire. It is the Western worldview that found it necessary to impose *spiritus* upon *mundus,* to forever make a mental metaphor of matter, to see swallows and immediately think of the ethereal, to see vultures and immediately invoke death and decay, to look at doves and assume domesticity and peace. And to give its very angels—wings.

A worldview so marked by a division of the physical and the metaphysical is ultimately alien to most American Indigenous cosmo-ontologies. There is no "up there and beyond" realm in the characteristic Native worldview, despite long-held cartoonish Western conceptions of that Indian happy hunting ground. Thus to call the *čanotila* "spirits" instantly and misleadingly invokes a Western dualistic metaphysics, positing a realm above and beyond all magpies and meadowlarks. For the Lakota, there is no need to conceive of "a place of contact between the natural and the supernatural world."[86] Whatever supernatural there is is inherent in the physical.

> They think heaven is so far away,
> beyond the farthest towns,
> not beneath the mortal sky,
> not the radiant fields of potatoes
> brown with dust,
> not the gold-eyed eagle perched
> in a tree,
> with perfect feathers and bones of air.[87]

To privilege a "heaven" that "is so far away" from real naturist matters, moreover, is to denigrate any rationale for saving *this* world, even to deny the value of this world altogether. As Linda Hogan has written, "the Western belief that God lives apart from earth is one that has taken us toward collective [ecological] destruction."[88]

And so the typical Native view is much more about the sheer mundane—and yet wonderfully magical—reality of physical landscapes like Spirit Mound, of Dickcissels and swallows and meadowlarks in the here and now. If there is a good deal of truth in the stereotype of the eco-Indian, the Native as naturist, this insistence on the greatness of *maka* (the earth) itself is its origin.

Let's return to William Clark's journal entry: "One evidence which the Indians give for believing this place to be the residence of some unusual spirits is that they frequently discover a large assemblage of birds about this mound. This is [. . .] a sufficient proof to produce in the savage mind a confident belief of all the properties which they ascribe to it." I would argue instead that it was an actively projective whitestream mind that made such an association, richly steeped in a 2,500-year tradition of associating the bird with spirit, of conflating flight with the human soul—of making the avian all-too-human.

The desperate need by the West to posit a metaphysics separate from the physical realm is reflected in A. Grove Day's introduction to his well-known compendium of traditional Native songs, *The Sky Clears*: "Even what seem at first to be poems descriptive of the beauties of nature are often found to be connected in the Indian mind with religion and worship." Day can only conceive of nature description per se and religious worship as two separate ontological realms. And so, for Day, "symbolism is the key to Indian poetry," since the apparently incredible privileging of other natural beings, such as eagles, coyotes, etc., must be symbolic of human spiritual strivings, not a mere celebration of these beings themselves and their essential roles in the biosphere. Day goes on to admit that "Chippewa songs," for instance, "reveal a knowledge of nature" arising "from the Indian habit, born of necessity, of scanning his environment with eyes that missed nothing." And yet, Day asserts, "there are almost no poems to be found" that "reflect in a lyrical manner the delight in nature for its own sake. The sort of white-man poetry exemplified" in Wordsworth's poetry "cannot be found among the North American Indians." In sum, "it was foreign to him [the 'Indian'] to scan a landscape seeking literary raw material."[89]

But such a culturally specific Euro-literary seeking is not necessarily a laudable thing; and in no way were the usual results of this "white-man poetry" some pure "delight in nature for its own sake." But Day must impose a Western division between aesthetics and religion, unable to conceive of a vision in which nature and spirit are conjoined as one immanence. And maybe the term *immanence* itself is too Western a term for what I would posit as a naturist-materialist worldview that yet allows for the magical synchronicity that characterizes the relationship between avian and indigene. This is the sheer-wonder-of-physicality that the subject conditioned by Western theology insists on translating as spiritual.

> God? [. . .] who the hell is he? There is nothing here, at the moment, but me and the desert. [. . .] Why confuse the issue by dragging in a superfluous entity? Occam's razor. Beyond atheism, nontheism. I am not an atheist but an earthiest. Be true to the earth.
>
> —Edward Abbey[90]

Early one summer morning several years ago, I gave a talk about Spirit Mound, offering some of these controversial ruminations above to a group of teachers involved in the Dakota Writing Project, after which we took a field trip to the Mound, walked up to the summit together, and then sat down and wrote. I no longer have what I wrote that day. I just remember the loud semiotics of the non-humans there, especially the Western Meadowlarks and the Dickcissels. I do remember wondering what impact such amazing sounds were actually having on English-teacher types who were probably trying to "write themselves," as they'd been trained, in as purply prose or poetry as possible. Unfortunately, probably not much—to the detriment of their writing and their writing selves.

After the three-hour drive home, I still had that rich two-species interplay in my head, which by that time I had reduced to a leaping, syncopated major-scale melody for the meadowlark, with the Dickcissel replying every other measure with percussive triplet quarter notes: *JICK-JICK-JICK*. I called it "Towards a Native Grassland Symphony," although it remains only two measures of music in my mind, with repeat signs.

That day, I recorded ten Dickcissels in eBird, though there were no doubt more; scouting the area the day before—I wanted no surprises during our group walk—I counted twenty. These are actually meager counts for me, as a spoiled Nebraskan: at my favorite birding venues only a short drive from Lincoln, I have recorded counts of 65 (twice) and 90: eBird continually flags me for such outrageous numbers for what is a supposedly declining species; but there's no mistaking almost a hundred mighty mites shouting *JICK-JICK-JICK* every few yards on a drive around a big lake. Maybe *these* are the real "little people" of Spirit Mound: and on a June morning on the Plains, there is just no shutting them up.

✳ MAY 2011, WILDERNESS PARK: *Veery*

I read the other day that "one of every four Americans is a birdwatcher."[91] That statistic is surely pure hyperbole, unless one includes, as this source apparently does, those who take a nature walk at least "once or twice a year." We real birders know that such people lack the requisite gumption to be one of *us,* a veritable MANIA that cannot be eased by the occasional nature excursion.

As an adolescent birder, I'd only kept a life list, and didn't even keep track of the dates of the first 150 species. That first childhood life list was handwritten in the back of my first "fancy" bird book—T. Gilbert Pearson's coffee-table tome *Birds of America.* The checkboxes in the index of my first bird guide, Robbins, Bruun, and Zim's *Birds of North America,* were duly filled in as a backup of sorts, with a few dates scribbled in for individual species.

Then as a young adult, I discovered the word *Big* and its seminal connection to birding: apparently there were Big Mornings, and Big Days, and Big Years that other birders kept track of. Ah, here my OCD list-keeping nature could truly *shine.* My Big Morning record, first recorded in 1987 as 31, is now 88—set one May morning in 2015 at Branched Oak Lake. My Big Day stats have evolved from a meager 55 in 1986, to 58 in 2003, to 66 in 2007, to 72 in 2009, to 90 on May 6, 2011. Ten days later I shattered that record with 103. I don't even do Big Days anymore: for one thing, I don't have the stamina that I did as a younger fellow; for another, the nature of the eBird database emphasizes specific locale counts, not total-day statistics. (The Big Year is another story, and if anything, eBird has made that more popular—and more competitive—than ever.) So 103 will probably remain my Big Day record until the day I die.

I began that day at dawn (of course), at one of the best birding venues in Nebraska, Branched Oak Lake: the 69 species total I got there by 12:20 was also a single-venue record for me at the time. (Yes, yet another list-and-record category!) May is *the*

month for birders, as the height of migration season—and for the
sheer *numbers* of birds: at Branched Oak that morning I recorded
45 Chipping Sparrows, 40 American Robins, 35 Yellow Warblers
and Common Grackles and Brown-headed Cowbirds, 34 Eastern
Kingbirds, 31 Canada Geese, 30 American White Pelicans and
American Goldfinches, 25 Bank Swallows, 24 American Coots, 23
Dickcissels, 20 Franklin Gull's and Black Terns and Cliff Swallows, 19 Brown Thrashers, 15 Baltimore Orioles, and 14 Gray Cat-
birds. (The counts for Swans a'Swimming, French Hens, Turtle
Doves, and Partridges in Pear Trees have been lost to posterity.)

However, my Big Day attempts were already in decline by
2011: the Big Year and that ever-expanding Life List had become
my central passions. But it was barely noon, and I already had 69
species, so I thought—what the hell, let's go for it.

I knew that I was doomed to be a lister from an early age. In
grade school, I even made a list of 15–20 Latin/scientific names of
familiar birds. To this day, I'm surprised how many I still remember, like *Spinus tristus* and *Tyto alba* and *Bubo virginianus* and
Parus bicolor and *Turdus migratorius*. I kept that list in a yellow
spiral-bound-on-the-top pocket notebook, along with a list of
bird poems I had memorized, and who knows what other cos-
mos-altering ephemera. I also memorized the state bird of each
of the fifty US states. Recently, I even had a dream that I had
started a list of bird species seen in my *dreams*.

I quickly headed west on Highway 34, to Seward County and
some favorite country-road and wetlands birding venues. Places
with such happy names as Crooked Mile Road and Straightwa-

ter WMA got me to 80 species, thanks in part to four different sandpiper species still around at North Lake Basin. Heading back east and then northeast of Lincoln, I hurriedly birded Jack Sinn WMA, and the Linoma Beach area, and Schramm State Park, along the Platte River. By this last stop, I was up to 87 species—thank you, Yellow-throated Vireo—and it was only 4:45 p.m.

At Platte River State Park, I saw three Blue-gray Gnatcatchers (#88) and a pair of Louisiana Waterthrushes (#89). Bird #90 was a Swainson's Thrush, tying my previous Big Day record by 5:14 p.m. (That I even recorded such mundane details is symptomatic of my obsessive-compulsiveness.) I broke the record, at 5:23, with the Eastern Wood-Pewee, a sentimental favorite of mine because of its plaintive whistled song—and its association with a significant other in my life. Species #92, #93, and #94 followed quickly. Number 93 was a Tufted Titmouse, seen at the usual place, I noted: near the park's (faux) Tepee Village. Ugh. Yes, my disgust at such an appropriative/ethnically insensitive name was also recorded in the day's original notes.

Record established, I drove back to Lincoln, satisfied. Or was I? I *was* pretty close to the BIG ONE HUNDRED, so I stopped at Holmes Lake in East Lincoln for species #95, a Green Heron. I might as well hit Wilderness Park for a look-see. All right: #96 was an Indigo Bunting; #97, a pair of Eastern Phoebes; and #98, two Tennessee Warblers. Bird #99 was a Northern Rough-winged Swallow, after which name I wrote, "finally," as too common a species to have resisted my efforts so long that day. Then finally, #100: a Great Crested Flycatcher: "ding-ding-ding-ding-$$$$," I wrote, dramatically—and noted that #100 came at approximately 8:00 p.m.

But as dusk approached, the day's avian bonanza didn't stop: a Wood Thrush was #101, and I wrote, romantically, what a "beautiful echoing song for the end of a long day." #102 was a Downy Woodpecker—another common "what took you so long?!" bird. Then the apotheosis, both species #103 and a new life species: a Veery in the bushes along Salt Creek. Since it was a rarity of a thrush for these here parts, I carefully noted, as documentation for eBird, "head pretty reddish, breast only slightly speckled; not much of an eye-ring." (Now that feels and reads anti-climactic as hell.)

"For all their skill as observers, the Indians do not qualify, in modern terms, as birders." Indeed, "as far as anyone seems to know," Natives "did not keep [birding] lists. The white man, as soon as he came to America, did."[92] Given my own psychopathological birding obsessions, one might wonder why a part-Indian fellow would even *want* to be a birder. Birding *is,* I have argued elsewhere, in good part yet another Western colonial act of *epistemic violence,* however seemingly benign. This makes it hard to be on the side of objectifying humans who want to chase birds down and—*count* them. Sometimes a fellow thinks too much and just wants to give up on the whole list-making enterprise. But not just yet.

✳ DECEMBER 2011, HIGHWAY 385:
Ferruginous Hawk

For much of my adult life, I have dreaded December. Each year, after rushing to finish up my grading chores to officially end the fall semester, I then had to turn right around, emotionally, and deal with family "celebrations" of a God that no one (in my family) really believed in anymore. This usually involved a day's drive to Rapid City, under rigid time constraints that didn't care whether the two-lane highways were experiencing blizzard conditions or not. "I may die on the road," I often thought bitterly, during white-knuckle drives up Highway 385, "because of a holiday for Jesus!?" Sometimes I would encounter what I called a cloud road: a road that, after a heavy snow, was bare black asphalt, except for the wind that blew the snow from the ditches back onto it, in great swirling, feathery swaths that made me feel as if I were a lost pilot, flying over unexpected cloudbanks that made me guess where every turn in the road was—a truly nightmarish journey.

But this is just me bitching. Christmas in Rapid was also one the few times a year I got to see Emma—even if I sometimes had to drive to Denver first to pick her up. It was also a glorious time when I could set my mind to auto-pilot, and go to stupid movies with my brothers and daughter, and watch my nieces and nephew play stupid video games for hours on end, my own psyche comfortably numb, far from the frenzy of Argus-eyed academia.

And then there was the birding, of course. I especially relished—road conditions allowing—the drives back home to Nebraska from SoDak, which I did a little more leisurely in order to watch the hawks and other raptors in the bare trees and on the power lines along the road. Running north and south through northwest Nebraska, Highway 385 usually doesn't have a lot of traffic, so if a man has to slow down to fifty, or   forty,   or   thirty   mph, it usually doesn't result in a five-car pile-up.

Late December 2011 was especially memorable in this regard because I kept a *list*, of raptors seen on my drive to Rapid and back. Not only are many raptor species more numerous in the winter months on the Plains, they are also more visible, given the bare trees and the birds' greater urgency for a meal. On this trip, I recorded 27 Red-tailed Hawks, 20 Bald Eagles, 7 American Kestrels, 5 Northern Harriers, 5 Rough-legged Hawks, 1 Prairie Falcon, and 1 Ferruginous Hawk. I saw a good majority of them along 385, taking my leisurely time: every few miles was a raptor in a bare tree or on a fencepost or on a power-line pole, saying, "Count me, Tommy. Count me. Just make sure you know that I'm a Rough-legged, not a Red-tail."

The Ferrugy (my own nickname for this particular bird, which I pronounce "Fer-OO-jee") was the coolest, rarest sighting: the largest North American hawk, the Ferruginous Hawk is a bird of the real out-West, and its eastern limits include western Nebraska. I'm lucky to see one a year. This year, I was just a few miles south of the South Dakota border when a huge, magnificent Ferrugy on a power-line pole came into view. Slow down some more? Hell, I just pulled right off the road, onto the emergency apron, and took photo after the photo of a hawk with a distinctive rust-stained "undercarriage," seemingly too large to move, or too superior to the ways of humankind to even have to. Perhaps because I've looked at my photos over and over since that cold but sunny morning, it remains a veritable spot of time in my avian life. All subsequent sightings of the species automatically evoke, in my mind's eye, that bird's big auburn eye looking back into my eyes as it finally flew away.

✳ MAY 2012, INDIAN CAVE STATE PARK:
Chuck-Will's-Widow

I just got back from Indian Cave State Park. Driving slowly, windows down, through the various campgrounds in the dark, I was stopped by a state Game and Parks guy, who asked me what I was doing. I replied, "Listening for goatsuckers." This answer did not appear to immediately satisfy him.

I could have replied, "Listening for nightjars," but that's nearly as strange and confusing; plus, I think the latter term is an even greater insult to this peculiar taxonomical order of birds (*Caprimulgiformes*). I'd rather be known as a clandestine sucker of goat teats than one whose nocturnal vocalization is deemed *jarring*. I could also have said, "I'm listening for Eastern Whip-poor-wills, Chuck-will's-widows, and Common Nighthawks," but that's too much of a mouthful. Besides, why and by whom is poor Willy being *whipped*? And under what mysterious circumstances did Chuck Will's wife become a widow? These are questions that inquiring birder minds want to know.

How fascinating it is that so many American bird names are yet another set of Euro-colonial, Euro-nominal acts. Collins's 1950s guide to North American wildlife describes the Whip-poor-will's song as "*whip-poor-WILL,* more accurately written *pur-ple RIB.*" But once again, we well might wonder how that rib got so purple and bruised? What sado-masochistic culture is making up all these supposedly descriptive syllables of other animals by projecting our own species's eons of cruelty and suffering? Yes, these birds—can I call them *caprimulgids* without sounding too pedantic?—are insectivores who feed in flight and thus, like cowbirds and Cattle Egrets, can commonly be found near livestock, and so the old European belief that they hung around goats to suck their milk behind peasants' plow-bent, pox-marked backs has at least a modicum of understandability. But there remains a whole discourse in their very names—of sucking, and whipping, and widowing—that smacks of a bad soft-porn romance and doesn't make the civilization that devised them look good to any objective alien observer.

My 2012 outing to Indian Cave was my first ever encounter with a Chuck-will's-widow—the 71st species I identified there that day. I'd waited until dark, and then waited some more, until, at exactly 9:19 p.m., I heard from the hill behind the cave itself just a few faint *widdow-widdow* calls at first, and then in a minute or two the initial *chuck* as the calls increased in speed and frequency. *Chuck-widdow-widdow, chuck-widdow-widdow.* Bird #70 was the Whip-poor-will, the first since I'd heard one in South Dakota way back in 1991. I recorded in my journal, "When they get started, they don't wanna stop, do they?" The third syllable (*will*) slap-echoing off the more distant hills was the most stunning aural event of the evening, the continuing announcements of poor Chuck's demise notwithstanding. I ended up seeing/hearing eight of them as I drove, slowly, out, of, the, park. Oh, yeah, I also saw/heard a first-of-the-year Common Nighthawk; so it was a three-goatsucker night, a phrase that will likely never be the name of a pop-rock band.

Yes, this was *Indian* Cave State Park. And I must point again to the ongoing irony that many of my favorite birding places on the Great Plains are also some of its worst closet-racist tourist-trap examples of Christo-Custer colonialism, the ideology of power that still permeates the very names of these places that have been the main venues of my birding journeys. For some reason, whenever I think of this place called Indian Cave, I hear in my mind's ear "Indian Joe State Park." And I feel the flash-of-a-moment hope that Tom and Becky are safe from that savage ne'er-do-well's dastardly doings. In other words, yes: there's something exotically sinister in the connotations of the very phrase "Indian Cave" that makes me sad.

Caprimulgids are

> secret birds with deep plaintive
> names like goatsucker, night-
> hawk, and chuck-will's-widow:
> who lay their eggs on flat-tar
> roofs, letting the sun's
> heat play mother

> laid her eggs on the flat-
> tar roof of McKinley
> Elementary, whose fifth-grade
> teacher was a dark-haired
> 32-year-old masturbatrice
> who loved deep plaintive
> names like goatsucker night-
> hawk and oh! poor chuck-
> will's-widow, who loved
> the darkly maternal,
> the very, sound of
> *caprimulgiformes.*

✳ JUNE 2012, CUSTER STATE PARK: *Canyon Wren*

A yellow-bellied marmot is earnestly trying to dig a hole in the middle of a packed-gravel mountain road. Driving slowly by does nothing to deter the varmint. I even stop the Forester right there and break out the spotting scope and tripod to check on some first-of-the-year Lewis's Woodpeckers circling bare trees high up on a peak: the black-faced bugger beside me just keeps on digging. One could learn from such dedication. Or be forewarned by such futility. Whichever the lesson, it happened in a wonderful place called Custer State Park.

The Black Hills of South Dakota, where I grew up, take a back seat to no place in its awful ideology of cowboy-and-cavalry celebratory hero-worship. The constant reminders of military brute force remain in the very names of its many venues. I grew up in these mountains—home of the Lakota *Wakinyan* or "thunder birds"—and it strikes me now on my various trips back how we longtime locals take the Anglo place names for granted, seldom or never considering their often untoward origins.

There's a town in the southern Black Hills called Custer, which lies about fifty miles northwest of the Pine Ridge Indian Reservation (as the vulture flies), a mild hamlet in the winter and a semi-torrid tourist trap in the summer, when tens of thousands of visitors flock to the place to recapture various hiker, biker, and Old West identities and ideologies. Of course the township of Custer is right next to Custer State Park. I've driven the highway between the two scores of times in my life, but only recently have I noticed that between the town and park is a business whose cuisine is, I'm sure, to die for: the 7th Cavalry Cafe. The sign, including the banner below, promises "OUTDOOR ADVENTURES." Rentals include "Bikes • Canoes • Kayaks • Fishing Gear." Yes, the elite can rent a kayak. The name of this establishment either brazenly or blithely and blindly celebrates one of the low points in American history. Scarier yet, the sign, at least, is pretty new, and I don't remember ever seeing this place until these last few years. In other words, the ideology underlying such a celebration lives on in this day and age. I don't expect that the town of Custer will ever change its name; but I can't help but react with sadness when I see new colonialist propaganda such as this continue to crop up in this, the twenty-first century.

My wife coordinated an annual week-long Holocaust conference for several summers at the University of South Dakota, in Vermillion. The conference considered in tandem the holocausts experienced by Jewish and Native American peoples. One summer, the main Native spokesperson had to give his main presentation via Skype, because he was in the Black Hills teaching another class. He said—as my wife relates, and I paraphrase—"Here I am in a town called Custer. What the fuck? It's as if I'm a Jew living in Germany, in a town called Hitler. Do you think *they'd* be able to get away with that?" Maybe the analogy is a touch hyperbolic, but the truth is there: beside the nearly completely victorious Christian churches on the Great Plains are these incredibly strident examples of Euro-American military conquest: the names of General Custer, General Sheridan, General Miles, General Crook, General Terry, General Harney, et al. infest many of the town, school, and other place names in South Dakota and neighboring states. The innumerable tourist traps laud the exploits of gold-lusting hooligans, at last. The "rah-rah" brainwashing continues on, creating a painful cognitive dissonance in the few of us who are birding—and just generally living—while Indian.

So I *still* can't get over Custer, really, here on the western Plains. South Dakota's official state tourism guide to the park that I have in hand is called *Tatanka: The 2011 Guide to Custer State Park*. It's hard to look at the cover and see "Tatanka" and "Custer" in the same title without experiencing more cognitive dissonance. The publication's byline states, "Tatanka is the Lakota word for bison. [. . .] The *Tatanka* is published by the S.D.

Department of Game, Fish & Parks."[93] Translation: we, the outfit who named this park after General Custer, feel blithely free to co-opt the language of a conquered people without feeling one ounce of hypocrisy.

Page nine has a section titled "Buffalo History Comes Alive": "Would you like to learn more about the history of the buffalo at Custer State Park? What about hunting buffalo with an 1878 market hunter? Do you want to see and touch buffalo body parts and learn the Native Americans [sic] uses for them?" No. I don't. But I feel confident that "they" used every damned part of the buffalo because that's one of the myths about Indians that get passed on to good white people from the fourth grade on.

The somewhat surprising gem of this text is a rather stunning admission: in 1874, Custer's exploratory expedition "discovered gold in the Black Hills. Under the 1868 Treaty of Fort Laramie, however, this region belonged to the Plains Indians, and white settlement was not allowed." But "word of the discovery spread quickly," and soon "a flow of fortune seekers came to these newly discovered mountains of gold. It was more than the army could control and within two years, nearly 10,000 settlers illegally inhabited the Black Hills." DeMallie's annotation of Black Elk's wonder at how the "yellow metal" discovered in the Black Hills "makes the Wasichus crazy" is as follows: "Despite the army's efforts to discourage them, by summer 1875 some eight hundred miners were working illegally in the Black Hills, an area reserved for the Lakotas by the 1868 treaty."[94] The stunning word in both sources is *illegally*. The phrase "more than the army could control" sounds like an empty gesture: of course the US Army was not going to protect Native rights against the ideology of Manifest Destiny, of good, civilized Americans. They were there illegally, but certainly one dare not call *them* "illegal immigrants."

In 1982, Mystique introduced an utterly reprehensible video game for the now antique Atari gaming system: Custer's Revenge. It was labeled NOT FOR SALE TO MINORS. The game's cover sleeve sports a stereotypical raven-haired Indian princess beside a tipi, looking both ravishing and ravished, apparently both loathing and secretly enjoying the groping of a pint-sized cartoonish Custer, whose eyes are mere inches from her private parts. Rape is a power trip, above all, as psychologists have long told us; but for the 1980s, this is one weird re-assertion of colonialist power.

"Get over it," my good white friends are forever telling me; but I can't, because it's not over. Ojibwe activist Winona LaDuke has encountered the identical admonishment: "'You guys should get over it, it happened a long time ago.' You cannot get over it if you are still in the same circumstance as a consequence of what happened a hundred years ago."[95] It's all part of the story of how a discourse of colonization of the American West has left its indelible mark upon language and visual representation, an epistemic imperialism that continues to this day, from Black Hills tourist traps to video games.

If these "GET OVER IT" people were *just* talking about a survival-of-the-fittest amoral social Darwinism, not an American-exceptionalist Manifest-Destiny racist colonialist genocide justified by a high Christian moral idealism, then I wouldn't be so upset—I could actually accept the "logic" of it all. That is, after all, how nature works. But if this "might makes right" is what these folks ultimately mean, that humankind is a mere animal, too—it also means that you have to surrender any lofty pretensions regarding your Western ethics and religion, and acknowledge Western theology (including its direct descendant, secular humanism) to be a hypocritical and bankrupt enterprise, a mere prop and rationalization for capitalist greed and colonialist thieving violence. Acknowledge, please, how much the Captains of Christo-Custer colonialism have lied to themselves for half a millennium that slavery, slaughter, and cultural deicide were fine Christian behaviors, against the apparently subhuman infidel "savage." To quote from a song by the Diné band XIT: in so many ways, we're "still playing a game called Cowboys and Indians." I'd also claim that the northern Great Plains are ground zero for this game, where the Indian Wars came to their climax and denouement, where the discourse of the Old West, of cowboys and Indians, and of "Pioneering New Frontiers"—the University of Nebraska–Lincoln's official motto since 2004—gets its biggest play: again, to the delight of tourists from both coasts and of rednecks on many a western South Dakota cattle ranch. What gets *lost in translation* in such a heavily commercialized and simulated milieu? The historical trauma of near-genocide, massacres, broken treaties, land theft—epitomized in that damned 7th Cavalry Cafe.

But I can't bring myself to an act of earnest political protest, of actually boycotting Custer State Park. Why? Its bi-annual pull on me is magnetic, as one of the best birding places in the Dakotas. As part of the Black Hills, it is one of the easternmost habitats for birds that are characteristically species of the Rockies, of the Mountain West, like the Golden Eagle, White-throated Swift, Lewis's Woodpecker, Red-naped Sapsucker, Prairie Falcon, Cordilleran Flycatcher, Plumbeous Vireo, Clark's Nutcracker, Violet-green Swallow, Mountain Bluebird, Townsend's Solitaire, MacGillivray's Warbler, Western Tanager, and Red Crossbill. Yes, to the lay reader, this is Tom making yet another list; but to the birder, this list is drool-worthy.

And it includes the Canyon Wren. I've only heard the Canyon Wren six times, five of them here in Custer State Park, usually in late May or June. I say *heard* because I don't remember if I've ever seen one or not, and I don't even care to check my records to see if I have: for the Canyon Wren is a *voice*—and what a voice. Edward Abbey describes it as a "tinkling music [. . .] like little silver bells falling across a glockenspiel—no, like wilderness lorelei—calling down to us from the rimrock, sweetest of all bird songs in the canyon country."[96] But all human discourse fails to capture the real song that has captured my heart for the last fifteen years.

In Custer's great park, I first heard the bird at a pull-off unpromisingly called the Fish Hook Picnic Area. Behind the narrow mountain stream is a steep granite cliff often pockmarked by mountain goats. In some hidden rock cranny a few yards above the creek sang a Canyon Wren, unmistakable, a long un-birdlike trill simultaneously descending and accelerating into an aural climax. Yes, I must deem the sound *erotic*. I also must admit that the song was unmistakable because I'd been playing it in one of my iPhone birding apps over and over, in preparation for the potential encounter of this unusual bird on the extreme northeast edge of its range. And I was truly, maybe inordinately, happy about my luck, beyond my visceral reaction to the song. I may have even smiled out loud. I know that I did want to shout at the other people who had pulled over, taking photos of the mountain goats: "Don't you HEAR that?! It's a fucking CANyon Wren!" But I didn't. The human fascination with large exotic mammals is mainstream; humans' rarer fascination for small vocalizing birds is still considered queer.

I heard a second Canyon Wren the next summer a little to the west, in the Grace Coolidge Walk-in Trail. Just a few hundred yards down the trail is another stretch of granite cliffs, where the hiker must ankle-wade or rock-hop over the small stream there. Only a few feet above the stream, to the left of the crossing point, another Canyon Wren was dropping its plummeting cascade on the world; again my spine and mind went numb.

My daughter Em and I camped out at Custer State Park in the summer of 2007—oh, the Mountain Bluebirds and Western Tanagers!—and we attended a camp-ranger presentation that evening, about the park's wildlife management, the state's control of the big-game populations. When the college student/ intern finished her talk, Tom the Terrible raised his hand: "I was just curious about the origin of the park's name. Why Custer? I recall that he ordered 800 Indian ponies to be put to death on the spot at one point in his storied career. Is this an example of good 'wildlife management,' perhaps inspiring the name choice?" She hemmed and hawed, and did her best at disavowing such past behavior, until I actually felt sorry for her. But then, Custer's bloodlust continued into the twentieth century in western South Dakota, so much so that most of the park's vaunted large mammals are re-imports, including the bison. (In fact, the park was originally created as a game preserve.) At least one mammal, the Rocky Mountain Bighorn Sheep, is a surrogate for a similar Black-Hills-native animal that was hunted to extinction (Audubon's Bighorn Sheep, all individuals having gone to animal heaven by 1916).

Lame Deer once said about the Black Hills, "We used to go there to pray. Here you can still see antelope, at Wind Cave and in Custer State Park. They have been put on a reservation like us Indians, but maybe they don't know it."[97] The analogy between Indian reservations and wildlife preserves—indeed, both have been called "reserves" in various times and places—is insightful enough in its dark humor; but that those in power have dared name an enclave of native bison and antelope, of native Mountain Bluebirds and Vesper Sparrows, after the man who led the gold-lust that resulted in their eventual diminishment and enclosure is another sad deal, indeed. And such names as "preserves" and "sanctuaries" are ironically sad in themselves, indicative of a mainstream culture whose destruction of habitat and other species has occasioned the need for such places. Moreover, "sanctuary" is from the Latin *sanctum*: i.e., sacred or holy. No irony here: these species and places only became "sanctified" when we realized that we had damned near killed them off through our anthropocentric ways.

In my first year as a college freshman, I was on a ROTC scholarship, because my high school counselor couldn't figure out any other way I could afford college. During the first semester, in Military Science I, I earned 1,024 out of a possible 1,000 total points, for an A+. (I must have done some extra credit?) I still remember my exact total with pride. We mostly studied the military tactics and strategies of famous US military conflicts, including the Custer fiasco. We learned that the good General's fatal mistake was dividing his forces. (Commandment #1 in Military Science: Thou shalt not divide thy forces.) But I was already divided *myself*. Implicit in the language of the textbook and the tone of the instructors was that Custer stood for—that he *was*—America, and that he *should* have won, by all *right*—given a better strategy, of course. Where did that leave me, a part-Indian student wondering which side I was supposed to be cheering for?

I did not make it through the second semester of ROTC.

✳ JUNE 2012, MILLWOOD STATE PARK:
Black-Bellied Whistling-Duck

I'm trying to check into a motel in Hope, Arkansas, but I've run into a major snafu. The desk clerk is telling me the Wi-Fi password for my room. She reads, "*V* as in *Victor*, *I* as in *AY-un.* . . ." I ask "What?" three times to this last piece of apparent gibberish. "*I* as in *AY-un*," she says again, and I finally get it. "Oh. '*I* as in *inn*!'" No, I didn't stop to wonder whether my thin, clipped vowel as I said *inn* sounded like some northern Satanic snake-talk to this southern sort-of-a-belle; I just wearily headed for my room, hoping that these people had "normal" channels like ESPN in their cable package.

This happened towards the end of my most extended road trip explicitly dedicated to birding. Seven states and three nights in motels earned me twelve new species, mostly of the southern/southeastern variety: exotics, to this northern Great Plains yokel. My original plan was to get all the way to the Gulf Coast, via some Louisiana roadway without too much traffic, which would have no doubt at least doubled that lifer count. But I always forget until, say, the second night of such trips how wearying it is to be on the road for too long and how much I dislike being away from my books and guitar. I was only able to dip into the very northern part of Louisiana before I headed happily back north, where people are usually less eager to act upon their religious beliefs in dealing with my heathen ass.

Heading south of Lincoln on June 18, 2012, my first stop was just into Missouri, at the wonderfully named Squaw Creek National Wildlife Refuge. (In defense of the South, we Great Plains folks take a back seat to no one when it comes to racist place names.) But it wasn't until some city park in a town called

Carthage that I got my first lifer of the trip, a Prothonotary Warbler—one of the most stunning US warblers, both for its exqui-
site lemon yellow and its loud, clear *seet-seet-seet-seet-seet-seet* of
a song.

I spent the first night in Cassville, Missouri, in an Americas
[*sic*] Best Value Inn & Suites, which was pretty much a Motel 6
with a longer name. My real target was a few miles south, Roar-
ing River State Park, in the southwest corner of Missouri, a
place I'll always remember fondly as the site of three lifers, the
Pileated Woodpecker (the large-crested bird that inspired the
"Woody the Woodpecker" cartoon), the Yellow-throated Warbler
(another brightly colored and loudly singing southeastern warbler), and the Fish Crow. I counted seventeen of the last, after
figuring out, with the help of my iPhone recordings, how to tell
them from your mundane American Crow. It was their French
accent, I told myself as a mnemonic device of sorts, a more nasal
ahr that distinguished them from the standard *caw* of the more
familiar corvid. In my longest walk through a streamside woods,
I also encountered some armadillos—I couldn't believe how small
and cute and tame they were, and how far *north* they were! Then
I recalled the people and accents in the motel and convenience
stores and realized that I was pretty far south already.

On the second day, I hit the same state park again early in the
morning, on my way to Arkansas and Louisiana. Unfortunately,
the most memorable part of the second day may have been losing my iPhone. Stopping at a stream along an Arkansas highway,
I became completely enamored by the syncopated explosives of
a White-eyed Vireo and got out of the car to see if I could get
a visual. Now let me tell you: getting out of the car is a tortuous act for a birder—at least, for this one—because it usually
involves grabbing your birding notebook, your binoculars, and

(in this day and age) your cellphone with its bird-guide apps; and frankly, after many hours and hundreds of miles of staring at power lines, et al., for birds, I can sometimes barely chew gum and quote Nietzsche at the same time, my mind has become so frazzled. Anyway, when I got back into the car, I couldn't find my iPhone—OH!—my birding apps, my GPS system, my email, my entire connection to twenty-first-century hyperreality. Complete panic, as my gut dropped, seven hundred miles from home. I don't know if it was five or twenty-five minutes before I found it where it had fallen, a black rectangle on a black floor under the seat, a place I had already checked innumerable times, but finding it was as if I had re-affirmed my faith in a deity whose loss had left my entire soul bereft of meaning. A deep breath of relief put my plummeted gut back into order. It strikes me now that this led to my resolution, more than anything, to just hit the top of the Pelican State and to turn back towards home.

My Louisiana let's-just-skirt-the-border compromise was lucky, nonetheless. In the Kisatchie National Forest, I got two lifers in the form of the Brown-headed Nuthatch and the Pine Warbler: I first saw both in the same stand of pines just a few miles into the forest. I later drove into one of those prototypical southern swamps that seem to drip with the heat of racial oppression and Faulknerian syntax, that seem haunted by what I assumed were the famous cypress trees, although I wasn't sure since, to this day, I can barely tell an elm from a cedar. The birding was pretty mundane, with various heron species I'd already seen often on the trip; the most notable sight was a park warning sign with a lot of explanatory text under the title "Alligator Safety." Cool, I thought, as I took a photo; now I'd had just enough of the South to head back north.

Driving back into southwest Arkansas, I headed to Hope, for

the second night, not because of its association with a former president but because it was next to perhaps my most anticipated birding target of the trip, Millwood Lake. I checked in, struggled with the clerk's pronunciation of *inn*, slept the whole night through (for the first time in years) from sheer exhaustion—but at least I had my iPhone!—and was on my way to Millwood Lake by dawn.

Millwood Lake is a huge manmade reservoir, and the thirty miles I recorded as my trip around it really only covered a few sections of its vast shore access. (I did want to be halfway back to Nebraska by the end of the day.) But I stayed there for three hours and saw fifty-one species, including SIX lifers. It wasn't much after dawn when I saw my first interesting bird, only the second Little Blue Heron of my life, barely a silhouette against the lake with the rising sun behind it, and my adrenaline was already in full rush. Then I saw a truly strange site: two birds flew into a tree beside the lake—pretty big, with weird pink legs and long orange bills, and they were . . . ducks?! White-wing patches: check; high, squeaky calls: check. Yep, the Black-bellied Whistling Duck was my first lifer of a day that had barely begun, and things were looking good.

On the northeast arm of the lake were Okay Road and Okay Landing, and they were more than okay, as I got three lifers in a row, in the space of ten minutes or so. First was the Common Gallinule, whose cackling calls I heard first, and then I saw what might best be described as a coot with a gaudy orange-red bill. The second lifer flew over my head, an Anhinga, looking like a cormorant with a large raven-wedge of a tail; I'd see a second Anhinga later along the lake, and hear its (also not un-raven-like) croaking voice. But I'm really a sucker for songbirds, and the highlight of the three lifers was no doubt the Painted Bunting.

First I heard the finch-like song, which I'd learned well listening to my iPhone recordings on the way there—for this bird was one of *the* target lifers I had envisioned acquiring on this trip. Then I saw the singer, a male brilliant with its glossy deep-hued-blue head, its red breast and belly, its lime-green back—a gaudily gauche coloration that would have been inconceivable, if not for the fact that I was long familiar with a painting of this bird: it graced the cover of both editions of my longtime main bird guide, *Birds of North America.*

However, I figured I only had time to skirt the lake's southeast and southern edges—a few more campground drive-throughs, for the most part—before heading out. At Millwood Overlook, three big birds flew over my head, white with black wingtips—like a pelican? No, their bills were long, thin, curved ibis beaks: White Ibises. Lifer. Check. Then, driving through Millwood State Park, on the southern tip of the lake, I saw a warbler, with a yellow front, a blue-gray back, white wingbars, and white tail-sides; a second look at the bird, when it responded to my iPhone recording, assured me that it was a Blue-winged Warbler. Lifer. Check.

Six lifers in three hours: such a rich place and moment, such a bonanza of "feathers of time" (if I can coin a phrase). And then, in a flash, what a hurry I was in to get the hell out of there, to grab a MacDonald's breakfast at the next hick town, to be on my way to somewhere else. And it's not just birding: I'm pretty sure I've wasted most of my life in this impatient, anti-Zen fashion, as if I were a migrating bird with no actual home.

Seeing my trip home as an act of acceleration, I recorded only a few highway-side species on my drive through Oklahoma. I mostly remember that Oklahoma Highway 75 is also called the Indian Nation Turnpike. I wondered, *which* Indian nation? Then I realized that most of the people driving the highway didn't give a flying fuck, mostly pissed off (as I was) in learning that this was a toll road. I rolled into southern Kansas, got a motel in Independence, and had time to bird the city park for a while before dusk. Another night of the sleep of the just. Or the just plain tired.

Having already abandoned (all) Hope, I left (my) Independence the fourth day of the trip, limping home emotionally exhausted. I did stop at this place called the Wilson County State Fishing Lake, not far north of Independence, and saw three more Painted Buntings, including a much less gaudy female. I took Highway 75 all the way out of Kansas, as fast as the law allowed—or: even faster, according to the Highway Patrol fellow who pulled me over. He took his sweet time writing the ticket in the comfort of his own vehicle, so I kept my windows down and listened for birds. And wrote down "NOBO /" and "DICK //" in my birding notebook.

Those are my shorthand for one Northern Bobwhite and two Dickcissels. By this point in my OCD life, I'd memorized the 4-letter banding codes for most of the species in my area. I even began thinking of bobwhites as NOBOs—pronouncing the abbreviation as an acronym. Seeing an Eastern Bluebird, my mind now thinks EABL, much as if I had immersed myself in a foreign language and begun to think in it. And then, oh, the mental games: seeing an Eastern Bluebird, I now have to recite in my head a paraphrase of the old "Weeble" toy commercial: "EABLs wobble, but they don't fall down." And laugh a little to myself like a shy madman. A Mourning Dove is now forever a MODO, or sometimes, when I'm bored, "Mr. Modo Risin'"—to the melody of the old Jim Morrison lyric. And the poor little Pine Siskins (PISI)?: they're "pissies," of course. Yes, I've spent way too much time alone.

✳ JULY 2012, NEWTON HILLS STATE PARK:
Yellow-Bellied Sapsucker

My second marriage has been mostly a long-distance one. Soon after we married, I moved to Iowa City to get my PhD; for economic reasons, my wife stayed in Vermillion to labor on as an adjunct professor at the University of SoDak. When I was hired by the University of Nebraska fresh out of grad school, she remained in Vermillion, "for economic reasons." Truth be told, from the feathers of time called retrospection, both of us were bookish introverts already set in our ways by the time of our marriage, and living apart has seemed to suit us both.

But she has always been more social than I in terms of our get-togethers. "Are you coming next weekend?" "You *have* to come Easter weekend!" And Thanksgiving, and Christmas, and . . . until at last, religious and national holidays have become both her annual set of excuses for our reunions and dots on the calendar that require a three-hour drive north.

"Are you coming next weekend?" Recently, my reply to this eternal refrain has become "Why? It's freaking South Dakota. There are even fewer birds there than here!" It's a testament to my passion for birding that my wife usually accepts this as a semi-rational excuse.

But there are the *de rigeur* times when I must make the drive, sit down at a family meal, whisper sweet (sardonic) nothings in . . . a movie theater showing a chick flick or Marvel movie. My saving grace is that I know, deep down, that SoDak has some damned good birding, and I'm quite willing to take advantage of that. Yes, my precious time with family now annually includes getting up at about 5 a.m. on Thanksgiving and Christmas mornings and driving thirty miles to Yankton's Gavins Point Dam to take photos of the Bald Eagles who winter just below the dam. It has become a holiday ritual for over a decade now, and—my wife is "fine" with it. She either just accepts that I'm a nut or has come to realize that being around such a nut unable to bird for too many hours in a row is not exactly a walk in the park.

On one wintery occasion, she jostled me awake, thinking that I'd called her someone else's name in my sleep. Who is this Glaucous?, she demanded of me, in the middle of the night. Huh? Oh. Glaucous Gull, I mumbled, still half-asleep. Reports of a possible lifer, at Gavins Point Dam, over by Yankton. You belong in Yankton, she replied. This last is a South Dakota joke. The state mental institution is there. I'll be heading there in an hour or so, I joked. Or maybe I've been heading there most of my life.

> Wife *[crawling into bed]*: Ouch! There's something sharp in this bed! *[Frantic foray through the sheets.]* It's a burr! Don't you take your dirty clothes off after you're done birding?
> Tom *[shivering]*: Usually. But it's too fucking cold in here!
> Wife: Wuss.
> Tom: Turn up the heat, you cheap hussy!

Summers are another story. Then I usually have the time to bird the more distant mythic realms of—oh, say, Kansas, and Wyoming, and Montana, so there's even less reason to hang around southeastern SoDak with my binoculars on the ready. But I did find, out of necessary desperation, at least one other birding gem in the area: it's called Newton Hills State Park, about halfway between Vermillion and Sioux Falls, a quick drive up I-29. Near the Big Sioux River, its riparian woodlands render it a smaller, more northerly, version of Nebraska's Fontenelle Forest and Indian Cave State Park. All are birder heaven-havens in terms of the eastern songbirds that manage to just barely get this far west in their range. Hot, humid, and tick-ridden, such places are indeed about all of the East I need for the year, great birding aside.

I've only been there a handful of times, all in the early 2010s, and my lists are highlighted by such vocal eastern birds as the Wood Thrush, the Yellow-throated Vireo, and the Ovenbird. One list counted eight Ovenbirds—all only heard, probably, their ringing *kuh-CHEE, kuh-CHEE, kuh-CHEE, kuh-CHEE, kuh-CHEE* echoing from the forest floor as if they were huge cicadas emphasizing the wrong syllable. A Scarlet Tanager or two can be found along the same low woodland trails, calling *CHICK-BURR* to make you look at him, to make you admire and wonder at a stunning deep-red bird with deep-black wings in the middle of a deep-green forest.

My second trip there, in 2012, got me only the second Blue-winged Warbler of my life, proof again that relatively rare south-eastern birds sometimes show up there. This trip also got me a lifer in the form of another eastern bird, the Yellow-bellied Sapsucker. The first one I saw was a more plainly colored juvenile, which complicated matters for a moment, until I saw an adult a short time later along the trail, the obvious large white vertical wing stripe sealing the deal, as did the mewing calls.

The Yellow-bellied Sapsucker is most famous for its very name, having long been something of a joke among non-birders as a putatively made-up name, as a satire on the long, ridiculous bird names thrown around by those goofy "birdwatchers." A similar misunderstanding exists among non-birders thanks to the campfire game called snipe-hunting, leading to the belief among many that the snipe is a mythical bird, when in fact there *are* real birds that go by the name of "snipe." And yes, Virginia, there *is* a Yellow-bellied Sapsucker.

✳ JULY 2012, MORRISON PARK: *Lesser Goldfinch*

The year 2012 marked close to a decade of visiting daughter Em in Denver almost every summer, in the suburb of Lakewood, to the southwest of Denver proper. Emma was now in her teen years and so, in the summer, she could sleep deeply until noon, while my middle-aged inclination was to rise earlier and earlier: in short—*cough, cough*—there was ample time to bird. My favorite birding venues on these trips, for several years, had been Kountze Lake and the wonderful Chatfield State Park to the south, but this summer I wanted to branch out a bit, habitat-wise. Farther southwest from Denver is the little touristy town called Morrison. On the edge of this town is Morrison Park, a small ravine of a streamside park on the foothills of the Rockies; it's just south of the more well-known Red Rocks Park, with the famous outdoor-concert amphitheater. But I avoided the latter as an untoward magnet of automobile traffic and noisy human sociability.

This first trip to Morrison Park was not unlike many of my more pleasant birding stops at a new place: the novelty of the terrain, for instance—in this case a stream with a bit of the coniferous Rockies on the one side and a bit of the scrub-shrub-hills of the US southwest on other, with a sprite of mountain water so quick and narrow that it reminded me of the Black Hills creeks back home. Then the novel combination of old and new bird species: yes, chickadees and robins and starlings were there, to remind me that I was still on the same planet. But there were also three first-of-the-year species, birds I'd only seldomly seen in my life, including two Broad-tailed Hummingbirds, the female among the flowers beside the stream, the male singing his metal-insect trill in zigzag flights. There was a pair of Lesser Goldfinches, the male with a black back that said as if in welcome, "No, Tom. I'm not your everyday American Goldfinch." Then an American Dipper, standing, amazingly, on a wet rock in the middle of the stream, followed by a few flights low over the water up and down the stream, a bird I hadn't seen for well over twenty years.

A good morning, in brief. My pleasure was redoubled by having arrived at 6:30 a.m., the sun already up, yes, but only the birds and one human—*moi*—active, a private communion I envisioned as usually only reserved for a select few British poets and even fewer saintly introverted naturalists. I returned to my trusty Toyota Corolla to drive a little farther up the park, only to discover . . . .

A flat rear right tire? No! A veteran of owning several older claptrap vehicles, I had no problem getting the rear of the car jacked up, and the lug nuts off, and then a simple tug on the tire itself . . . availed nothing. Huh?! Why couldn't I get the bloody tire off?! How stupid (or what did my wife call it?—"not mechanically inclined") could I be? After some more ineffectual tugging, it crossed my mind to break out the owner's manual to see if I was missing something, but the impulse quickly passed.

Morrison itself was only a few blocks away, so I walked into town to buy a can of Fix-a-Flat™. It was still early in the morning, and a Saturday, so not much was open, including the first gas station or two. The third Broad-tailed Hummingbird of the morning buzzed by, and I dutifully noted it in my little notebook. Already a ball of summer sweat from the walk on what promised to be a hot day, I finally found a little mom-and-pop general store with the necessary can of salvation on the shelves. Oh, please, let this work, I prayed to no god in particular as I made my way to the cashier. A local erstwhile hippy with long gray hair was buying the morning *Denver Post* and pondering the selection of homemade scones wrapped in cellophane at the counter. He was going to walk leisurely back to his car, and drive leisurely home, and have a leisurely read of the newspaper on his leisurely weekend morning. I envied him to the point of hatred. I decided that I'd better buy two cans of Fix-a-Flat™ just to make sure.

I made it back to car as the sun became less and less pleasant and injected the great foam hope into the afflicted tire. I had been dreading the alternative if it didn't work: call Emma's mom? And have my car towed, eight hundred miles from home? And it wasn't so much the shame: above all, I dreaded the hit that the time delay would put on my birding efforts. As a veteran of this canned remedy, I also knew it to be only a temporary respite, so after a quick search on my iPhone Maps app, I immediately drove to a Walmart on the westside of Denver and bought a new set of tires. As I paid the large, unexpected expense with my credit card, I stubbornly refused to ask them if they'd had any problems getting the right rear tire off. Even a non-mechanically inclined birder has a modicum of pride.

I see that my eBird report still includes the bitter note: "Spent most of time fixing flat tire!" But things could have been a lot worse. So—thank you, Morrison Park, for the three FOYs. And thank *you*, Fix-a-Flat™.

✳ MAY 2013, PAWNEE LAKE STATE RECREATION AREA: *Bonaparte's Gull*

As I write this, I'm as avid a birder as ever, if not more so. Bird lists are now more than ever the epitome and *ne plus ultra* of my obsessive-compulsive disorder. Then there's the news, of humans and politics. I see no quick end to the developed nations' capitalist hegemony, to white privilege, to Christian epistemic violence—the latter two subtly reinforced and enforced by global capitalism's mass media. The "information age," moreover, has become the "dis/mis-information age": our growing inability to veritably ascertain the "truth," via social media, etc., is fulfilling French postmodern theory's greatest dreams of discursive play and worst nightmares of discursive coercion. At last: I'd rather be birding.

Birding Pawnee Lake, I take a left to the first "Day Use" turn-off on the south side of the lake. The sandy beach at road's end is sometimes a profitable setting for late migrating shorebirds and gulls. Luck: there's a gull there, and on inspection, it doesn't seem to be one of the abundant and ubiquitous Franklin's Gulls. Ah! Its pinkish-orange legs announce it as a Bonaparte's Gull, a rarity for me, and I break out my Canon Rebel and jump out of my car. My luck continues: the bird remains standing where I found it, as I walk closer and closer, firing off photo after photo.

In fact, I finally become curious—why won't it fly away? Just a few yards from the bird, I see a second, a companion; what I had presumed to be a piece of refuse stands up awkwardly on the sand and flies weakly for a short distance. The first bird is apparently its mate, attending to its companion's last minutes of life, and it will soon be in mourning, I figure.

I'm too emotional now myself for any more ambulance chaser photos. I drive back towards Lincoln, simultaneously doing a search on my iPhone for the local bird rescue organization. There it is, complete with phone number: I stop at the one gas station in the tiny town of Emerald and call an outfit called the Wildlife Rescue Team. But the person answering the phone must be the spouse or friend of a volunteer or something. She says, "You want us to save a *what?* A *gull?*" Yes. I give her detailed directions, but to this day, I don't know whether her question meant, "What's a gull?" or "You seriously want us to save a stinking seagull?!" Neither possibility, frankly, was reassuring.

I assumed, as I said, that the first bird was soon to be in mourning. And I also assume that his/her partner died well before any human rescue team ever got there. Take mourning as a metaphor, if you will. I certainly don't mean that I think the bird's emotions and cogitations were *anything like* what we humans (of whatever culture) think and feel in the face of such loss. And frankly, I'm rather sick of naturist writers—even contemporary ones—trying very hard to make them analogous, via appeals to elephant's tears, et al. I prefer to give birds, to leave birds to, their sheer *other*ness. At last, what do I know of Bonaparte's Gulls, really? I have no idea what that bird was experiencing, and I know that probably everything I have made the reader feel—regarding the poor bird's loss and mourning—is ultimately human projection. And yet, and yet—one still is called to feel, to act, on behalf of even the non-human other:

> If I am responsible for the other [human], and before the other, and in the place of the other, on behalf of the other, isn't the animal more other still, more radically other [. . .] than the other in whom I recognize my brother, than the other in whom I identify my fellow or my neighbor?[98]

And yet again: how can we know another animal when we

don't even know ourselves, we who are ourselves pretty much mixed-up and botched subjects to capitalist hegemony and epistemic violence? Yes, and so some of us, at the dawn of the twenty-first century and the fall of Western civilization, have turned to list-making in some out-of-humans'-way swamp or beach or forest. And yes, there is a good deal of guilt involved in my choice to dance on this particular Titanic.

And yet, and yes: I'd still rather be birding.

✳ MAY 2014, EL SEGUNDO BEACH: *Brown Pelican*

I have been to California twice: for my daughter's high school and college graduations. As much as I have lauded Great Plains birding, my few trips to Texas and California have created one of the great regrets of my life. Why haven't I traveled more? Even better, why don't I just *move*?! Oh, say, to California. Out there, around Los Angeles at least, the hummingbirds just sit on the power lines like so many starlings and House Sparrows. My two-night visit to LA for Emma's graduation from USC had me wondering, "Hey, is there an opening at some directional California state college? Sign me up."

For the trip, being totally Beverly-Hillbilly-hick-stupid, I simply booked a place as close to LAX as possible, a reasonably priced motel with a shuttle to/from the airport. Ah, perfect: the Hacienda Hotel, in beautiful downtown El Segundo. Well, this so-called hotel was a pretty rundown hole-in-the-wall, and the jumpy elevators with peeling walls looked as if they were ready to transport me to *The Shining* at any moment. But I did like El Segundo in general, a small, unassuming city just south of Los Angeles: not only could I walk the length of the town—birding, of course—but it ended at a *beach*. (I may have neglected to mention that I had never seen the ocean. And I haven't since.)

Arriving Wednesday night, I awoke in the lovely Hacienda Hotel before dawn (4:15, to be exact) because entering my open hotel window were the warbles of—? Huh. I love being new to a place and feeling like a beginning birder. It took me a while—until later that morning, actually, when I saw one on my walk—to figure out that it was the song of a Western Bluebird. (I should have guessed it was a thrush of some sort, at that early hour.) First of the year. A good start.

Then the early a.m. walk around the neighborhood, including a tiny park: apparently, California's idea of a park is a thin strip of lawn under great rows of Iron-Giant-sized transformer towers. I heard these *pit-SEE* calls, flycatcher-like, and then saw the bird fly over my head, to a power line: Black Phoebe. Lifer. Then there were the hummingbirds, who enjoyed my iPhone recordings of hummingbird songs: one came over and started making semi-circular courtship flights right beside me. Allen's Hummingbird. Lifer. These tiny, feathered cyclones are truly social beings. A few blocks later there were three more engaged in what could only be described as a "flight-fight"; I guess ocean-front breeding territory is worth battling over in these parts. A brilliant orange-and-black Hooded Oriole in the top of a palm tree was only an FOY, not a lifer, but I still felt as if I were at a birder's Disney World, a brave new world that had such strange birds in it.

Checking my iPhone map, I decided to walk to the city's Library Park and back, before Emma and the Ex were to pick me up for an evening at USC. Yep, just as I'd hoped and planned for: a noisy Western Scrub-Jay. Lifer. A couple more Allen's Hummingbirds and Black Phoebes reinforced their presence in my lifer memory banks, but there were also these small, busy-buzzy birds I couldn't place. They were tiny and flitty and high-pitched like a chickadee, but I couldn't get a good look, even though they seemed to be following me. . . . Finally: oh, Bushtits! FOY, and such cute little fuckers.

Unfortunately, the Bushtit is cursed with one of the most atrocious double-entendre names in birddom. Indeed, thumbing through the names in any bird guide, the cultural critic might reasonably argue that many of the species' names were intentionally made up by a coterie of old patriarchal letches hellbent on sexual innuendo. Another bird cursed in this regard is the Brown Booby. When the Nebraska Ornithological Union recently emailed me, asking permission to use my photo of this bird in their quarterly journal, it tore me up inside to have to respond in complete seriousness. Because part of me is apparently still fourteen years old.

The afternoon drive to USC with Emma and the Ex was highlighted by another lifer, a Western Gull flying around some shopping center. But I was pretty distracted during the trip because Emma was driving. I remembered letting her try to drive my car in Rapid City, and then Lakewood, and I remember fearing for all the mailboxes in both neighborhoods. Now she was driving on an LA freeway, waving her arms to yap at her mom and me as she drove, handling the on- and off-ramps with practiced equanimity. She had a lot more guts than I did. I was so proud. But still very, very frightened.

That night, I attended a screening with Emma and the Ex of a short film Em had written the screenplay for, as a capstone activity for her screenwriting BA. It was called *Campbells*, about a single woman who suffers through a rough day at work—in a prison, where her very raison d'être is called into question by a Black inmate. She finally comes home, close to a nervous breakdown. She is homesick for her childhood, for her mother. Near tears, she slowly opens a can of tomato soup, and the film fades out as the woman finds some ritualistic communion and comfort in this return-to-her-home-and-family meal.

Friday morning: since Emma's graduation ceremony wasn't until mid-afternoon, I had time to walk to El Segundo Beach, a healthy several-mile jaunt with binoculars and camera in tow. On the way, I recorded three more Allen's Hummingbirds, another scrub-jay, ten Bushtits, and seven ravens. As with my previous California trip, I was shocked at how assimilated these last birds had become to human presence, even urbanization: here were these huge black corvids in El Segundo's trees, in humans' front yards. I even came across a raven fledgling that had fallen onto someone's lawn, the adult pair squawking beside it, probably trying to keep the domestic cats away. Good luck on that, I thought, and headed on towards the beach.

El Segundo Beach was a disappointment immediately. It was deserted, for one thing, which is usually a good thing for a birder. But the cynic in me wondered why. Well, the hazardous waste markers may have been one reason; the discarded rubber gloves and syringes scattered about the sand may have been another. My first time seeing the ocean. Christ. Manifest Destiny had gotten here before me and ruined everything.

But I had come all this way for lifers, dammit, and lifers I would get, even if I contracted some blood-borne disease from carelessly stepping on a stray needle. (Okay, I was feeling dramatic in my despair.) I walked closer to where the beach met the ocean. I picked up a small seashell and put it in my pocket, for posterity. I scanned the rocks along the shore for Black Oystercatchers— one likely lifer on a SoCal beach this time of year, according to my pre-trip research. No luck. I walked along the beach towards the north, with Emily Dickinson's "I never saw a Moor— / I never saw the Sea" racing through my mind. Somehow I felt that I still hadn't.

Then I trained my binoculars on some commercial ship a few hundred yards offshore, as if to check whether my binocs were still operational. Along the waves just this side of the boat were—*ta-dah*—about eight Brown Pelicans. Lifer. They flew back and forth horizontally to the shore, as if willfully denying me any chance at a decent photo. But that was fine with me. I just watched, and watched, and thought, "Finally. The OCEAN." I watched one of them coast in the air without wing-flaps, just above the surface of the water, as if it could float forever like a child's dream.

The final lifer of the trip was a bit farther north, this time on the beach itself: beside the semi-familiar Caspian Terns were some smaller terns, with more yellow-orange bills: ah, about twenty-five Elegant Terns, calling *kitt-er-ick* just like the bird guides said. I was especially tickled by the loose, shaggy feathers on the backs of their heads. I remember thinking that they looked like 1960s "long-hairs." I thanked these avian Beatles silently for redeeming my walk, my first and only trip to the ocean, and walked back for one more night in the Flea-Hotel California before catching an early flight back to Lincoln.

Six lifers on this California trip, all told. I pretty much birded through Emma's high school graduation. I pretty much birded through Emma's college graduation. I may have pretty much wasted my life birding. I could use some Campbell's tomato soup right now.

✳ MARCH 2015, PAWNEE LAKE STATE RECREATION AREA: *American Robin*

Dead robin in the middle of a two-lane county asphalt road. Oh, a live robin right beside it, mourning, if you will. (And it may be just as anthropocentric to refuse this possibility as to embrace it.) I turn the car around to get the sun at my back, grab my camera for this touching scene—and a local yokel in a pickup drives around me and promptly runs over the second robin. Damn.

I'd already counted probably seventy-five robins that fine spring morning driving around Pawnee Lake, since robin migration was still in full flow, and they stood in fields and on country-house lawns in good-sized flocks. I had eventually resorted to counting them by fives and tens, as annoying dirt-common interruptions to my hoped-for rarities and first-of-the-years, the birds of real awe and wonder. But and so—let's admit it, birding had become, for me, all about the numbers, if it hadn't always been so from the very beginning.

Now I gazed, still a bit stunned, at two feathered charcoal splotches trimmed in red, the longer-lived bird with one wing still pointed to the sky, as if the last bemused and futile gesture of a human in a Stephen Crane story.

Numbers. . . .

Damn.

✳ JULY 2016, MEDICINE BOW NATIONAL FOREST—VEDAUWOO: *Dusky Flycatcher*

After driving my Toyota Corolla for over ten years, I finally grew weary of slogging its front-wheel drive through muddy back roads. So I broke down and bought a new Subaru Forester, blessed with all-wheel drive, seventeen-inch tires, and—most importantly—a certain cachet among veteran birders as an outdoorsy back-road vehicle par excellence. I even splurged on a set of customized license plates that read "GN BRDNG." Some of my Facebook friends teased me that they read the plate as "Gone Brooding" or even "Gone Barding" (damned English-major types, of course), but I remained fairly gleeful about my new acquisition and couldn't wait for summer to arrive.

Dare I go back to Wyoming? On my previous trip, I'd brought back bedbugs in my luggage, which had made my life a living hell for six months. Hey, this time I'll book a much less bedbug-likely motel, I told myself, not some locally run flophouse in Laramie—you know, a place worthy of a new car with custom plates. (Oh, the hubris! Certainly, Tom, after all your reading in the Greek classics, you should have been prepared for a fall.)

The first eventful birding of the trip was a stretch of road called, wonderfully enough, the State Line Road, where Kimball County, Nebraska, turns into Laramie County, Wyoming. It was an early Thursday afternoon, and the highlights were two FOY Cassin's Kingbirds—a pair, just north of some railroad tracks. This western species is hard to distinguish from the more common Western Kingbird, unless you hear the *ch'beer* calls; but the lack of white outer tail-feathers sealed the ID for me. There was also a pair of Blue Grosbeaks: not that unusual in such a country-road setting, but I think it was the first time I'd ever seen the male and female together. I headed into Wyoming in high spirits. "Gone Brooding," indeed.

Right before Cheyenne proper—it wasn't even 2:00 p.m. yet, thanks to gaining an hour because of the time change—I took a left off the interstate, to check out the vaunted Campstool Road and Wyoming Hereford Ranch, whatever that was. It was over-cast, and windy, and even rainy the last fifteen minutes of a nine-mile stretch of road, but I still managed thirty species. The two singing Brewer's Sparrows (FOY) were one highlight; I remembered them from my last Wyoming trip, although I had to jog my memory via an iPhone recording. A radiant Bullock's Oriole was the other special sighting; I recognized its rattly calls first, and then I saw the bold-white-wing-patched male. I was birding the Mountain West once again, damn it! It felt good.

From my last trip, I knew exactly where to get two FOY long-spur species: Chalk Bluffs Road, straight south of Cheyenne. First decent photo, in years, of a Swainson's Hawk—check. A great visual of a male Chestnut-collared Longspur on a barbed-wire fence: check. Two McCown's Longspurs—I heard them first, but then I finally got a few decent photos. Finally, the starkly black-and-white Lark Buntings—the state bird of Colorado—were rampant and voluble, another reminder, if I needed one, that I wasn't in Nebraska anymore.

I checked into my motel—and yes, I immediately pulled down the bedspread to look for bed bugs—and took a short nap. A *short* one: I had birds to see, and photos to process. I finished the birding day at the Vedauwoo district of the Medicine Bow National Forest, a short drive about halfway to Laramie. The real highlight wasn't a bird at all, but a young Moose—big as fuck, yes, but with spindly excuses for antlers. I followed it around for a good while, getting plenty of bad photos of the strangest North American member of the deer family. I only had time to bird the areas accessible from the main south entrance, with names like Box Canyon and Beaver Ponds Day Use. I planned on driving through the whole range from the north the next morning. But I was fortunate enough, in the two hours allotted, to see another

Broad-tailed Hummingbird, a male in the same Turtle Mountain Trailhead parking lot where I'd seen one two years ago. FOYs— the holy grail of birding by this point in my life, next to lifers— included a raspy-voiced Steller's Jay, eight Common Ravens, and three Mountain Chickadees, whose more hoarse-throated *dee-dee* calls distinguished them from their eastern Black-capped kin.

I pulled out of Cheyenne by 6:00 a.m. the next morning, hoping for a good Friday. But damn, I immediately hit a Pronghorn,

> the sound of living
>   flesh and bone
>   meeting man-
> ufactured metal,

damaging my front left fender and quarter panel pretty good. Or rather, the Pronghorn hit *me*: I hadn't really got up to speed on the short service road that would take me to Highway 210, the back way to Vedauwoo, and the poor creature ran up quickly from behind my left side, leaping ahead of me like some crazed gazelle, right into the corner of my new Subaru. Yes, that's exactly how it happened. I'm pretty sure. DAMN. I pulled over as soon as I could, maybe a half-mile down the road, and examined the damage. Besides a very cracked up front left fender, some type of fluid was leaking out onto the ground. A quick look revealed that the windshield-washer-fluid reservoir had been damaged, too. Then I looked back, scanning for the Pronghorn, hoping it either was only grazed—hard to believe, frankly—or had died a quick death. A pickup truck—maybe two?, I don't remember for sure— of local yokels had already parked beside what I guessed to be my recent contact. I then perhaps too quickly assumed that they were already doing what seasoned Wyomingites do when they come upon a freshly killed cervid. The human psyche's powers of rationalization and self-justification are glorious things. My great guilt about the dead (or wounded?) Pronghorn was confronted head-on by my good ol' American materialist concern about my damned inanimate hunk of metal. My idealistic pride as a post-human environmentalist was rendered moot and pathetic.

I believe that I was still in shock as I decided to keep up my day's itinerary. First, the eight-mile, two-and-a-half hour drive on Vedauwoo's Happy Jack—oh!—Road. Driving into eastern Colorado or eastern Wyoming is inevitably a pleasure because they are such wonderful hybrid zones—as the Great Plains turn into mountains, as the meadowlarks turn into magpies. But now a great emptiness, a continual sinking of the gut, accompanied my simultaneous pleasure of seeing mountain species for the first time in a long time: a Red-naped Sapsucker taunted me by calling *Pronghorn*, as did a Steller's Jay, or so I imagined. A Mountain Chickadee was clearly whistling the tones 2—2—2—2—2—1, an unusual number of repeated major second tones. I usually would have found this piece of ornithological musicology to be heartwarming, or at least intellectually stimulating; but all I really heard was the taunt of *Pronghorn!*; all I really felt was the fear that I wouldn't make it back home without my fender or front quarter panel falling off. All I really heard was

the sound of living
    flesh and bone
        meeting man-
ufactured metal.

I stopped at some parking lot with a sign for Headquarters Trail, partly to scan the pines for woodpeckers and jays, partly to see if my cracked-up front left was still there. From the tall pines, I heard the three-part song of a Dusky Flycatcher. A lifer! I mean (a lifer)—heard in parentheses, as it were, by a crestfallen fellow with a wounded Subaru Forester. I verified its song on my iPhone, duly recorded it in my notebook with a star and a circle, and proceeded on my way, driving as carefully as I could on the bumpy mountain gravel road. I realized that I was being dangerously stupid, in terms of making it home mechanically and psychologically intact, but decades of obsessive birding had made my behavior fairly intractable.

I even had the nerve to proceed to my next planned venue, the other branch of the Medicine Bow National Forest, a much more steep and mountainous area southwest of Laramie. "Highlights" no longer qualified as a term, as I inched my way up steep inclines that dwarfed my home Black Hills, stopping every few miles to check the status of my quarter panel. A Broad-tailed Hummingbird, a Red-naped Sapsucker, three Common Ravens, four Hermit Thrushes, and three Red Crossbills somehow found their way into my pocket birding notebook. I also heard, then saw, four White-crowned Sparrows at a mountain pond south of some place named Foxpark. I imagined living in in a nice, quiet place called Foxpark—in another, less obsessive-compulsive life.

On my way to my next planned stop, Hutton Lake National Wildlife Refuge, I took a county dirt road again, as if tempting fate to toss my fender into a ditch in the most remote of all possible boonies. The avian gods teased me back with a Swainson's Hawk, a raven, and a lugubrious Wilson's Snipe standing on a fencepost, saying, "See? Life ain't so bad! Take my picture!" I couldn't. Since I am an inveterate pouter, I wouldn't give that snipe the pleasure.

Hutton Lake included several lakes and thus also at least a

few waterbirds to slake the thirst of this now forever-cursed-to-me semi-arid region. Besides the several duck species on the several small lakes, I mechanically recorded five Eared Grebes, a pelican, four White-faced Ibises, three Willets, and two Forster's Terns. I heard some McCown's Longspurs and a Brewer's Sparrow singing. I saw a male Northern Harrier being mobbed by Red-winged Blackbirds. I saw two more Swainson's Hawks. I heard over and over, in my mind's ear,

> the sound of living
>   flesh and bone
>   meeting man-
> ufactured metal,

as I headed back to Laramie.

In town, flying above a rundown Dairy Queen was a lone California Gull: FOY. I realized that I had better spend the second night in Laramie, to emotionally reconnoiter. The crack in my car had seemed to have spread, or at least the big, flapping-loose piece was drooping closer to the ground. So, before getting a motel room, I stopped at a Hardware Hank's and bought a roll of duct tape, hoping it would hold my fender on until I got back to Lincoln. I also prayed for no rain: muddy roads might well prevent me from driving anywhere at all, since I had no working wiper-fluid dispenser.

But I did have to hit Old Laramie River Road to finish the day—by now, out of sheer dumb stubbornness. However, I *refused* to count the Pronghorns—"that'll show 'em"—although I usually try to keep track of any interesting mammals on my birding outings. I counted thirty-seven bird species on the drive and was surprised (again) by the good number of waterbird species. But

I was forever worried, as I conscientiously noted each sighting, that my duct-taped fender would fall off at any moment. As I came upon a beautiful pair of Swainson's Hawks, I tried to recall whether I could call 911 even when my phone said "no service"— which it did say, intermittently, here in yet another back-road boondocks.

The Swainson's Hawks remain my greatest memory of this drive: I saw five in all, including a pair on a power-line pole and my first ever dark-morph of this species. I got by far my best life photos of this species, and I couldn't wait to get back to Lincoln to process them on my real computer. An FOY Prairie Falcon zoomed by like a bat out of Hades. *(Pronghorn!)* I recorded seven now-old-hat McCown's Longspurs. *(Pronghorn!)* I saw only one Brewer's Sparrow but heard six: their elaborate songs were quickly becoming a favorite, truly a sparrow's song among sparrows. *(Pronghorn!)*

I limped up the long interstate hill out of Laramie the next morning, stopping once more at Vedauwoo. "It's on the way home," I reasoned. A Broad-tailed Hummingbird was waiting for me at the usual place (Turtle Mountain Trailhead), and I got a truly wretched photo. Four more zipped around Box Canyon. Seven Common Ravens chanted *Nevermore*—and I knew exactly what they meant. Two singers were the final FOY tallies for the trip: a Townsend's Solitaire and a Cassin's Finch.

I only got twelve FOYs on the trip, but for July, that was still a decent accomplishment. The year 2016 was the first year that I would top the magical 300 bird species mark (301, to be exact)— a goal I'd had for over a decade—and so these twelve western/mountain birds were integral to that achievement. But it's that one poor Pronghorn that I will never forget. In his/her memory, I now keep a roll of duct tape in the back of the Subaru.

❋ NOVEMBER 2017, LEWIS AND CLARK LAKE:
Snowy Owl

> Finally! A Snowy Owl—in Alaska. But now I can't find
> my camera. . . .
>
> —my dream, 20 Jan. 2013

My December 2011 raptor count in an earlier section was incomplete: "27 Red-tailed Hawks, 20 Bald Eagles, 7 American Kestrels, 5 Northern Harriers, 5 Rough-legged Hawks, 1 Prairie Falcon, and 1 Ferruginous Hawk." I forgot to add: *zero* Snowy Owls. Yes, I struck out on the never-yet-seen Snowy Owl again. It had become a mythic bird to me, the true God and Reason for the Season, the real impetus for any winter road trip, each of which inevitably ended with "Snowy Owls: 0." But let me just say that, on that trip, I never noticed so many WHITE plastic baggies littering our fine fields and roadsides in my whole life.

At several winter nadir points of frustration in this regard, I considered resorting to "phenomenological" birding: "In the process of scanning the horizon as I drove a dirt county road, I thought for at least one second that an interesting clump of snow might be a Snowy Owl. Therefore it was." I have also long and frequently lamented: why *isn't* my next lifer a Snowy Owl or a Whooping Crane? How come every new species I get is a bird that no one else (that is, no normal, non-birding-fanatic person) has ever heard of? Christ, I could just start making them up. "Yeah. I saw a Ruby-Headed Prothonotary Godwit the other day. Quite the sight. No, you wouldn't know it. Pretty damned obscure."

Obviously, most of my thoughts and writing about this species have involved the vast majority of my life when I had never seen one—and had faint hope of ever doing so. In 2012, during the last major winter influx of Snowy Owls into the Lower 48 until 2017, I even grew bitter on Facebook, lamenting the 140 Snowy Owls that had been reported in Nebraska in the previous month or so: "I don't *want* to see a Snowy Owl. If I did see one, I wouldn't even record the sighting. If I got a photo of one, I'd erase it from my SD card. So there."

The 23rd of November 2017 was Thanksgiving morning, so I had made my obligatory trip "home" to Vermillion, SD, to be with my wife. Which meant that I was actually already in Yankton, by dawn, scanning Yankton Lake for birds, and Lewis and Clark Lake for birds, and driving across Gavins Point Dam, the huge hydroelectric dam that divided the two lakes. A Long-tailed Duck on Lake Yankton, a Horned Grebe scoped on Lewis and Clark Lake, and a flock of about twenty Snow Buntings scattering below the dam to the west, along the Lewis and Clark Lake riprap, had been the highlights so far. It wasn't until my second drive along this north-south dam road that I saw it. About half-way along the road, at exactly 8:59 a.m., Central Standard Time, there it was, standing on the riprap below, along the lake, not far from where I'd seen the buntings maybe a half hour before: a Snowy Owl. "Big as life," and all that shit. "This is what you've waited for for so long," I said to myself, and I rather half-ruined the moment, as usual, by over-thinking the present by introjecting too much of the past.

Two cars had already stopped along the road before me: would I even have seen it if they hadn't led me to look? I'd just bought a new super-telephoto camera and so I got lots of photos, without having to worry about over-stressing a rare, perhaps health-compromised bird. The heavy dark moon-disc markings on its breast marked it as an immature bird, as are most of the Snowies that wander this far south during certain special winters. Tears did come to my eyes, goddamnit, and I drove away after only about five minutes, not even knowing why, I was so flustered.

I checked out Lewis and Clark (why does that pair of names continue to haunt me?) again for a few minutes until I thought, fuck, what the hell am I doing? I drove back to the owl, which had flown a mere few yards farther north, but seemed not all interested in leaving. I took more photos, taking more time to relish the moment.

Then ego pride struck, and I wondered if anybody had reported it on eBird, or on the sd-birds or NEBirds listservs. Sure enough, someone in the local birding community had already spread the word, which may have explained the number of cars lined up on the road. So now I blessed my usually cursèd luck that I'd seen the Snowy *before* I checked my mobile notifications and saw that it had been reported: this lack of knowing had made the experience all the more thrilling, all the more "authentic." Finally, a lifer that had lived up to the vaunted lifer moment.

I kidded later in my eBird report, when I got home, that the bird seemed so tame that it was probably still there. And of course, and ironically, the bird stuck around for several more days, right on that riprap, so that every beginning birder and probably half the snot-nosed kids in Yankton saw it, just for the novelty, and I felt somewhat pissed and cheated. But you know how I am.

✳ MARCH 2018, WEST PLATTE RIVER DRIVE: *Whooping Crane*

A few months later, on the single day of March 7, 2018, I saw both a Whooping Crane and a Snowy Owl. The first was in Nebraska and the second in Kansas, but how many people—even lifelong avid birders—can say that they have accomplished that feat? Whooping Cranes have long been the most famously rare, most endangered species of North America. And the arctic Snowy Owl's intermittent appearances in the continental US?—well, you know my long frustration regarding ever seeing this bird.

My first Whooping Cranes had been in October 2015. Scoping that rare and new species: priceless. Getting my car dusted by a duck hunter's stray buckshot: not so much. Nor was I pleased that the Avi-Auto—my too-cutesy name for my new Forester—received its first speeding ticket trying to get the hell out of Kansas as quickly as possible.

But for this later trip, for once, I will omit the interminable details. Maybe from a certain sense of jadedness, even ennui. It's done, a *fait accompli*: I saw both a Whooping Crane and a Snowy Owl on the same freaking day, and so—there. Okay, the former was a football field away in the middle of a flock of thousands of Sandhill Cranes along West Platte River Drive, one of the more well-driven touristy stops for Sandhill Cranes, a few miles south of Grand Island, Nebraska. The latter—much more unusual, given the place—was on the riprap rocks bordering the wetlands of Cheyenne Bottoms, Kansas. I got really bad distant photos of both.

Early the next morning, I hit my second favorite Kansas birding venue, Quivira National Wildlife Refuge. I immediately head to the gravel road bordering the north edge of the Big Salt Marsh, where I come upon a Rough-legged Hawk sitting on an historical marker sign. I pull up more closely and shut the car off (rule #1 of bird photography, a lesson learned the hard way). After taking a few shots, I get out of the car and walk—slowly—towards my deific subject, and—snap off a few more shots, getting closer—and—closer. Damn. Is this fucker even alive? On or near his/her deathbed? I get close enough to touch said deific subject. I feel really lucky, even blessed (in a secular way, of course), but I'm worried about the bird. I finally decide to drive around the Wildlife Loop of the marsh, as usual, and then come back to the sign, and—*whew*—the bird has flown. A few moments later, I see my old buddy hovering above the road, as rough-leggeds are wont to do. It lives! Oh, dying and reviving gods! I feel relieved—that I can now justifiably enjoy the great photos I'd just taken of my now-favorite raptor. . . . And this, the day after the Whooper and Snowy—it's as if the bird gods are saying to an aging man: here, Tom, enjoy yourself. Enjoy Us. You're not long for the world.

It has really struck me recently that I don't have a hell of a lot longer to live. And my values system now is such that I prefer to spend much more of that time, from here on out, outside instead of inside. And much more time living among and experiencing birds than reading and writing about them. Or about anything else. And now it's as if all the birds keep lining up for photos, as if they sense my mortality. It has also struck me that, in the second half of my life, I have taken much more earnestly to birding as a compensation for my general bookish introversion. It has been birding, above all, that has forced me to look up from my books, to look around once again, to see anew, and even more, to hear anew. In short, birding is wonderful therapy for a person so chronically brain-addled by books that he usually barely *senses* anything real. Birding, ultimately, is one lone human being being real with the Real.

Furthermore, birding may be one of the few *ethical* avocations left to postmodern humankind. It's often just one human individual and his/her birds and bird list. Pondering my avocation, my second wife once asked me, "How do you know that people just don't *lie* about the birds they've seen?" I looked at her with both shock and amusement. (And that's a hard look to pull off.) Okay, unconscious wish-fulfillment may have talked me into an FOY or two in my life that I may have looked back on later as perhaps a wee bit problematic: but the conscious LIE thing is sheer blasphemy, anathema to any true birder.

To frame my situation more perversely, birding may also have long been the only thing that has kept me from checking out of a world full of fucked-up human animals, a group that includes myself. But now, to my own surprise, I want to delay the checking-out, want one more birding trip, one more bird list, one more bird. Faced with this new greater sense of personal ending, I now rise before dawn and yell (silently), "Once more unto the beach!" Or marsh, or wherever.

Such thoughts may also stem from the fact that my mom died recently, after much of this book had been written. Over a decade of COPD and biannual hospitalizations from pneumonia—each one a near-deathbed event—finally took its toll on her body to the point that her mind must have been just too emotionally exhausted to go on. On her real deathbed, in March of 2017, she seemed almost happy to be going. I realized, somewhat bitterly, that this was in good part due to the heavy pain-killing medication she was on, and I wondered how many terminal patients in the US were being thus medicated into their graves, and I even wondered if I would eventually gladly embrace the same fate.

There remained that last drive from Lincoln to Rapid while Mom was still alive. (I hoped she was still alive. My brother's last phone call had been cryptic.) Repress. Repress. . . . Okay. Well, next to birds, I get off most on place names when I'm driving. Flashing back to a recent Texas drive, I don't think the folks of Bovina, Texas, thought out their name too well: yes, I know your name proudly declares that you're a cow town, but I don't think that you thoroughly considered the negative connotations of "bovine"? And I don't even have the heart to Google how the next county I drove through—Deaf Smith County—got its name. I imagine some Wild-West boxed-ears-brutal scenario that the locals now look back upon fondly as quaint Old-West justice. And even the radio is weird down there. On the way back from Texas, I came upon a broadcast of two Kansas high school baseball teams on the radio: the Redskins are playing the Red Demons?! Cue the song "Savages," from *Pocahontas*. The Wild West continues, and Custer lives! Jesus, neither team could call themselves the Dirty White Boys?

The Texas reminiscence has also been a round-about way of trying to say that I've recently taken up the latest rage among birders, county-list birding. Once you've birded so long that adding birds to your life list and even your state list becomes more and more prohibitive, seeing how many species you can see in a particular county is the next logical step in this general madness. So, on various recent road trips, I've been recording the various common-as-dirt species I see in every new county I drive through—at eighty mph. (Yeah, I may be missing a few species.) And sometimes, far from home, I get this sudden weird elegiac feeling, knowing that I will probably never see this particular dirt-road-rural county ever again: "I'll miss you, Deaf Smith County! Yes, to me, you'll always be just nine Great-tailed Grackles and a Eurasian Collared-Dove! Oh! The memories!"

Mom asks the nurses, "How much longer is this gonna take? . . . Let's just get it over with." Their answers are clouded in great medical mystification, and so Mom misunderstands and becomes exasperated: "Another whole day?!" Deep disappointment. She wants to go now.

After a few minutes of a scene from Kafka, it finally becomes clear—to Mom and the ten or twelve family members scattered around the hospital room—that things are moving along swimmingly, really, that we are just waiting on the priest, for some Episcopalian version of Extreme Unction, the last rites. Mom's medicated good spirits return, and she even has the peace of mind to joke, "Well, I made it to eighty, huh?" She even chuckles a little. Such an off-handed realistic statement to make, part of me thinks. Another part of me feels that I am participating in some theater of the absurd, or some Aldous-Huxleyan future in which we all go gently into that good night according to such a regimented formula.

The plot complications continue as, surrounded by family— some in their teens negotiating their way through their first public demonstration of grief—Mom has someone tear the wrapper off a grape popsicle, as her last meal of sorts. She slowly edges it into her mouth and finally says, "It's cold. It feels good." Waiting for Godot—I mean, the Episcopal priest—she even eats a second popsicle, which brother Terry unwraps and put in her hands: "See how good a boy he is? I got him trained well." Nervous laughter.

What pisses me off most, this day of her dying, is that Mom has "trained" me in such a way that I can't even attend to her death properly. Ironically, Mom was the one who instilled in me a near psychopathological obsession about not missing work—for fear of being deemed a "lazy Indian," of "living on Indian time." I even made two different day-long drives to Rapid, one for her death and one for the funeral, so that I'd miss as few of the classes I was teaching as possible. And yet she'd also continually told me and my brothers that we were no good. What kind of self-esteem does a boy acquire having to hear that every other day of his childhood? Better question: what kind of racist work environment, how abusive of a white racist husband, did Mom suffer to make her project the pain of her internalized racism upon her kids? Thank the Lord—no, I don't think so—that she also used Catholic guilt to keep me wanting to be a good boy, despite my bad-faith feelings as I did so. During one of my trips home for Christmas in my late forties, she said of her dog, "Midget's like you when you were a kid, Tommy. *I didn't have to punish you when you did something wrong—you punished yourself.*" Good times, Mom. Good times.

With her hair unruly, obviously unwashed and unbrushed for days, she looks like one of those old photos of untamed old Indians as she lies there, waiting to die. Or, better, she looks like Great-uncle Percy when he'd grown old and took on the look, deserved or not, of having suffered long for his race.

We're interrupted by two more medical people, who are there, strangely enough, to lead Mom through some physical therapy. More than strange: it's a truly painful moment for the rest of us in its sheer incongruity. But Mom is now Ms. Equanimity even here: "Don't bother," she tells them. "I'm leaving the country tomorrow." I would even like to detect an understated humor in this marvelous retort, but I'm not sure. Either way, I love the metaphor. Mom had rarely been a metaphorical person.

The morning before her funeral, I drove to some dirt roads southeast of town, to do a little birding. I thought, by way of tentative conclusion, that Rapid City had been a pretty cool place to spend a childhood, and to bird. Thanks, Mom. I waited to get among the meadowlarks and lark sparrows before I started blubbering. As one part of me bawled, another part of my schizoid psyche more calmly reasoned, with even a certain sense of self-righteous satisfaction, that there was no more appropriate place for my momentary breakdown than here among the birds of the western Plains.

There is a chalkboard in the room so that the nurses can keep each other informed regarding the room's current occupant. It now reads: "Discharge date estimated *[in a different handwriting]*: TBD." We all assume, even *hope*, it will be "determined" today.

Brother Terry arrives again with today's newspaper from home, so that Mom can do her last crossword puzzle, one of the daily pleasures of her last several decades. But there's a major snafu: she has forgotten her glasses at home, so she won't be doing any more crosswords in "this country."

The chalkboard also lists the doctor's name: "Dr. Labrie." Mom keeps telling the nurses, "I'm ready to go any time," and she repeats the same when Dr. Labrie shows up.

"Of course, Marie." Again, I find the matter-of-factness of the whole affair impossible to imagine. "We'll just put you to sleep." As if he were saying, "We'll just change your oil and rotate your tires, and you'll be good to go."

Once, in my twenties, I hurriedly bought Mom some plastic

flowers from Safeway for her birthday. She told me, "Tommy, don't you know those are flowers for gravestones?" No. I didn't.

Mom's seemingly newborn radiant self continues to blossom: she is incredibly magnanimous with the nurses, saying goodbye to each one, thanking each one for her help. Once again, I can't help thinking, this is the woman who trained her sons by making them feel guilty for being no good?

Maybe that's why she's always been a dog person, loving each one passionately as a safe surrogate object for the love she couldn't give to humans. Her mind wondering from point to scattered point, she starts talking about her current—her last—dog now. She'd talked to him right before they'd taken her to the hospital: "I said to him, 'You *know*, don't you, Duke?' He knew." More nervous laughter. But yes, we all knew that Duke knew that she knew that he knew.

Now one of the nurses is discussing with all of us the procedure of increasing the level of the opium drip—once the priest gets here and has done his Heavenly duty. "The most important thing right now," she tells us, "is that she goes peacefully." I'll just *bet* that's the most important thing: you, the medical attendants, the whole medical system, certainly most want that. And we, the family survivors, certainly most want that. My only objection, all along, has been, well—should Mom certainly most want that? But I quickly realize that I'm probably being selfish.

The greatest ordeal is the final long wait for the Episcopalian priest. Of course, Christianity *would* still be fucking with me. There is some confusion, even an argument about whether the priest has even been called: is he even aware that it is—*time?* We find out just before he arrives that Mom is only one of a whole handful of folks in need of Last Rites that the good fellow has had to administer to today. He is as infuriatingly matter-of-factly good-natured as the doctor when he walks in, and he breaks into his practiced "spontaneous" spiel immediately. Because of my own experiences from Catholic Indian boarding school on, I can only half-listen, full of anger, full of selfish sorrow for myself. I change the channel in my own ruined mind by trying to remember what godless philosopher I was teaching in my crit-theory course right now. Was it Derrida? Or Foucault? And how is this crazy superstitious death-bed scene still happening, in the freaking twenty-first century, on the peripheries, at least, of an "enlightened" society?

Then I wonder if it occurs to this Episcopalian priest that the reason he is looking down at an Indian woman for last rites is that his church was an early missionary competitor, with the Catholics, for Indian souls in the Dakotas. During my interview of Mom some years ago, I asked her why Grandma was Catholic and she was Episcopalian. Years before, Mom had simply told me she'd chosen the Episcopal Church because of the prestige of the local church. (In sum, it was a class thing: the hip kids went there.) During this interview, she clarified that, since Grandma Mollie was a Catholic and Grandpa Art was a Methodist, they let their kids pick their own religion. Mom and most of her sisters chose to be Episcopalian because, yes, it was the cool thing to be. But I'd still emphasize the crux of this transaction, that it was all about grabbing Indian "souls," one of the less obvious but more pernicious grabs of the winning of the West.

Vine Deloria has treated this subject most earnestly: since Christian missionaries in the Americas "came to preach and stayed to rule," land "acquisition and missionary work always went hand in hand in American history." And it hasn't been just the one Book, but a whole library of competing dogmas and denominations, as Deloria wittily points out:

> Churches began lobbying early in the 1860's [. . .] for franchises over the respective reservations. Thus one reservation would be assigned to the Roman Catholics, one to the Lutherans, one to the Methodists, and one to the Episcopalians. [. . .] It always bothered me that these churches who would not share pulpits and regarded each other as children of the devil, should have so cold-bloodedly divided up the tribes as if they were choosing sides for touch football.[99]

"In Dakota Territory" specifically, according to John Lauck, "reservations were allotted to the Episcopalians, the Catholics, and a joint Congregational-Presbyterian organization"; moreover, as non-Protestant papists and thoroughly associated with those damned late-immigrant Irish trash, the Catholics had to fight the hardest: "When Catholic bishop Marty visited the Pine Ridge and Rosebud reservations to conduct missionary work, 'Episcopalians working under Bishop William Hobart Hare would get federal officials to run him out, but he would return in secret'"! In sum, "Bishop Marty 'faced and participated in vigorous, sometimes vicious, interdenominational competition for souls in Sioux Country'"[100] One almost pities a denomination that was itself reviled by its competitors in good part out of ethnic bigotry; but the Catholics, too, were in earnest pursuit of the Indian "soul," and were of course some of the most eager participants in deicide and cultural genocide.

Finishing up the Last Rites—I *think*. I hadn't been giving him my undivided attention—the priest starts talking to Mom about Heaven and the afterlife. Here Mom stuns me again with another metaphor. She has no worries regarding the matter; in fact, "I'm going to go up like a bottle rocket." Lord. First of all, I'm amazed at the metaphor itself and wonder if she'd read it somewhere, or more likely, heard it on TV one Sunday. Secondly, I find it yet another incredibly incongruously irruptive event, this from a woman who had never expressed a heart-felt religious sentiment in her life. But at this moment there is a small, small part of me that envies her (however sudden) faith; another part of me, I guess, is half-relieved that she is dying in the comfort of this illusion, just as she is dying in the comfort of an opium drip. The best part of me—although this may be open to debate—shakes a clenched mental fist at the vacuity of an entire worldview.

Well over a decade before she died, Mom had arranged with the cemetery that her tombstone be adorned with that hackneyed graphic "The End of the Trail": the design is based on a statue by a long dead white guy, of course: an Indian with bowed head and spear, on a horse just as downcast. Sadly, Mom never realized that the image was part of a dominant ideology in which the dying Indian was really another cog in the machine of colonial imperialism and genocide and Christianization. Ah, *this* whole metaphor—for the Native cowered and conquered by Western theology?—is truer than she could have imagined.

The priest gone, the drip is increased, and it takes a good hour or so for Mom to die, her breathing becoming more and more shallow. There is a literal death rattle, as her lungs struggle for their last gasps, one last rise and fall. No need to mention which of her several sons and several grandchildren put their heads on her body, one by one, and cry. I am one of them, but I mostly remember the long minutes afterwards, watching the fitful rise and fall of the blanket on her belly, as the time between each final breath became greater, and greater, until . . . bottle rocket. Or not.

I returned to Lincoln with too much OCD to handle. Pictures from the past and angst over the future. And a big hole in the middle of the two. They'd told me to take whatever sentimental items I wanted. Fuck that, I said. But I did end up with a few hundred photos, her Chicago Bears coffee cup, her two small stuffed Eeyore toys, a set of four wall-hanging saucers with mostly unidentifiable paintings of British(?) birds made in China, and my own first book that I gave her when it was first published. The scribbled dedication to Mom is too . . . for words.

I am even more of a slave to petty details now since Mom died, as if completing one small item from my architectonic set of TO-DO lists were a respite from grief, a bulwark against mortality. And I guess it is. I'm sure it's why I became a list-maker in the first place: it's that wonderful false sense of order and control against the chaos of the real, the immutable. My first task was scanning all those photos. What this several-day scanning exercise—and my review of that interview of Mom, as emotional accompaniment—actually achieved was the realization that this semi-memoir should have been much more a tribute to my mother than some whiney-ass testament to Tom-as-victim, of Indian boarding school, et al. Her life was so much more a suffering and struggle and triumph; mine is more a more of a latter-day "philosophical" pissed-offèd-ness, at last. Some glitter and sputter here and there. But no bottle rockets.

So it is now with great shame that I remember being utterly ashamed as a child of being seen with my mom in public: "Wanna go to K-Mart with me?" "*Huh*-uh." But when my hard-drinking, ne'er-do-well Irish dad came to visit, I leapt at the pleasure of being part of the dominant culture again, and riding through town in his big car. Meanwhile, my mom eked out our existence on welfare and food stamps; got job training and then a job; and worked her ass off for us kids. And still we were ashamed. I even remember being relieved that Mom was a working-8-to-5 single mother who could never make the parent-teacher conferences. Whew: they'd have found out "we was Indian"!

When Mom told my youngest brother, Tracy—a first-grader—that he was Indian, he started crying from the shock. About twenty years later, when I tried to explain to daughter Em, "Your grandma is an Indian," she exclaimed, "NO!" and also began to cry. And so taking Emma as a small child—raised by her white mother—to see her dark-skinned grandma was pretty much an eggshell proposition:

> my five-year-old told me as we walked today,
> "you know, Daddy, Indians are only
> half-human"—and my heart fell
> to see the mind of my golden girl
> turned by a Disney, fucked-up world
> that's made the Native some great animal,
> or a totemic, gut-felt god—

and to think, my golden-hair, they used to
call your daddy "Ganjun" (as in "Injun"),
and your grandma who made you that blanket: they called
    "squaw"—
after they'd also laughed your great-great-
uncle Percy into his grave
of a gutter on 5th & Bourbon—

(And yet she WILL WEEP and KNOW WHY)

She's innocent—hates no one, but the blight
Eats at the edges of this damned, botched species—
"My daughter! (—oh, her grandma—) Oh, my daughter!"
Old Shylock rises, draws on Shakespeare's art,
And argues that an *Indian* has a heart. . . .
No need for words: this golden-hair runs down
The sidewalk so fast today—her arms surround
That grandma that she loves, whose skin is brown.

Then, several years later when Emma was a pre-teen, we were
tubing on the Guadalupe River near my brother's place in Texas:
a stranger floated by and said, "Hope you got suntan lotion on, or
you'll burn." I flippantly replied, "Ah, that's okay. I'm part Indian."
But my heart rejoiced when towheaded Emma yelled from a few
yards away, "I'm part Indian, too!"

Dream (April 17, 2017): I'm in a strange house. I feel a hand on
my shoulder—and then my mom's voice says, "It's me, Tommy."
I shiver.

✳ MAY 2018, LITTLE BIGHORN BATTLEFIELD:
Red-Tailed Hawk

> Some of our young Indians have bumper stickers on
> their cars—"Custer Died for Your Sins!"—but I'm tell-
> ing you Custer is alive! Not one but many Custers are at
> work at their trade, which is beating down on the Indi-
> ans. Custer's spirit is in all those tourist traps which des-
> ecrate these mountains.
>
> —John Lame Deer[101]

One major player in the history of Christo-Custer colonialism
was, of course, that fellow named George Armstrong Custer.
Maybe the worst thing he ever did was order the murder of
almost 800 horses just so that Black Kettle's Southern Cheyenne
people couldn't get them back. Immediately after their dawn raid
on Black Kettle's camp along the Washita River in 1864, Custer
and his men find themselves with a whole lot of horses—875
"captured ponies," to be exact. "What we were to do with them
was puzzling," since, "even if we could take them with us," the
tremendous herd "would have been too tempting a prize to the
[Native] warriors," and "to effect their recapture they would have
followed and waylaid us day and night [. . .] until we should have
arrived at a place of safety."[102]

His decision is coldly calculating: "We did not need the
ponies, while the Indians did." Custer's subsequent rationalizations for his eventual decision are long and tortuous, as if he were
semi-conscious of how reprehensible that decision would be. He
finally concludes, "I decided neither to attempt to take the ponies
with us nor to abandon them to the Indians, but to adopt the only
measure left—to kill them. To accomplish this seemingly[!]—like
most measures of war—cruel but necessary act, four companies

of cavalrymen were detailed [. . .] as a firing party." Almost ten pages later, after some of the horses were culled from the herd to "transport" the "prisoners,"

> The work of destruction began on the remainder and was continued until nearly eight hundred ponies were thus disposed of. All this time the Indians who had been fighting us from the outside covered the hills in the distance, deeply interested spectators of this to them strange proceeding. The loss of so many animals of value was a severe blow to the tribe, as nothing so completely impairs the war-making facilities for the Indians of the Plains as the deprivation or disabling of their ponies.[103]

What strikes me here is how Custer can only understand these horses and their loss in terms of their use-value in warfare; he is incapable of comprehending that the Native observers may well have been "deeply interested" in this mass murder for other—dare I use the word *humane* or even *kinship?*—reasons; in sum, that they likely deemed all this a very "strange proceeding" for reasons other than mere utility.

So is it totally fitting that Custer's racism towards the Natives he found on the Great Plains very much concerned their *animal* or bestial nature. Custer's attitude reflects a general colonialist ideology here: if "we" can see these human others as non-human, as a "lower" *animal*—why, then, our political agenda of stealing their land and making them one of us via boarding schools, etc., can be all the more justified. This is from the very first chapter of Custer's *My Life on the Plains*:

> Stripped of the beautiful romance with which we have

been so long willing to envelop him [. . .] the Indian for-
feits his claim to the appellation of the *noble* red man. We
see him as he is, and [. . .] as he ever has been, a *savage* in
every sense of the word [. . .] one whose cruel and fero-
cious nature far exceeds that of any wild beast of the desert.

According to N. Scott Momaday, if Custer never really saw the
true nature of the Great Plains, he also "could not see the people" who lived there, filled as he was with a racist-colonialist
ideology.[104]

For Natives, a holocaust of the mind continues today. In the
northern Plains, it is epitomized, as I've said, by Custer's very
name.

On my May 2011 visit to the Little Bighorn Battlefield, I came
upon a Red-tailed Hawk, gliding above those rolling grasslands
of bloody history. Instead of soaring farther and farther away, as
is usually the case, it flew towards me, then right to me, finally
hovering over my car for a good while, flapping and flapping as
if—(OH!—I tingled)—as if to say "we are still here!" And I didn't
know at the time whether the bird meant avian raptors, or human
Natives, or both. This uncertainty no doubt contributed to the
uncanny tingle. On my long drive home to Lincoln, I decided
that I had to return someday to the site—and to that sight.

In May 2018, the place seems even more full of tourists. I
have returned this second time for another Red-tailed Hawk—
I think—or for a similar avian message, for perhaps just a little
healing for my lifelong bitterness towards Holy Rosary Mission
and all it stood for, my lifelong bitterness towards my abusive
then absent Irish dad, towards—well, the whole works. Yes, I am

thinking, expecting, a heavy Joycean epiphany here. But there is no Red-tailed Hawk, no cool ornithic icon to serve as a synchronistic Rorschach test for my welling-up emotions. And as you may well guess by now, I am also so busy looking for FOYs—especially a Brewer's Sparrow, if you must know—that I may not be, one might say, entirely in the proper spirit, in Wordsworth's "blessed mood" of quietude. Worse yet, I also strike out on FOYs. In a way, then, the Red-tailed Hawk in the title of this section is really a lacuna, a lack. The bird never shows; the epiphany never happens. I do hear about twenty-five Western Meadowlarks, and I imagine these birds' ancestors singing the same song before the coming of Custer, or even the coming of the Lakota: through all this human racial politics bullshit, the Real goes on; the avian abides. On my drive out of the Memorial, I see a bunch of tourists sitting outside on fold-up chairs, listening to a Park employee's talk on the history of the site. I see that he is Native, and I smile a little inside. A Lark Sparrow forages in the grass nearby, unperturbed. Three Cedar Waxwings whistle their sibilance from the pines right next to the chairs.

> When [. . .] the songs of his new neighborhood differ from those of the father, the yearling [Bewick's Wren] always rejects his father's variant and sings the local songs. [. . .] Once he left home, he was eager to replace Dad's songs with songs that would match those of the males who would be his neighbors for the rest of his life.
>
> —Don Kroodsma[105]

For some reason, this passage pleases the hell out of me. I didn't learn many of my father's songs, either, though I did wake up first, or fell into the world, interpellated as an Irish boy, I guess, with both my dad's first and last names. Then I woke up again,

Thomas P. Gannon, Abilene, TX, 1955?

as I listened to my drunken Irish dad beat my French-Lakota mother down the outside stairs. I really woke up when I heard the police officer call her a "squaw" who had probably deserved it all. Yes, I woke up then—if only intermittently, for a bit. In one real sense, I remain the hybrid walking wound of my Irish "cowboy" Dad beating my Indian mom. Yes, he was inevitably dressed in Western regalia, complete with cowboy hat, and cowboy boots, and one of those usually plaid Western shirts that had fake-pearl snaps instead of buttons. One of my earliest memories was one late summer night at Grandma's house, listening from my bed to

Dad and Uncle Billy—Mom's brother—beat the hell out of each other in Grandma's backyard, both obviously just home from the bar, as a crowd of mostly Mom's relatives egged Billy on. I never found out why they were fighting, but did it really even matter? It was Cowboys and Indians all over again, the Lone Ranger and Tonto fist-fighting in Fort Pierre, South Dakota.

In his defense, Dad was a product of the American mid-twentieth century, marrying my mom in the oh-so-special 1950s, that decade of American gloss and chrome and a contrasting very dark underside, despite the conservatives who would idealize the decade as a monocultural American Eden. For there always already lurked the specter of race: in a set of photos of me in a Lemmon, South Dakota hospital, I was a one-year-old close to dying of bronchitis. My dad's parents wouldn't even bother driving a mixed-blood baby to the hospital, until Mom started walking me there—thirty miles. Obviously, my Irish grandparents were none too happy with the two other creatures my dad had "done drug home."

I've neglected to mention that Dad ultimately sobered up and came back to live with my mom for about the last twenty years of his life. But I remained suspiciously distant, and he remained a card-carrying latter-day cowboy, a semi-truck-driving sonofa-gun, who loved his old-time religion as much as he used to love his Old Granddad, who still assumed that Indians were shit, who thought that making the almighty buck was more important than anything else.

At Dad's burial at the Pine Lawn Cemetery, I was told that just two Marines were there to fold the flag—not the seven needed for a twenty-one-gun salute—because so many had been called away to the Iraqi conflict. And in fact, it was the 7th Cavalry, Custer's old unit, that was leading the attack into Baghdad. This is an historical fact, not a metaphor. Some things never change.

I am still and always constantly bemused by my day-to-day personal and professional encounters in which I am told that "Indians should just get over it," as if all this Hotchkiss-Gatling-gunfire-and-brimstone is over-and-done-with history, Bad River water under the bridge. Then why is there still a 7th Cavalry Cafe, and a dominant whitestream attitude reflected in the fact that plenty of people apparently still want to eat there? And again, what kind of cognitive dissonance is occasioned by the fact that I teach at a university whose official tagline is still "Pioneering New Frontiers"? For my various students who interminably repeat the same "get over it" to me, and who offer the common justification that *they* didn't do it and don't blame *them* for what great-great-grandpa did—I feel it incumbent almost every semester to post on my course web page a parable that I wrote a few years ago:

> My dad raped a woman. And when he was done, he took this great diamond from her dresser drawer, a diamond beautiful beyond imagination. When my dad died, I used that diamond to make my fortune on Main Street, and on Wall Street. But later, the sons and daughters of that raped woman came to me and said that they wanted the diamond back. "Go to hell," I said. "*I'm* not the one who raped your mother or stole your diamond. Take your claims elsewhere!" Proclaiming all this with a mighty harrumph of triumph, I walked happily away to enjoy all the more my profits and my privilege.

I can't really blame Dad for being pretty much a victim of this attitude and ideology. But I can wish that he had been more consciously aware that he'd grown up white on a fairly middle-class SoDak cattle ranch and that this was not entirely *un*related, power-wise, to the fact that my Indian mom grew up in poverty on (or near) the Cheyenne River Rez. I can only wish that, before he died, he had been struck by some *deus ex machina* bolt of lightning—or the surprise appearance of a Red-tailed Hawk—and that he suddenly saw the mad presumption of his ways, and said just once to Mom, "Marie. I'm sorry." And I wish that just once, my father's people would truly apologize for what they did to my mother's people. *Hečetu lo.*

❊ CODA: *Birding While Indian*

A long-running joke among Native Americans in South Dakota is that the criminal charge of DWI—Driving While Intoxicated—actually means "Driving While Indian." There are variants: "Driving With Indians," "Drinking With Indians," and the like, depending upon the speaker and audience. But the general meaning of the Indian reinscription, whether uttered by Native or white, is that South Dakota has been—hell, it *is*—a pretty racist place for its original inhabitants.

As a part-Lakota who has also been a lifelong birder—who has been "*birding* while Indian"—I can safely assert that the birding world, too, is a "pretty racist place." No, it's not through some conscious official dictate by some plutocratic ornithological cabal of little old white women in tennis shoes, with a home office in Central Park. Rather, it's another (however subtle) example of institutional racism: that is, given the very structure of American society, itself determined by and large by an ongoing history of racism, Native Americans are much less likely to become birders. And while a rather inchoate group of hobbyists—let's call them Birder Nation—may not wield the same disciplinary power as a school system or a workplace, the subtle forces of white privilege are at work all the same, both in the vast literature about birds and birding and through such organizations as the American Birding Association.

The ABA is now aware of this problem. A recent ABA blog bears the title "Moving Forward: Increasing Racial Diversity in Birding" and voices birding officialdom's interest in "expanding the appeal of birding to a non-white audience." A comparable *National Geographic* article is boldly titled "Colorful World of Birding Has Conspicuous Lack of People of Color: More Diversity among Bird-Watchers Is in Everyone's Best Interest." Understandably, it focuses on the problems of being an African American birder and begins, "If you're a black bird-watcher, 'be prepared to be confused with the other black birder'"! Such black humor (pun intended) scenarios have already been brilliantly treated in YouTube videos: we can sadly easily imagine "how onlookers might react to seeing a black or Hispanic man with binoculars wandering the woods—or a suburban neighborhood—at dusk, dawn, or night."[106] My own excursions have sometimes been almost as uncomfortable, as a long-haired fellow of uncertain ethnicity. On a birding trip to the US South a few years back, I discovered that such a person driving slowly through Arkansas graveyards, binoculars in hand, received enough evil glances from the locals that I quickly stopped the practice.

As for the bare statistics, a 2011 federal survey found that only 5 percent of American birders "were Hispanic [. . .] 4 percent were black, 1 percent were Asian American, and 2 percent were 'other.'" It's very hard to express what it feels like to be that *other*. I do like the ultimate reason for this call for greater human diversity or social justice. It's for greater *bio*-diversity and for greater *environmental* justice at last: "Developing more diversity among birders will broaden support for measures needed to protect birds."[107] Birders—minority or not—are (or should be) more conscious than most people that, in the grand order of things, it's finally *not* all about human intramural politics.

Of course—as always in the US—this structural racism is inextricably tied to socioeconomic inequities; moreover, among US ethnic groups, Native Americans are the poorest of all. If classism and racism are the two great *bêtes noires* of US history, they are also harder than hell to tell apart; sometimes I suspect that they're pretty much one creature. So, if you're one of those people who adamantly believes that racism is over, that we live in an Edenic post-racial society, you can simply read this whole section as about birding while *poor*. But you would only be half-right.

The classism of birding is more manifest. Growing up on welfare and food stamps, I eventually managed to acquire a $5 bird guide and a $20 pair of K-Mart binoculars—which I got for Christmas but which I don't think were *ever* in alignment; and as a grade-schooler, I walked miles and miles, freezing or sweating, to a few select birding venues on the outskirts of my hometown of Rapid City, South Dakota. And I enjoyed every minute of it. But I was really missing out on many of what are now considered the *de rigeur* pleasures and privileges of being a birder. It took me many years into adulthood to realize that 1) you have to spend a good several hundred dollars on a pair of binoculars that are functionally worth a damn; and 2) you can't identify all those tiny distant look-alike shorebirds without a spotting scope, a decent one of which will run at least $1,500; and 3) you can't really bird with any genuine freedom without a reliable car and a wallet with enough money to buy tank of gas after tank of gas. I really didn't have all of these privileges until well into my fifties. To be able to jump on a plane and visit some tropical island for a few lifers now seems to be another assumed privilege of the birder. I'm still waiting to afford this one.

As for the average Native on a reservation, of course, such requirements are inexorably prohibitive. I feel guilty about this all the time, as I blithely wake up and drive off towards some fairly distant birding destination whenever I have a free morning: how many inner-city minority or rural reservation kids and adults have even the leisure to look at birds? At last, birding is ultimately very centered in class, and white, privilege.

Birding while Indian, on the Great Plains in particular, can be difficult because of language itself. The dominant discourse is replete with the dark shadow of colonialism and genocide. An ongoing colonialist ideology still permeates the Great Plains region, in terms of both place names and good ol' boy attitudes, be they conscious or unconscious. Birding the back roads around Lincoln, Nebraska, I am always struck at how inordinately symptomatic the names of the lakes and State Recreational Areas are: names like Stagecoach, and Wagon Train, and Conestoga. (As I drag my binoculars out of the car upon my arrival at one of these venues, I half-expect Hoss Cartwright or Rowdy Yates to show up on a fast horse and ask me, "Boy. *[Dramatic pause.]* You from 'round these parts?") And so, in just my own county, you can relive the glory and excitement of Manifest Destiny by hitching your stars to a stagecoach, or a Conestoga wagon, or an entire wagon train; you can also brave the savage dangers of—*play Native tom-tom in the background*—Pawnee Lake. And on the edge of Lincoln is Pioneers Park, if you haven't had enough cowboying up.

Yes, there are also the apparent acknowledgements to a Native American legacy nearby, evidenced by the names of Ponca State Park and Indian Cave State Park. But at last, such place names are really guilty elegies, insincere half-tributes to a supposed race long gone. Just a short drive south of Indian Cave is the Squaw Creek National Wildlife Refuge, just across the Missouri border. Oh, wait, they *just* recently changed the name of that area to the less colorful Loess Bluffs NWR. It was the least they could do.

> My bird is a genuine little savage, doubtless, but I value him as a neighbor. [. . .] [Nature] is an Indian maiden, dark, subtle, dreaming, with glances now and then that thrill the wild blood in one's veins.
>
> —John Burroughs[108]

Burroughs's conflation of bird and human Native—both metonyms for a more general "wild" American "Nature"—is a ubiquitous trope in Euro-American literature. And so again, the "birding Indian" always already inhabits a very liminal place, a double stance of both imperial Self and specular Other. Certainly, many American tribal peoples were very skilled in observing their environment, in closely studying the behaviors of other species, including—and maybe especially—avian life. And yet, "for all their skill as observers, the Indians do not qualify, in modern terms, as birders."[109] Why? It's ultimately a matter of *worldview*, of ideology. Birding per se has been historically embedded in a Western way of seeing and knowing the bird from its outset. Anglo-American popular interest in ornithology began circa 1800, fostered both by a newfound infatuation with natural sci-

ence in general and by the special social and symbolic status that
birds had acquired through the centuries. Soon "ornithology
became the most popular scientific discipline," supplemented by
a good many "handbooks and periodicals" for its new tag-along
hobbyist public.[110]

Meanwhile, this same ever-curious Western "I" or "eye" had
already well established itself in the New World, looking around
and seeing mere/empty landscape, or seeing Native Americans as
little-more-than-non-human-animals ready to be colonized, to
be penned up on reservations (à la wildlife reserves). It also saw
other indigenous animals as fit fodder for the same taxonomical
classification it had applied/would apply to other, human races.
The West's natural-history taxonomical system initiated by Linnaeus must indeed be seen as the regime of knowledge behind
the power of the actual ships and gunpowder of New World colonization—and an enterprise to be continued in the gun-and-
easel collecting and categorizing of nineteenth-century American
ornithologists like Alexander Wilson and Audubon. This colonizing, taxonomical "I" finds ample ground for its vision even in
such supposedly objective and scientific texts as Peterson's *A Field
Guide to the Birds.*

One doesn't have to have been birding while Indian to come
to the conclusion above, that the glorious pastime of birding is
itself necessarily complicit with Western ideology. My problem is magnified, however, in also realizing that the notion of
"Indian birder" is fraught with an inevitable cultural hybridity.
All protests aside, I am still a lover and slave to birding in its
full Western sense, and especially to the list-making and ordering
that the hobby entails. And it is not ironic at all, at last, that my
own academic writing refers as often to Baudrillard as it does to
Black Elk.

But on the other hand, birding while Indian remains a peculiarly enlightening—or disillusioning—lens through which to view my lifelong hobby. There is, for instance, that annual pain of being an Other every December when the local birding groups tout their Christmas bird counts—as if believing in a particular Old World desert-sand-tribe deity had some essential connection with identifying those invasive finches from Canada that show up at the winter feeders. "That's not what the name means at all!," they will object; but these people are working within an ideological frame in which Christmas is a natural—though it's really a cultural—given. Then there is also the weird feeling I get when coming upon No Trespassing signs and wondering about the whole enterprise of (mostly white) privately owned land, of fences, and borders, and even of the Dawes Allotment Act of 1887, which was ultimately aimed at assimilating Natives into bowing before the ideological might of fences, and of borders, and of No Trespassing signs.

One might even wonder why a part-Indian would ever *want* to be a birder. Birding *is,* as I have argued, yet another Western colonial act of *epistemological* violence, however seemingly benign. This makes it hard to be on the side of objectifying humans who want to chase birds down and—*count* them. And then there's the whole whitestream discourse, as we've seen, that has historically conflated avians and Indians as two wings of the same wild and savage bird, a discourse that played no small role in the fact that several American bird species and many human Native tribes have met the same fate at the hands of Euro-American colonialism—extinction—and that the remaining Native tribes, like the bison, have just barely avoided a similar end.

But then I wake up to a clock that says 5:30 a.m., and I am on my way out the door. I still want so much to "qualify, in modern terms," as a birder.

I dreamed recently that I was working on this book, but it was a different book, which I thought I'd begin as follows: Imagine *Tatanka Iotanka* (Sitting Bull) sitting next to you in a car parked along Mount Rushmore Road in Rapid City, South Dakota. If he recognizes his likeness on any of the billboards for the tourist traps scattered among his sacred Black Hills, he shows no indication. His attention is focused on the big sign announcing Shakey's Pizza only a few yards away, and he admits to himself that he is a bit hungry. Back in the day, he had been at Custer's Last Stand at the Little Bighorn. He had been murdered two weeks before the slaughter of his Lakota brothers and sisters at Wounded Knee. He had been warned of his death by a Western Meadowlark who sang his death song in a vision. His world had been a world of talking birds, of sacred cottonwoods, and of eager streams illumined by the high prairie sun. Now he turns slightly and looks you in the eye for a good while, as if to ask—was it worth it all, for this? Was it worth it, for so many choices of toppings on a Shakey's goddamned pizza?

✳ NOTES

Notes to Preface

1. Wordsworth, *The Prelude*, 213.
2. Silko, *Politics and Poetics*.

Notes to Essays

1. *Half of Anything*, Hogan, "The Two Lives," 237; Crow Dog and Erdoes, *Lakota Woman*, 5.
2. Silko, *Yellow Woman*, 179.
3. DeMallie, "John G. Neihardt," 265; Vizenor, *Manifest Manners*, 50.
4. Neihardt, *Black Elk Speaks*, 329fn3, 166.
5. Foucault, *Discipline and Punish*, 141.
6. Vizenor, *Bearheart*, 106.
7. Deloria, *Custer Died for Your Sins*, 105.
8. Levchuk, "Leaving Home for Carlisle Indian School," 185.
9. Foucault, *Discipline and Punish*, 166.
10. Crow Dog and Erdoes, *Lakota Woman*, 32.
11. Cook-Lynn, "New Indians, Old Wars," 196–98.
12. McNickle, *The Surrounded*, 102–03, 192 (emphases mine).
13. Lauck, *Prairie Republic*, 81, 62, 82.
14. Quoted in Collins, *Complete Field Guide*, 137.
15. Derrida, *The Animal That Therefore I Am*, 37.
16. Wordsworth and Coleridge, *Lyrical Ballads*, 41, 42 (emphases mine).
17. Stevens, *The Collected Poems*, 154, 93.
18. Sanders, "Speaking a Word for Nature," 188.
19. Rice, "How the Bird that Speaks Lakota Earned a Name," 425; Lincoln, *Sing with the Heart of a Bear*, 35, 404; Vestal, *Sitting Bull*, 278.
20. Rice, 439; Standing Bear, *My People the Sioux*, 39.
21. March, *A Reader's Companion*, 420.

22. Cather, *The Song of the Lark*, 433, 168, 187, 186–87.

23. Cather, *My Ántonia*, 7–8 (emphases mine).

24. Fire and Erdoes, *Lame Deer*, 9–10.

25. Johnsgard, *Crane Music*, 38.

26. Johnsgard, *Earth, Water, and Sky*, 111–12.

27. Welch, *The Death of Jim Loney*, 116.

28. Crow Dog and Erdoes, *Lakota Woman*, 22; Power, *Roofwalker*, 43.

29. "Gannon honored as Indian employee for month."

30. Welch, *The Death of Jim Loney*, 20, 116, 163, 167, 122.

31. Welch, 122.

32. Collins, *Complete Field Guide*, 220.

33. Hogan, *Dwellings*, 27.

34. Shepard, *The Others*, 59, 60, 61.

35. Hogan, *Dwellings*, 71, 65.

36. Derrida, *The Animal That Therefore I Am*, 64.

37. Johnsgard, *Earth, Water, and Sky*, 64.

38. Samsel, "Bird Poems."

39. Wordsworth, *Poetical Works*, 2.142–43; 199.

40. Wordsworth and Coleridge, *Lyrical Ballads*, 41.

41. Stap, *Birdsong* 30, 80; quoted in Stap, 81.

42. Pearson et al., eds., *Birds of America*, 2.28; quoted in Herkert, Vickery, and Kroodsma, "Henslow's Sparrow."

43. Gibbons and Strom, *Neighbors to the Birds*, 214; Burroughs, *The Birds of John Burroughs*, 44–45.

44. Standing Bear, *Land of the Spotted Eagle* 38, 165.

45. Ehrlich, Dobkin, and Wheye, *The Birder's Handbook*, 632, 646.

46. Neihardt, *Black Elk Speaks*, 18–19.

47. Gibbons and Strom, *Neighbors to the Birds*, 216; Ehrlich, Dobkin, and Wheye, *The Birder's Handbook*, 633; Farrar, *Birding Nebraska*, 86; Pearson, et al., *Birds of America*, 2.238, 2.236, 3.18.

48. Stap, *Birdsong*, 142.

49. Stevens, *The Collected Poems*, 93.

50. Neihardt, *Black Elk Speaks*, 104.

51. Wordsworth, *Poetical Works*, 2.236.

52. Fire and Erdoes, *Lame Deer*, 5.

53. Krech, *The Ecological Indian*, 149, 147.

54. Shepard, *The Others*, 328, 198.

55. Quoted in Lincoln, *Sing with the Heart of a Bear*, 104.

56. Welch, *The Death of Jim Loney*, 20–21, 104–05, 179; Stevens, *The Collected Poems*, 70.

57. Deloria, *For This Land*, 257.

58. Fire and Erdoes, *Lame Deer*, 136, 166–67.

59. Nash, "Indian Reservations in Texas & Tours."

60. Lee, *To Kill a Mockingbird*, 90.

61. Latour, *Pandora's Hope*, 172.

62. Blake, "Auguries of Innocence," 481.

63. Rowland, *Birds with Human Souls*, 64, 63.

64. Fire and Erdoes, *Lame Deer*, 85.

65. Fire and Erdoes, 84.

66. Fire and Erdoes, 86.

67. Neihardt, *Black Elk Speaks*, 316fn1.

68. Fire and Erdoes, *Lame Deer*, 82.

69. Latour, *Pandora's Hope*, 280.

70. Quoted in Melmer, "Crazy Horse Wins—Again."

71. *Devils Tower/Northeast Wyoming.*

72. Lauck, *Prairie Republic*, 59.

73. Deloria, *For This Land*, 207.

74. Janiskee, "National Park History."

75. Fire and Erdoes, *Lame Deer*, n.p.

76. Farrar, *Birding Nebraska*, 64.

77. Farrar, 60.

78. Custer, *My Life on the Plains*, 15–16, 3.

79. Johnsgard, "Birds of the Prairie."

80. Sharp, Silcock, and Jorgensen, *Birds of Nebraska*, 291.

81. Walker, *Lakota Belief and Ritual*, 242.

82. "August 25, 1804." All subsequent quotations from Clark's journal are from the same day.

83. Burroughs, *The Natural History*, 256.

84. Mussulman, "William Clark (1770–1838)."

85. Hogan, *Dwellings*, 98.

86. National Park Service, *Spirit Mound.*

87. Hogan, *The Book of Medicines*, 77–78.

88. Hogan, *Dwellings*, 85–86.

89. Day, *The Sky Clears*, 7, 19, 147.

90. Abbey, *Desert Solitaire*, 184.

91. Farrar, *Birding Nebraska*, 144.

92. Kastner, *A World of Watchers*, 7.

93. South Dakota Game, Fish & Parks, *Tatanka*, 2.

94. South Dakota Game, Fish & Parks, 11; Neihardt, *Black Elk Speaks*, 49, 308fn5.

95. LaDuke, *The Winona LaDuke Reader*, 145.

96. Abbey, *Desert Solitaire*, 158.

97. Fire and Erdoes, *Lame Deer*, n.p.

98. Derrida, *The Animal That Therefore I Am*, 107.

99. Deloria, *Custer Died for Your Sins*, 105–06, 109–10.

100. Lauck, *Prairie Republic*, 79–80.

101. Fire and Erdoes, *Lame Deer*, 86.

102. Custer, *My Life on the Plains*, 350–51.

103. Custer, 355–57, 365–66.

104. Custer, 21–22; Momaday, *The Man Made of Words*, 106.

105. Quoted in Stap, *Birdsong*, 53–54.

106. Retter, "Moving Forward"; Hamilton, "Colorful World of Birding."

107. Hamilton, "Colorful World of Birding."

108. Burroughs, *The Birds of John Burroughs*, 49, 134.

109. Kastner, *A World of Watchers*, 7.

110. Gaull, *English Romanticism*, 369.

✳ WORKS CITED

Abbey, Edward. *Desert Solitaire: A Season in the Wilderness*. Simon, 1968.

"An Abused Family." 1915. *Birds of Nebraska*, edited by James E. Ducey and the U of Nebraska–Lincoln Libraries, 2004, http://birds-of-nebraska.unl.edu/view?docId=DJ.00003.xml;query=;brand=default.

Alexie, Sherman. "Avian Nights." *New Letters*, vol. 69, no. 4 (2003), pp. 21–23.

"August 25, 1804." *Journals of the Lewis and Clark Expedition*. Center for Digital Research in the Humanities and the U of Nebraska P, https://lewisandclarkjournals.unl.edu/item/lc.jrn.1804-08-04#lc.jrn.1804-08-04.03.

"Aunt Bea's Medicine Man." *The Andy Griffith Show*, season 3, episode 34, Mayberry Enterprises, 11 March 1963.

Benét, Rosemary, and Stephen Vincent Benét. "John James Audubon." *A Book of Americans*. Farrar and Rinehart, 1933, p. 63.

Blake, William. "Auguries of Innocence." *The Poetry and Prose of William Blake*, edited by David V. Erdman, Doubleday, 1965, pp. 481–84.

Burroughs, John. *The Birds of John Burroughs: Keeping a Sharp Lookout*. Edited by Jack Kligerman, Hawthorn, 1976.

Burroughs, Raymond Darwin, editor. *The Natural History of the Lewis and Clark Expedition*. Michigan State UP, 1961.

Cather, Willa. *My Ántonia*. 1918. Houghton Mifflin, 1995.

———. *The Song of the Lark*. 1915. Edited by Sherrill Harbison, Penguin, 1999.

Collins, Henry Hill, Jr. *Complete Field Guide to American Wildlife: East, Central and North*. Harper, 1959.

Cook-Lynn, Elizabeth. "New Indians, Old Wars." *Native American Voices: A Reader*, edited by Susan Lobo, Steve Talbot, and Traci L. Morris, 3rd ed., Prentice Hall, 2010, pp. 194–99.

The Cornell Laboratory of Ornithology. "Why Do Some Birds Mimic the Sounds of Other Species?" *All About Birds*, 1 April 2009, https://www.allaboutbirds.org/news/why-do-some-birds-mimic-the-sounds-of-other-species/.

Crow Dog, Mary, and Richard Erdoes. *Lakota Woman*. HarperPerennial, 1991.

Custer, George A. *My Life on the Plains.* 1874. U of Nebraska P, 1966.

Day, A. Grove, editor. *The Sky Clears: Poetry of the American Indians.* 1951. U of Nebraska P, 1964.

Deloria, Vine, Jr. *Custer Died for Your Sins: An Indian Manifesto.* Avon, 1969.

———. *For This Land: Writings on Religion in America.* Edited by James Treat, Routledge, 1999.

DeMallie, Raymond J. "John G. Neihardt and Nicholas Black Elk." Neihardt, pp. 242–66.

Derrida, Jacques. *The Animal That Therefore I Am.* Edited by Marie-Louise Mallet, translated by David Wills, Fordham UP, 2008.

Devils Tower/Northeast Wyoming. Revised ed., Devils Tower Tourism Association/Crook County Promotion Board, 2009.

Ehrlich, Paul R., et al. *The Birder's Handbook: A Field Guide to the Natural History of North American Birds.* Simon, 1988.

Farrar, Jon. *Birding Nebraska. NEBRASKAland Magazine,* vol. 82, no. 1 (Jan.–Feb. 2004), Nebraska Game and Parks Commission.

Fire, John (Lame Deer), and Richard Erdoes. *Lame Deer: Seeker of Visions.* Washington Square Press, 1972.

Foucault, Michel. *Discipline and Punish: The Birth of the Prison.* Vintage Books, 1977.

Gannon, Genevieve Marie. Personal interview. 7–8 Feb. 2011.

"Gannon honored as Indian employee for month." City of Rapid City news release. 18 Sept. 1985.

Gaull, Marilyn. *English Romanticism: The Human Context.* Norton, 1988.

Gibbons, Felton, and Deborah Strom. *Neighbors to the Birds: A History of Birdwatching in America.* W. W. Norton, 1988.

Half of Anything. Directed by Jonathan S. Tomhave, Native Voices, 2006.

Hamilton, Martha H. "Colorful World of Birding Has Conspicuous Lack of People of Color: More Diversity among Bird-Watchers Is in Everyone's Best Interest." *National Geographic,* 23 Sept. 2014, https://www.nationalgeographic.com/travel/article/140923-bird-watching-diversity-environment-science.

Herkert, J. R., et al. "Henslow's Sparrow (Centronyx henslowii)." *The Birds of North America,* edited by A. F. Poole and F. B. Gill, version 1.0, Cornell Lab of Ornithology, 2020, https://doi.org/10.2173/bow.henspa.01.

Hogan, Linda. *The Book of Medicines.* Coffee House, 1993.

———. *Dwellings: A Spiritual History of the Living World.* Simon & Schuster, 1995.

———. "The Two Lives." *I Tell You Now: Autobiographical Essays by Native Writers,* edited by Brian Swann and Arnold Krupat, U of Nebraska P, 1987, pp. 231–49.

Izaguire, Frank. "Introducing: The Lifelook." *ABA Blog,* American Birding Association, 13 Feb. 2014, https://blog.aba.org/2014/02/introducing-the-lifelook.html.

Janiskee, Bob. "National Park History: Renaming National Parks Can Show Respect for Native Cultures." *National Parks Traveler,* 3 July 2008, https://www.nationalparkstraveler.org/2008/06/national-park-history-renaming-national-parks-can-show-respect-native-cultures.

Johnsgard, Paul A. "Birds of the Prairie." 22 April 2003, U of South Dakota, Vermillion, SD. Lecture.

———. *Crane Music: A Natural History of American Cranes.* Smithsonian Institution Press, 1991.

———. *Earth, Water, and Sky: A Naturalist's Stories and Sketches.* U of Texas P, 1999.

Kastner, Joseph. *A World of Watchers.* Knopf, 1986.

Kenny, Maurice. "Reading Poems in Public." *On Second Thought: A Compilation,* U of Oklahoma P, 1995, pp. 130–31.

Krech, Shepard, III. *The Ecological Indian: Myth and History.* Norton, 1999.

LaDuke, Winona. *The Winona LaDuke Reader: A Collection of Essential Writings.* Voyageur Press, 2002.

Latour, Bruno. *Pandora's Hope: Essays on the Reality of Science Studies.* Harvard UP, 1999.

Lauck, John K. *Prairie Republic: The Political Culture of Dakota Territory, 1879–1889.* University of Oklahoma Press, 2010.

Lee, Harper. *To Kill a Mockingbird.* 1960. Warner Books, 1982.

Levchuk, Berenice. "Leaving Home for Carlisle Indian School." *Reinventing the Enemy's Language,* edited by Joy Harjo and Gloria Bird, Norton, 1997, pp. 177–86.

Lincoln, Kenneth. *Sing with the Heart of a Bear: Fusions of Native and American Poetry, 1890–1999.* U of California P, 2000.

The Lone Ranger. Directed by Gore Verbinski, performance by Johnny Depp, Disney, 2013.

March, John. *A Reader's Companion to the Fiction of Willa Cather.* Edited by Marilyn Arnold and Debra Lynn Thornton, Greenwood Press, 1993.

McNickle, D'Arcy. *The Surrounded.* 1936. Fire Keepers, 1998.

Melmer, David. "Crazy Horse Wins—Again." *Indian Country Today,* 12 Sept. 2018, https://indiancountrytoday.com/archive/crazy-horse-wins-again.

Midge, Tiffany. "Mt. Rushmore & the Arm of Crazy Horse." *Outlaws, Renegades and Saints: Diary of a Mixed-Up Halfbreed,* Greenfield Review Press, 1996, p. 18.

Momaday, N. Scott. *The Man Made of Words: Essays, Stories, Passages.* St. Martin's, 1997.

Mussulman, Joseph A. "William Clark (1770–1838)." *Discovering Lewis & Clark,* https://lewis-clark.org/members/william-clark/clarks-biography/.

Nash, John Cagney. "Indian Reservations in Texas & Tours." *USA Today: Travel Tips,* 17 Nov. 2017, https://traveltips.usatoday.com/indian-reservations-texas-tours-60348.html.

National Park Service. *Little Bighorn Battlefield.* US Department of the Interior, 2007.

National Park Service. *Spirit Mound.* US Department of the Interior, 20 April 2020, https://www.nps.gov/mnrr/learn/historyculture/spiritmound.htm.

Neihardt, John G. *Black Elk Speaks.* 1932. Bison Books, 2014.

Pearson, T. Gilbert, et al., editors. *Birds of America.* 1917. Illustrated by Louis Agassiz Fuertes, Doubleday, 1936.

Peter Pan. 1953. Platinum ed. Walt Disney, 2007. DVD.

Peterson, Roger Tory. *A Field Guide to the Birds: Giving Field Marks of All Species Found in Eastern North America.* Illustrated by Roger Tory Peterson, Houghton Mifflin, 1934.

Power, Susan. *Roofwalker.* Milkweed, 2002.

Red Cloud Indian School. "History." https://www.redcloudschool.org/page.aspx?pid=429.

Retter, Michael. "Moving Forward: Increasing Racial Diversity in Birding." *ABA Blog.* American Birding Association, 13 Aug. 2015, https://blog.aba.org/2015/08/moving-forward-increasing-racial-diversity-in-birding.html.

Rice, Julian. "How the Bird That Speaks Lakota Earned a Name." *Recovering the Word: Essays on Native American Literature,* edited by Brian Swann and Arnold Krupat, U of California P, 1987, pp. 422–45.

Rowland, Beryl. *Birds with Human Souls: A Guide to Bird Symbolism.* Knoxville: U of Tennessee P, 1978.

Samsel, L. A. "Bird Poems." Received by Thomas C. Gannon, 7 March 2010.

Sanders, Scott Russell. "Speaking a Word for Nature." *The Ecocriticism Reader: Landmarks in Literary Ecology,* edited by Cheryll Glotfelty and Harold Fromm, U of Georgia P, 1996, pp. 82–195.

The Savage Nation. Hosted by Michael Savage, Talk Radio Network, KFAB, Omaha, 29 Aug. 2007.

Sharpe, Roger S., et al. *Birds of Nebraska: Their Distribution and Temporal Occurrence.* U of Nebraska P, 2001.

Shepard, Paul. *The Others: How Animals Made Us Human.* Island, 1996.

Silko, Leslie Marmon. "Poetics and Politics: A Series of Readings by Native American Writers." Tucson, 6 April 1992. Seminar transcript.

———. *Yellow Woman and a Beauty of the Spirit.* Simon, 1996.

Snyder, Gary. "It Pleases." *Turtle Island,* New Directions, 1974, p. 44.

South Dakota Game, Fish & Parks. *Tatanka: The 2011 Guide to Custer State Park.* State of South Dakota, 2011.

Standing Bear, Luther. *Land of the Spotted Eagle.* 1933. U of Nebraska P, 1978.

———. *My People the Sioux.* 1928. Edited by E. A. Brininstool, U of Nebraska P, 1975.

Stap, Don. *Birdsong.* Scribner, 2005.

Stevens, Wallace. *The Collected Poems.* 1954. Vintage, 1990.

Vestal, Stanley. *Sitting Bull: Champion of the Sioux.* 1932. U of Oklahoma P, 1989.

Vizenor, Gerald. *Bearheart: The Heirship Chronicles.* U of Minnesota P, 1990.

———. *Manifest Manners: Narratives on Postmodern Survivance.* U of Nebraska P, 1999.

Walker, James R. *Lakota Belief and Ritual.* Edited by Raymond J. DeMallie and Elaine A. Jahner, U of Nebraska P, 1991.

Welch, James. *The Death of Jim Loney.* Harper, 1979.

Whitman, Walt. "The Dalliance of the Eagles." 1880. *Poetry and Prose,* Library of America, 1996, p. 412.

Wordsworth, William. *Poetical Works.* Edited by Ernest de Selincourt and Helen Darbishire, Clarendon, 1940–1954. 5 vols.

———. *The Prelude or Growth of a Poet's Mind (Text of 1805).* Edited by Ernest de Selincourt, rev. ed. by Stephen Gill, Oxford UP, 1970.

Wordsworth, William, and Samuel Taylor Coleridge. *Lyrical Ballads.* 1800. Edited by R. L. Brett and A. R. Jones, 2nd ed., Routledge, 1991.

XIT. "Reservation of Education." *Silent Warrior,* Sound of America Records, 1973.

MACHETE
Joy Castro, Series Editor

This series showcases fresh stories, innovative forms, and books that break new aesthetic ground in nonfiction—memoir, personal and lyric essay, literary journalism, cultural meditations, short shorts, hybrid essays, graphic pieces, and more—from authors whose writing has historically been marginalized, ignored, and passed over. The series is explicitly interested in not only ethnic and racial diversity, but also gender and sexual diversity, neurodiversity, physical diversity, religious diversity, cultural diversity, and diversity in all of its manifestations. The machete enables path-clearing; it hacks new trails and carves out new directions. The Machete series celebrates and shepherds unique new voices into publication, providing a platform for writers whose work intervenes in dangerous ways.